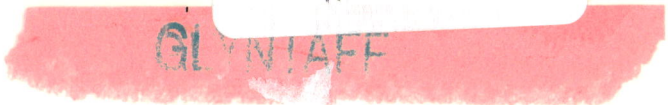

Law in Society Series

Law in the Balance
Legal Services in the 1980s

Law in the Balance

Legal Services in the 1980s

Edited by

PHILIP A. THOMAS

Law in Society Series

edited by

C. M. CAMPBELL and PAUL WILES

MARTIN ROBERTSON · OXFORD

© Martin Robertson and Co. Ltd., 1982

First published in 1982 by Martin Robertson & Company Ltd.,
108 Cowley Road, Oxford OX4 1JF

British Library Cataloguing in Publication Data

Law in the balance
    1. Legal aid – England
    2. Law – England
    I. Thomas, Philip A.
    344.2   KD512

    ISBN 0-85520-444-3 (Case)
    ISBN 0-85520-482-6 (Paper)

Typeset by Oxford Verbatim Limited
Printed and bound in Great Britain by Book Plan Ltd, Worcester

Contents

Contributors

Richard L. Abel is Professor of Law at the University of California, Los Angeles, USA. He has been editor of the *Law and Society Review* and *African Law Studies* and has written on African legal systems, dispute institutions, the sociology of family law, the sociology of lawyers, and the sociology of the legal protection of health and safety.

H. W. Arthurs is Professor, and former Dean, of the Osgoode Hall Law School, York University, Toronto, Canada. He has written a number of articles on the legal profession, and legal education, and is a Bencher of the Law Society of Upper Canada.

Colin Campbell is Professor of Jurisprudence in the Faculty of Law of The Queen's University of Belfast. He has carried out research into legal services and the legal profession. He has contributed numerous papers to journals and books and is co-editor (with P.N.P. Wiles) of *Law and Society* (1979).

Phil Fennell is Lecturer in Law at University College, Cardiff. He is the secretary of the Law Centres Federation, and is also a member of the editorial board of the *British Journal of Law and Society*.

Philip Lewis is a Fellow of All Souls College, Oxford. He has written extensively on the legal profession and legal needs. He prepared a research paper for the Royal Commission on Legal Services.

Martin Partington is Professor of Law at Brunel University. He has written in the areas of housing law, social security law, and legal services. He has been on the Executive Committee of the Legal Action Group and assisted in drafting the evidence of the group to the Royal Commission on Legal Services.

Mike Stephens is Lecturer in the Social Sciences Department at the University of Loughborough. He is completing his PhD on neighbourhood law centres which is his area of special interest.

Philip A. Thomas is Senior Lecturer in Law at University College, Cardiff. He is the founding and present editor of *The British Journal of Law and Society*. He has written extensively in the area of the legal profession and legal services.

William Twining is Professor of Law at the University of Warwick. A former president of the Society of Public Teachers of Law he has a special interest and expertise in legal education in the United Kingdom and abroad.

Ian Willock is Professor of Jurisprudence at the University of Dundee. He is editor of the *Scottish Legal Action Group Bulletin* and Chairman of the Dundee Legal Advice Association. He was the co-ordinator of the Scolag Evidence to the Hughes Commission.

Preface

The 1960s and 1970s in the United Kingdom were periods of change, development and trenchant criticism of the legal profession and legal services. For example, the legal profession almost doubled in size, an enormous increase in public funding of the private practitioner occurred to produce the rapid growth of civil and particularly criminal legal aid, new legal services such as the duty solicitor scheme were introduced and a radical alternative to private practice emerged in the early 70s in the form of neighbourhood law centres. However, the level and nature of criticism outpaced the piecemeal change that the legal profession was able to offer. The Prices and Incomes Board and the Monopolies Commission produced reports which were, in part, critical of legal services while the public often felt that the cost, accessibility, efficiency, service and speed of practitioners was unsatisfactory. For some this dissatisfaction culminated in an announcement by the Prime Minister, Mr. Harold Wilson, on the 12 February 1976 that a Royal Commission would be established with wide terms of reference to investigate all aspects of legal services. The terms of reference were:

To inquire into the law and practice relating to the provision of legal services in England, Wales and Northern Ireland, and to consider whether any, and if so what, changes are desirable in the public interest in the structure, organisation, training, regulation of and entry to the legal profession, including the arrangements for determining its remuneration, whether from private sources or public funds, and in the rules which prevent persons who are neither barristers not solicitors from undertaking conveyancing and other legal business on behalf of other persons.

The Royal Commission on Legal Services reported in October 1979 (Cmnd. 7648) and was followed in May 1980 by the Royal Commission on Legal Services in Scotland (Cmnd. 7846). In March 1980 a conference occurred, organised by the *British Journal of Law and Society* in conjunction with the Faculty of Law. University College, Cardiff, on 'Legal Services in the 80s'. The aim was to use the Commission's Report as a peg on which to hang substantive questions of theory and practice which test both academics and practitioners in the UK and abroad in this turbulent decade. These papers represent an edited and revised selection of contributions given at Cardiff.

In this book the Royal Commission on Legal Services is referred to as the Commission, and its recommendations as the Report. References to chapters and paragraphs of the Report are placed in brackets in the body of the text. The 765-page Report appeared in two volumes, each volume having two parts. Volume one contains the main text and recommendations while volume two carried the invaluable surveys and studies. The authors' references to material found in volume one cite only chapter and paragraph (4–16), chapter 4, paragraph 16, which deals with the nature of legal services. References to volume two include the volume number (II table 2.1).

Those who attended the Cardiff conference were generous in their praise of its conceptual basis, implementation and administrative efficiency prior to and during the meeting. Such plaudits must be shared between the members of the editorial board of the *British Journal of Law and Society*, a few faculty colleagues, graduate and undergraduate law students and in particular Richard Lewis who was principally responsible for the administration of the conference. The measure of its success was directly related to the level of his commitment. Finally I wish to thank the Nuffield Foundation for its generous financial support towards the conference.

Philip A. Thomas
Faculty of Law,
University College Cardiff
May 1981

Introduction

Philip A. Thomas

The contributors to this book have addressed themselves to the issues of legal services in the 1980s. Necessarily they have considered the findings and recommendations of the Royal Commission on Legal Services, but their terms of reference are much wider. Implicit in that decision was the recognition of the limitations of the Commission and its Report. This shortfall was produced in part by the Commissioners themselves, but more generally there are important structural constraints which guide commissions unobtrusively towards certain predictable conclusions. It is to these two matters that I wish to address myself, albeit briefly, for they explain the more expansive approach of the authors of this book, but more importantly provide a warning for those liberal social reformers who believe that centrally controlled institutions of change, purportedly independent of the state, are an effective and dynamic way forward. Certainly there were those who felt that the case for reform of legal services was total and that its achievement would be promoted and possibly fulfilled by the establishment of a Commission. For such people I hope this Introduction has special meaning.

The mass media, and public and professional response to the Report's publication in 1979 varied from antagonism, frustration, disappointment and cautious approval, to euphoria. On the day of the Report's publication Lord Goodman wrote: 'The arguments with which it supports its more important conclusions are lame beyond orthopaedic help,'[1] while the popular press commented variously on a 'damp squib on law reforms,' 'high price for hot air,' and 'fury at "carry on" law report.' The Legal Action Group was tempted to ignore the Report[2] while Professor Zander 'counted well over a hundred recommendations' which he thought 'would amount to valuable changes.'[3] Finally, the Chairman of the Bar, Mr. Peter Taylor, greeted the Report as 'thorough, honest, balanced and constructive'[4] which were sentiments echoed by the President of the Law Society, Mr. John Stebbings, when he described it as 'magnificent.' I recognise that each of these parties made a qualitative judgment of the recommendations from a particular and different perspective. What I echo are the words of Sir Cyril Phillips, Chairman of the Royal Commission on Criminal Procedure[5] when he said: 'If we cannot or do not try to understand or examine or illustrate or relate our problems or proposals in terms of some underlying principle or principles, we are bound to find ourselves in difficulty.' I do not assume a group of 15 Commissioners, supported by an administrative staff, who over several years met 141 times, travelled extensively in the UK and abroad, received evidence from 3,500 people and produced a 765-page Report did not reach their conclusions without recourse to theory, whether articulated or not.

It is my contention that the Commissioners adopted wholeheartedly the ideology of the legal profession which has been characterised as the trait or functionalist approach. It has an impressive lineage and numbered amongst its exponents Carr-Saunders, Wilson, Marshall, Parsons, the Webbs, Tawney and Whitehead. The common features attributed to lawyers were skill based upon theoretical knowledge; training and education; demonstration of competence by passing a test; integrity maintained by adherence to a code of conduct; a professional organisation and service for the public good. Though such ideology is discredited in contemporary sociology of law it was forcefully proposed by the Law Society in its evidence and accepted by the Commissioners as a working model which guided their thoughts and dealings (3–18). For example, it resulted in a high level of consultation between the Commissioners and the Law Society, which even included the solicitors organising the remuneration survey on behalf of the investigating body. Such liaison is perfectly proper if lawyers are seen to be operating in the public interest (1–36). The level and nature of possible change then becomes private, internal and incremental. Thus, the professions themselves are seen to be the appropriate bodies to institute change, as to some extent they have, and scant attention is given to the provision of alternative and professionally distasteful forms of legal services. For example, in this huge Report a derisory half page is devoted to the discussion of a nationalised legal service (5–7). The autonomist 'independence' of the legal profession, which excludes the participation and scrutiny of lay people, remained · inviolate and the suggestion that elected lay people should sit on the Council of the Law Society was rejected (29–40).

This Report was not atheoretical. It was prepared according to an ideology based upon a relationship of law, state and the people which incorporates such notions as independence of the legal profession from the state, the desirability of minimal external interference with the professional bodies, the idea that lawyers are altruistic and can be trusted to identify and cater for client and public interests, and finally that the profession is trying to satisfy – and is basically achieving – those goals which it has laid down. With further support, such as that provided by the Report, and additional financial assistance from the state it will theoretically move itself and legal services closer to self-fulfillment.

My second point is that those who threw themselves wholeheartedly into the pressure group working for the establishment of a Commission did not appreciate the dangers of an 'unsympathetic' Report which was likely given the structural nature of Royal Commissions. To them the reform case was unanswerable. This position represents a level of false consciousness which recognises Royal Commissions as the practical apotheosis of democratic pluralism. Thus, when a disappointing report appears it is explained away as the product of a dominant chairman, inadequate research, pressure of time or one of a number of unusual factors. Whereas these factors may play a part in producing a report unacceptable to liberal reformers, they divert attention away from the commission as an institution. R. A. Dahl has argued that 'all the active and legitimate groups in the population can make themselves heard at some crucial stage in the process of decision.'[6] The Commission presents an image of an independent body of randomly selected lay people with no political commitments, brought together to investigate a specific issue and ultimately recommending certain courses of action to the government of the day. But the chairman is appointed by the Prime Minister and there is an unrelenting similarity in the types of people who are appointed, as Cartwright has tabulated.[7] Recurring recruitment patterns are also found in the general membership of the commission which is itself selected incrementally from the 'list of the great and the good'.[8] Thus, although a public attempt is made to ensure a balancing of interests in the composition of the commissioners' pool, it is stocked only with well-bred varieties: 'Interests will be carefully balanced; the right professional and administrative groups; Scotland and Wales; the North and the South; women and men; the left and the right – all will be carefully matched, though the representatives of each will generally come from the middle of the political road.'[9] With such a composition it is easier to understand why evidence received from solicitors or barristers was specially noted on the receipt record card. No other cards were so marked.

The realistic boundaries of the debate are laid down not by the commissioners but by the politicians who establish the commission. By bringing a socially sensitive issue within the format of a commission it becomes possible to argue that something is being done and indeed action is occurring, but the speed and direction is predictable and possibly controllable. The terms of reference, choice of chairman and commissioners, the community of values between the commissioners and the 'insiders' – such as the legal profession – giving evidence, combine to produce a set of factors which to the uninitiated might appear like democratic pluralism, but to others will reflect the use of power to protect and entrench a series of values which might be in conflict with those shared by the 'outsider' to this process.

The government's response to the Benson Report for England, Wales and Northern Ireland and the Hughes Report for Scotland, is at the best studied indifference. But then perhaps they were intended to stimulate the professions and not the politicians, or assuage the public and the activists through the appearance of dialogue, investigation and recommendation. Perhaps one of the lessons learnt by those concerned with the nature and quality of legal services is that you cannot wait for central authority to change unilaterally that which is being questioned and rejected by the periphery. Though the other contributors to this book do not necessarily share the views expressed in the 'Introduction', there is a unanimity of concern that we have yet to realise that principle embodied in the Magna Carta: 'To no-one will we sell, to no one will we deny or delay right or justice'.

Notes

1. *The Evening Standard*, 4 October 1979.
2. LAG Bulletin, November 1979, p. 246.
3. 33 Current Legal Problems 1980, p. 33.
4. Law Society Gazette, 1979, p. 1069.
5. (1981) Cmnd. 8092.
6. (1965) *A Preface to Democratic Theory* p. 137–8.
7. (1975) *Royal Commissions and Departmental Committees in Britain* p. 70.
8. Sir Gilmour Jenkins, Oral Evidence, (Non-Parliamentary Paper 1957) 4th day, question no. 931.
9. D. V. Donnison, Committees and committee men, *New Society* (1968), 18 April, p. 558.

CHAPTER 1

The Politics of the Market
for Legal Services

Richard L. Abel

How should we read the Report of the Royal Commission on Legal Services? First, it is the most comprehensive single account of a contemporary legal profession despite its numerous oversights. Second, and as important, the Report is a political event in the continuing struggle over control of the market for legal services, even if its significance is sometimes ambiguous. For whom does it speak? I offer what seems the most plausible interpretation, as a necessary foundation for analysing the contents of the Report.

Although the Commissioners did not have identical backgrounds, they were socially rather homogeneous: virtually all would probably style themselves 'professionals,' of which the largest subgroup was lawyers, and the extremely influential chair was a leading accountant, a profession closely allied with (though occasionally a competitor of) lawyers. They did not agree about everything, as evidenced in the body of the Report and the notes of dissent, but nevertheless managed to reach consensus about the vast majority of issues. The Commission was certainly not the creation of the legal profession but it may have become its creature. The profession totally dominated the collection and submission of evidence and both branches greeted the Report with unqualified praise – they were the only interested parties to do so. I take these facts as sufficient to justify me reading the Report as expressing the interests of the professional class generally, and legal professionals in particular. Such a global statement naturally requires qualification: the interests of professionals often mask those of their most powerful clients, capital and state; the professional class must sometimes sacrifice the concerns of a particular profession; and the legal profession, like all others, is internally divided. I will try to take account of both what unites and divides the actors in this debate over the future of the profession.

My analysis is predicated on the fact that all occupations under capitalism are compelled to seek market control. The struggle this generates is political as well as economic. Those occupations that produce legal services became a profession in the course of the nineteenth century, when they attained a high degree of control over supply. In recent decades that control has been endangered and eroded. The profession's response has been two-fold: to defend and recapture control where possible and to turn increasingly to the creation of demand. Both strategies have had a significant impact on the structures within which legal services are produced. This constellation of changes has required, and elicited, new efforts to legitimate control of the market for legal services, and these legitimations have reacted upon professional behaviour. I take up those topics in turn – supply control, demand creation, the transformation of productive relations, and legitimation – while noting their important interrelations.

Supply Control

Occupations struggle for market control under capitalism by seeking to control the factors of production. Those that produce goods concentrate on control over land (and other natural resources), capital, and technology. Those that produce services usually can control only the remaining factor – labour – by controlling the production *of* and *by* producers (Larson 1977). The various occupational categories engaged in the provision of legal services had largely attained that goal by the mid-nineteenth century through consolidation into two branches each of which enjoyed a state-protected monopoly (Larson 1977, Abel-Smith and Stevens 1967, Reader 1966, Millerson 1964, Carr-Saunders and Wilson 1933). Despite continuing competition between barristers and solicitors, occasional encroachments by other occupations e.g. accountants, and repeated attacks by critics in academic life and government (e.g. Zander 1968), the professional monopoly remained largely intact for nearly a hundred years.

Since World War II professional control over the supply of lawyers has weakened as academic education has progressively displaced apprenticeship and professional instruction as the dominant mode of entrance. In the period 1970–78, the number of universities and colleges offering law courses more than doubled, growing from 29 to 71, the student body increased by 50 per cent, and the proportion of new entrants with university or college degrees increased from 40 to 60 per cent in the solicitors' branch and from 64 to 70 per cent among barristers (38–13, 39–18; see also II: table 1.2). The profession exercises virtually no influence over this first stage; even at later stages its control has declined. Whereas apprentices used to pay handsomely for the privilege of learning their trade (Abel-Smith and Stevens 1967, p. 349), today articled clerks receive a substantial, if still inadequate, salary (II: table 16.19), and the pupillage fee of 100 guineas was abolished in 1978 (38–14, 39–67). Neither apprenticeship nor professional examinations pose serious barriers to entry today: attrition at this stage has become almost insignificant.[1]

This loss of control is dramatically confirmed by changes in the size of the profession. The number of practising lawyers per 10,000 population rose from 5.3 at the beginning of the century to 7.8 in 1978, an increase of nearly 50 per cent (4–12). Most of this expansion has occurred in the last two decades, during which the number of barristers rose six times, and the number of solicitors twelve times, as fast as they had done in the first sixty years of the century: a period when the ratio of solicitors to population actually declined (3–9–12). These changes are not felt equally throughout the profession. They affect barristers almost twice as severely as solicitors (growth rates of 106 and 67 per cent during 1965–78) (II: tables 1.6, 12), as the Commission recognizes (18–41–55). Furthermore, control over supply is still exercised more effectively at the top of each branch than at the base: the number of QCs increased only 22 per cent between 1973–8, while the rest of the Bar grew 37 per cent (Annex 33.2 table 33.8); principals in solicitors firms increased only 25 per cent between 1968–78, while assistant solicitors grew 120 per cent (II: table 1.7). Yet it will only be a generation before this demographic bulge is felt among senior practitioners.

Supply control through limitations on production *by* lawyers was also under siege during this period. Competition between the two branches intensified and constraints against competition within each were removed, e.g. barristers from one circuit could appear more easily in the courts of another (32–51–52), and the abolition of scale charges allowed solicitors to engage in price-cutting for conveyancing (21–30).[2] Some laypersons have sought to dispense with legal representation (21–28), perhaps expressing the widespread discontent with professionals (Illich 1977). Even more important, other occupations constantly challenge the monopoly of lawyers: accountants have largely pre-empted the field of tax law (4–6) and trust companies wish to increase the services they offer in the administration of estates (19–25).

One response of the Commission is to resist further erosion of the three most salient controls over production by producers: the divided profession, rights of audience, and the conveyancing monopoly. The divided profession gives solicitors state protection for their monopoly as intermediaries between clients and barristers. The Commission endorses this monopoly, rejecting the claim of accountants that they be allowed to brief barristers themselves (19–12, cf. 19–8–11). It supports this decision with mere conclusions: denying that the divided profession contributes to inefficiency or delay, maintaining that only solicitors are competent to select barristers, although the lay public are capable of choosing solicitors, asserting that it is necessary to preserve the quality of legal representation, and judging, and dismissing the data it collected on the relative costs to the client of divided and fused professions, without even presenting them (17–15, 18–40). Its arguments ultimately reduce to tautology: the present arrangements are necessary 'to maintain an effective two-branch profession' (19–6).

If the divided profession makes work for solicitors, rights of audience benefit both branches. Their shared monopoly in the lower courts is justified by the ritual invocation of technical complexity (18–11) and the reminder that courts possess formal legal authority over solicitors, though no evidence is offered of its exercise (19–17). But the real reason is that continued control over supply is the precondition for creating demand (discussed below): 'it would be inconsistent to propose increased effort and expenditure on a skilled legal service and at the same time propose that, when the protection it confers is most needed, it may be discarded' by the public for self-help or the assistance of a competing occupation (18–11). The exclusive right of barristers to appear in the Crown Courts is also rationalized on the ground of technical competence (18–37). But here, too, the better explanation is demand allocation: because solicitors have more work than barristers (compare 8–41 with 18–55), they were neither united nor energetic in challenging the latter's monopoly (Glasser 1980, p. 31, Zander 1980) and therefore did not persuade the Commission (18–51–56). If exclusive rights of audience are essential to barristers, the conveyancing monopoly has been the economic foundation of solicitors for the last hundred years (Spring 1977, Offer 1977). Three out of every ten clients consult solicitors about conveyances (II: 8–68); in 1975–6 conveyancing fees totalled nearly £300 million, or 61 per cent of solicitors' non-contentious work (II: table 16. 56). The dramatic increase in home ownership (4–2), mobility, housing prices, and the number and value of mortgages (II: 5–5 and table 5.1; Bowles and Phillips 1977, p. 640; Glasser 1979, p. 202) are largely responsible for the capacity of the solicitors' profession to absorb the large increase in numbers in recent years. For the same reason the Commission concludes that the monopoly must be preserved (21–60; but see Notes of Dissent 3, 4, 5) and even strengthened to include executory sales contracts, exclude notaries public, and carry increased penalties for unauthorized practice (21–59–61–63). Of course, it justifies this on totally different grounds: the monopoly is necessary to prevent dishonesty and incompetence (21–21; but see Joseph 1976); true competition within the conveyancing industry is impossible (21–32–34).

These restrictive practices are not equally valued by all strata of the profession. Loss of control over entry primarily affects those who compete with new entrants: sole practitioners and small firms. Hence the Commission recommends the retention of controls over production by qualified producers: for their first three years, solicitors cannot practise on their own or enter a partnership without the permission of the Law Society (38–33; cf. 39–69). A unitary profession would also threaten the competitive position of smaller firms of solicitors in provincial cities, for these would lack litigators (17–33–34). It is the younger barristers who would lose most if the Bar were deprived of its exclusive rights of audience. The conveyancing monopoly accounts for 60 per cent of the fees of sole practitioners but only 33 per cent of those of firms with 10 or more principals (II: tables 5.3, 16.50). These facts explain both why the base of the profession appears more 'conservative' on issues of economic self-interest and why the Commission is solicitous of its fears; we will see this pattern repeated with respect to demand creation.

If supply control is to be preserved it may be necessary to shift to more subtle, informal methods. Thus the Commission repudiates explicit rationing of entry (33–39, 39–7) but endorses the requirement of a first degree for barristers (38–40) and efforts to discourage potential recruits (33–44–45). One such deterrent, the difficulty of finding a permanent seat in chambers, is a function of several factors: the considerable expense involved in opening a new set of chambers; the control exercised by the Senate in lending money only to a 'balanced' set and in granting or denying permission to practise at home and employ a spouse as clerk; and the economic and social disadvantages of practising outside the Inns (33–9–11–13–21–29–30–33 and table 33.5). As a consequence, while barristers increased 97 per cent between 1965–78, sets of chambers increased only 18 per cent in England and Wales as a whole, and a mere 9 per cent in London, where just one of the 200 sets of chambers moved outside the Inns (table 33.6). This explains, in turn, why approximately 100 young barristers were unable to find a permanent seat (33–21) and why, during the same 13-year period, 551 barristers with less than ten years experience left practice (II: tables 1. 13. 14).

Since the solicitors' branch is less overcrowded the Commission recommends against all-graduate entry, which would reduce recruitment by only 9 per cent and exclude a category whose lack of credentials may already render them less competitive (39–13–15). But the remaining constraints on entry to both branches remain considerable: the cost of an undergraduate education; fees for professional education and examination (£900–£1,500) (Annex 39.2 tables 39.2.3); and abstention from full-time work for a period of 4 to 7 years (38–37–42).

Control over production by producers is probably more significant in preserving the market position of solicitors. Here, too, there is a shift from formal to informal mechanisms. Conveyancing scale charges established in 1883 were finally abolished in 1973, yet the result was hardly an outburst of price competition (21–30). Solicitors still preferred not to compete (21–93), encouraged by the official 'Guide to the Professional Conduct of Solicitors' (quoted 21–78) and aided by the exchange of price information among firms (22–54), a practice that would almost certainly be unlawful in other occupations. Nevertheless, the Commission recommends the readoption of a new scale of 'standard' charges (21–92–99). The net result of this deformalization of restrictive practices seems to have been a steep increase in the cost of conveying smaller properties (Bowles and Phillips 1977, pp. 642–3).

There are several independent measures of the consequences of this loss of supply control. First, the income of all lawyers has failed to keep up with the rate of inflation in recent years (though this is also true for most wage-earners) (table 36.1, II: tables 18.32, 38; but see Glasser 1979). More significantly, relative economic position within the profession correlates closely with the extent to which supply control has eroded: solicitors have done better than barristers, and the more junior members of the Bar have fared worst of all (II: table 16.35). Another index of market control is the way in which fees are set. One definition of a profession (if not a definition most professionals would choose) is that it establishes the price of its services unilaterally and after the fact rather than by negotiation before they are performed. The Users' Survey ascertained that three-quarters of its client-respondents had no clear idea at the outset what their legal services would cost; most did not ask (perhaps because they suspected no answer would be forthcoming); 9 per cent did ask and received an unsatisfactory response (II: 8–306–309). Barristers bill solicitors and not clients but even though barristers are not supposed to accept a brief unless the fee is marked in advance, clerks frequently set the fee afterwards or renegotiate a fee already marked (37–71–72, 78). The Commission accepts the profession's view that solicitors, unlike other providers of services, cannot give binding estimates in advance (37–16). The truth, of course, is that supply control allows them to refuse to do so.

But the critical test of market control is whether lawyers extract a monopoly profit by virtue of their control over supply. Gross income strongly suggests they do. The income of solicitors increased more than 400 per cent between 1966–76, a rise of 5 per cent a year at constant prices (Glasser 1979, p. 202). A more precise measure is the difference between the actual price and the price that might be expected in a free market. Conveyancing generates 55.6 per cent of solicitors' income but represents only 40 per cent of their costs (21–73) and is the most remunerative form of work after company law (II: table 16.58). Although the Commission rejects international comparisons (21–82), conveyancing fees in Australian states where solicitors have a monopoly are approximately twice those in states where they do not (II: table 7.1). Even after the abolition of scale charges, conveyancing fees are almost invariably proportional to the price of the property transferred (Bowles and Phillips 1977, pp. 646–9). The Commission justifies this practice on the ground that value is an accurate index of the amount of time necessary to perform the conveyance (21–75–97), but its own data contradict that claim (tables 21.7.8). Rather the *hourly charge* for conveyancing varies directly with the value of the property conveyed; it is almost twice as high for property worth more than £30,000 than for property less than £5,000 (II: table 6.23). The hourly charge also appears to vary directly, if not as strongly, with the size of the firm (II: table 6.10) – the opposite of what one would expect in a competitive market since larger firms ought to be able to achieve economies of scale (Muris and McChesney 1979).

Demand Creation

If the 'rise of professionalism' (Larson 1977) through the attainment of supply control was a concomitant of the 'great transformation' (Polanyi 1957) that accompanied the emergence of competitive, industrial capitalism in the nineteenth century, the present era of monopoly capitalism and the welfare state appear to be effecting equally significant changes in the market for legal services (and others). Because the profession has lost substantial control over the production of and by providers of legal services, it is compelled to turn to another strategy to absorb the consequent overproduction – namely, demand creation.[3]

This is not a new strategy. The divided profession (which requires a client, who wishes the service of a barrister, to purchase also those of a solicitor) and the Bar's exclusive right of audience (which requires a client, who might be content with a solicitor, also to purchase the services of a barrister) both have long histories. But though these practices have survived and receive the imprimatur of the Commission, other forms of professional featherbedding are under attack. The Bar Council modified the 'two-counsel' rule in 1977, under pressure from the Monopolies and Mergers Commission, although barristers continue to enforce the practice without formal sanction (33–73–74, 83–86). And the Commission recommends that a single solicitor should be allowed to act for both buyer and seller or mortgagor and mortgagee in most ordinary conveyances (21–64–65), though once again solicitors probably would co-operate to defeat such a change.

The real limitations upon a strategy of creating private demand are not the rules of professional conduct (which can be frustrated by tacit understandings); they are external. First, the profession does not control private demand, which is a function of changes in the economy (the business cycle), the society (e.g. marriage stability), and substantive law (e.g. the response to injuries, the structure of taxation). For instance, the number and value, at constant prices, of residential transactions dropped dramatically in the slump of 1973–5, with the result that conveyancing as a proportion of solicitors' income was ten per cent lower in 1976 than it had been ten years earlier (Bowles and Phillips 1977, pp. 640–41, Glasser 1979, p. 202). Second, the profession can do little to stimulate private demand. The needs of the business community are already fully satisfied (4–21) – with the helpful stimulus of a tax deduction for legal expenses, a form of *public* demand creation (5–4). Efforts to increase individual consumption – the 'whatsisname' campaign in the UK (4–25, 27–5; see Fennell pp. 144–160), the promotion of an 'annual legal checkup' (ABA Committee on Professional Ethics, Opinion 307, 1962), and of open-panel group legal service plans by the American Bar Association (Goodman 1979) – have been largely abortive.[4] Third, attempts to augment private demand can backfire. If the public come to perceive the profession as excessively greedy they can support other occupations that wish to challenge the professional monopoly or advocate reforms that would eliminate the need for any professional assistance. Continuing criticism of the conveyancing monopoly (Glasser 1980, p. 31), recommendations for change in the system of compensating injuries (Pearson Commission, 1978), simplification of divorce and probate procedures (Abel 1979b), recent interest in alternatives to courts (Abel 1981) – all threaten to reduce private demand.

As a consequence, legal professional energies have turned to public subsidization of demand.[5] The close connection between loss of supply control and state-created demand can be seen by comparing the degree to which different professional segments rely on the latter. Legal aid as a proportion of gross income is a 6 per cent for solicitors but approximately 50 per cent for barristers (36–41, 86), more than half for the junior Bar but only a quarter for QCs (II: table 18–17).

It is important to recognize just how recently the profession embraced demand creation. Although legal aid has roots in the nineteenth century, and even earlier antecedents, the goal of the profession until recently was to furnish the bare minimum of service necessary to legitimate the legal system in terms of liberal ideology (Abel-Smith and Stevens 1967, Chap. 6), rejecting any scheme which might tend to make people more litigious' (10–6). But the last thirty years have witnessed a complete about-face in professional attitude (13–6) and a phenomenal growth in legal aid: the number of civil applications granted, for instance, rose from 38,000 at the beginning of the scheme in 1950 to 211, 337 in 1976–7 (12–4) and the pace has accelerated in recent years (Annex 2–3). Furthermore, several significant institutions have been created or fundamentally restructured within the last decade: legal advice centres, the 'green form' scheme, duty solicitors, and law centres (7–28, 10–13, 8–1, 9–1).

To what extent *can* demand be created? The necessary precondition is the progressive legalization of social life (see Schuyt *et al.* 1977). The Commission observes that whereas in the nineteenth century the law's reach was largely limited to property, possessed by only a few, and crime, committed by only a few, today the state intervenes everywhere (4–3–15). The welfare state places novel obligations upon the older forms of property (realty, natural resources, income, capital, labour power) through laws governing planning, revenue, contract, and industrial relations, and it also creates the 'new property' (Reich 1964) – numerous forms of entitlement that derive entirely from public law.[6] The regulatory apparatus of this new welfare state is not the courts but the tribunals, which the Commission therefore sees as the largest untapped source of demand (4–5; see also 3–13, 28–5).

But if statutes and subsidiary legislation constantly proliferate, other indices suggest a more ambiguous picture of the legalization of daily life. Although civil litigation and criminal prosecution both increased dramatically during 1960–75, they actually declined in the subsequent three years (Annex 2–3). Furthermore, if we normalize for population growth, the rates of both activities are lower today than they were at the beginning of the century (4–1, excluding motoring offences). Finally, the ratios of civil and criminal cases to practitioners decreased over this period for barristers, although they rose for solicitors – once again illustrating the relative success of the two branches in the project of market control (4–1 and Annex 2–3).

The Commission read these figures as suggesting an 'unmet need' for legal services.[7] It therefore conducted the Users' Survey to investigate such need and thereby lay the social scientific foundation for public demand creation. The survey revealed that use of lawyers by individuals was 'infrequent': 15 per cent of the respondents had consulted a lawyer within the previous year, 22 per cent within two years, a third within five years, and slightly more than half over a lifetime (4–15, II: 8–14). On the other hand, only 9 per cent of respondents recalled any occasion during the previous year when they thought a solicitor might have been helpful but did not consult one; of these, one quarter resolved the matter satisfactorily on their own and another quarter decided to drop it (II: 8–371, 373). One interpretation of these figures might be that less than 5 per cent of the population experienced 'unmet need' in any given year.

The Commission, however, concludes that demand can and should be stimulated and addresses three possible dampers that may contribute to the present low level of use. The first is geographic distribution: the ratio of population per lawyer varies regionally between 2,000 and 66,000, creating disparities that may be augmented by the refusal of many solicitors to accept legal aid clients (4–28–29–31). Therefore the Commission recommends that the state provide interest-free, delayed repayment loans to solicitors who set up practice in deprived areas (16–25–26). Yet physical inaccessibility is not clearly a problem: the Users' Survey revealed no significant variation in lawyer use by region, or between urban and rural settings (II: 8–37, 58, 64).[8]

The second obstacle is information – when are legal services appropriate and who can provide them? The Users' Survey suggested that existing sources of information generally do not recommend lawyer use:[9] only one-quarter of those who first sought the advice of a layperson were encouraged to see a lawyer, and three-quarters of those who consulted lawyers had not been urged to do so by anyone else (II: 8–122, 372). Nevertheless, there are a large number of mechanisms that do serve to transform troubled individuals into clients. In 1977–8 the 750 Citizens Advice Bureaux received 3 million enquiries, of which they identified one-third as legal; in 1976 they referred 250,000 matters to solicitors (2–6, 7–7).[10] The profession clearly sees the CABx as an important source of business, for 3,300 solicitors a year contribute their services (2–21). The Commission recommends that such participation be regularized, expanded, and supported by public funds, in preference to the use of salaried lawyers or the provision of legal advice by government lawyers, both of which might withdraw business from, rather than create it for, the private profession (7–13, 16, 26, 27). Similarly, on the criminal side, the Commission recommends that the duty solicitor scheme should expand and engage in the aggressive stimulation of business by means that would have been unthinkable in the very recent past: solicitors should be situated in every magistrates' court, approach prisoners in remand cells before trial, and be available after conviction to advise prisoners of their rights on appeal and in civil matters unrelated to their prosecution (9–1, 14, 23–24, 14–14–17). Once again these services should be provided through a rota rather than by salaried lawyers, in order to create business for private practitioners (9–23–24). Finally, solicitors themselves educate potential clients about the utility of legal services: they provide advice under the 'green form' scheme not because such work is profitable (the average payment was £21) but because more than a quarter of those consultations generated legal aid matters; and many offer a half-hour consultation at a reduced rate of £5 as a kind of loss leader to drum up business (11–7, 13–2–4).[11] The Commission urges that this 'loss' be underwritten by the state so that all solicitors can offer such advice free of charge and without the impediment of a means test (13–4).

The third obstacle to increasing the demand for legal services, and the one the Commissioners (together with most other observers) believe to be paramount, is cost (3–37). The data, again, are ambiguous: only 3 per cent of the population sampled said they had failed to consult a solicitor during the previous year because of the expense (II: 8–373); yet if all these people had done so, use would have increased 20 per cent (II: 8–15). The Commission therefore recommends a large number of reforms designed to expand legal aid.[12] First, it notes that many potential clients are mistaken about eligibility and expense and urges greater dissemination of information about the programme (13–51).[13] Second, because legal aid is an unattractive form of work for most solicitors

(4–29–31 and table 4.1), it recommends changes that would reduce the administrative burdens and increase both the range and level of remuneration (5–20, 7–15, 9–9–20, 13–2–4–66–68, 16–21).[14]

But most important of all, the Commission recommends major expansions of eligibility. The number of courts in which legal aid is available has increased steadily to encompass almost the entire structure (12–4). Nevertheless, whereas 80 per cent of the population were eligible for some assistance when the programme was initiated in 1950, only 40 per cent were still eligible in 1973 because the means test was not adequately indexed to account for inflation (12–5).[15] An adjustment was made in 1979 and the Commission recommends that this become a regular practice (12–6–24). It also proposes numerous liberalizations in the means test (13–12–22), removal of the ceiling so as to render the entire population eligible (12–29–32), and elimination or reduction of contributions, which discourage a significant proportion of those eligible from using legal aid (11–13, 12–22–48, 14–31).

The Commission also advocates relaxation of non-economic restraints on legal aid. There is little room to expand criminal legal aid – it already pays for most representation and constitutes up to three-quarters of the income of criminal defence specialists (table 14.1, II: 16–117 and table 16.53) – though the Commission recommends curbing the discretion of judges to deny assistance, as well as other minor extensions (9–11, 23–24, 14–6–10, 16–17).[16] In the civil area, by contrast, the Commission recommends liberalizing the test of when legal aid is appropriate, extending legal aid to substantive areas previously excluded, and authorizing the representation of additional parties (13–25–26, 70–72, 14–25). But the most significant expansion proposed is that legal aid committees have discretion to authorize representation in administrative tribunals (15–28), which held *six times* as many hearings in 1978 as there were contested civil cases in the Crown Courts (15–1). There are two reasons for interpreting this as demand creation. First, it has been proposed many times in the last 30 years but has never before received official endorsement (15–4–5). Second, the Commission recommends legal aid payments only to solicitors even though it justifies that recommendation by arguing that tribunal outcome is related to the nature of representation and then offering evidence that lay representatives are sometimes more successful than solicitors (15–10–21, II: table 4.5; see also Notes of Dissent, (2–4–6).

If public demand creation appears to be the only way for the profession to preserve market control, it introduces its own problems – pre-eminently the need to distribute business.[17] True, even a strategy of supply control required some attention to how qualified producers would divide the market (discussed further in the next section). But demand creation brings this issue to the forefront, for several reasons. First, control of supply increases the business available to all producers indifferently, but demand can be created only for *specific* producers – the same mechanism that generates demand also allocates it. Second, when the state creates demand there is a norm that all producers are entitled to share equally in satisfying it, an expectation that overrules the inconsistent ideology of competitive capitalism.[18] Third, the demand thus stimulated cannot simply extrapolate existing patterns of consumption because most individuals have no established habit of lawyer use: half have never seen a solicitor; two-thirds have not seen one in the past five years; even those who have used a solicitor at least once rarely have a longstanding relationship (4–15, II: 8–14, 123); and individuals prefer to use a different lawyer each time (Curran 1977, pp. 190–91). Finally, the creation of demand among a distinctive clientèle for new kinds of services inevitably contributes to growth of a differentiated professional stratum to satisfy it, first through functional specialisation but ultimately along lines of ideology, economics, and socializing (see Katz 1978, Brennan 1968).

Interest in distributing demand, and especially in distributing it equally, appears to account for a good deal of professional behaviour and many of the Commission's proposals. In seeking to remedy the geographic maldistribution of solicitors, the Commission recommends against a guaranteed income for practitioners in deprived areas, and for Law Society control of subsidized loans to such practitioners (16–23–29), implicitly conceding that equality among solicitors is more important than equality among clients. But this issue has been aired most fully, of course, in debates over the structure of legal aid. The decision thirty years ago to provide legal aid through private practitioners rather than full-time salaried poverty lawyers, which is vehemently reaffirmed by the Commission (5–7–8), ensures that virtually all publicly generated demand will be spread throughout the profession. It is hardly surprising that every professional association except the Legal Action Group endorsed this *status quo*. Today debate revolves around the law centres. Although professional hostility toward the centres has often been expressed in political terms, it was actually based on economic fears. But the profession has since re-learned the old story: that a single lawyer in town may starve but the arrival of another virtually guarantees the prosperity of both (8–3). The Commission seeks to strengthen this symbiosis by recommending that law centres charge the same contributions as private lawyers rendering legal aid (thereby eliminating any competitive edge) and urging the centres to refer paying clients to private practitioners (8–22–32 ff.).

Spreading demand is an expensive process. The Commission makes two recommendations that would substantially increase such public expenditures: central government support for the law centres which would provide a basis for controlling competition between them and the private profession, and state subsidy for free half-hour consultations by potential clients (so that solicitors do not use that inducement to gain competitive advantage) (8–23, 13–2–4). But far more important are the administrative costs of operating the legal aid system. In 1977–8, the Law Society spent £7.3 million to administer civil legal aid payments of £39 million – an overhead of 16 per cent (11–10);[19] and this would increase substantially if the government were to accept the Commission proposal that it assume many of the administrative costs presently borne by lawyers (13–68).

Legal aid relies on public choice to distribute demand widely. Two other institutions confer that function directly on lawyers or their subordinates. More than one hundred duty solicitor schemes presently handle in excess of 100,000 cases a year[20] and they are ultimately to be extended to all magistrates' courts (9–1–4). The Commission acknowledges that their primary purpose is to spread business among participating solicitors (9–7). This function is also visible in the contrast between the Commission's recommendation that duty solicitors or their subordinates directly approach every defendant in the cells and its condemnation of similar behaviour by police, court staff, or jail wardens as 'touting and corrupt practices' because the latter might give certain solicitors a competitive edge (9–14–17). In other words, soliciting business is wrong if a few do it on their own initiative but proper if all agree to do it in turn.

If the duty solicitor scheme is concerned to allocate criminal business at the first moment that the accused is aware of the need for legal representation, the CABx perform the same function at the threshold of contact with the civil law (2–12).[21] In order that the CABx may help to distribute business equally, the Law Society presently publishes lists of solicitors' firms willing to accept legal aid clients, which it sends to all Bureaux (7–13, 27–9). But precisely because their purpose is to spread business (and because solicitors anxious for business hold themselves out as competent in areas where they are ignorant) those lists contain insufficient information to permit clients to make intelligent choices. Furthermore, the Bureaux are now authorized to recommend individual solicitors (which could concentrate business). Therefore the Commission proposes that all CABx emulate those 40 per cent in which solicitors presently serve in a rota (which would render the CABx an exact civil parallel of the duty solicitor scheme) (7–16). And just as the Commission condemns individual lawyers who solicit criminal business, so it urges the absorption of the 130 voluntary legal advice centres, which would deny the enterprising lawyers who set them up any competitive advantage (7–28–29, cf. Leat 1975).

Yet despite the variety, ingenuity, and magnitude of these devices, the concentration of publicly created demand seems inevitable. Among solicitors' offices doing any legal aid work in 1977–8 (and many did none), 60 per cent received less than 15 per cent of their income from legal aid, whereas 20 per cent received nearly 70 per cent (table 4.1, see also II: 16–110 and table 16.52). The disparities among barristers are even greater: junior practitioners before the London criminal courts earn 92 per cent of their gross fees from public funds, whereas QCs engaged in London Chancery and specialist practice earn less than 2 per cent (II: 18–37–42 and tables 18.17–21).

If state subsidized demand is seen as the primary remedy for diminished professional control over supply, the stimulation of private demand is not ignored. But here again problems of distribution shape these efforts and sometimes even argue that opportunities to create demand should be foregone. Thus the Commission recommends against the contingent fee despite evidence that without it many personal injury victims with legitimate claims go uncompensated (Burman *et al.* 1977, Harris *et al.* 1981) because (among other reasons) 'it would reward some lawyers disproportionately' (16–6), perhaps leading to such distasteful American phenomena as the self-styled 'king of torts' (see Belli and Kaiser

1976) or the 'Inner Circle of Advocates', membership in which is limited to attorneys who have secured verdicts in excess of $1 million for a single plaintiff (Bernstein 1978). Similarly, the Commission notes that 'pre-paid legal services schemes of various kinds, have not been attempted in this country and seem unlikely to become established here' (16–1) 'but in the last few years some insurance companies have begun offering legal cost insurance to individuals as well as to companies' (16–13). This strikingly parallels the (ultimately unsuccessful) efforts of the American Bar Association and state bar associations to promote 'open-panel' plans, in which a client is entitled to retain *any* lawyer, thereby encouraging the spread of business, and to discourage or even prohibit 'closed-panel' plans in which a single firm contracts with a group to provide legal services to its members, thereby concentrating business (Deitch and Weinstein 1976, pp. 21–26, 39–42).

But the tension between demand creation and distribution is greatest, and most visible, in the controversy over advertising. Although the legal profession, and all others, maintained for decades that any form of advertising was fundamentally inconsistent with 'professionalism', the Commission now entertains the possibility that some advertising may be permissible, even desirable. The Report, however, is filled with contradictions. It favours institutional advertising but opposes that by individual solicitors or firms; it tolerates local advertising but not regional or national; it acknowledges the need of the public for information but insists that solicitors should not be able to say anything about quality, number of staff, fee income, caseload, clients represented, or fees charged (unless these are fixed); it recommends the solicitation of business within the structure of the CABx and duty solicitor schemes but condemns that by individual lawyers (27–2, 31, 36, 37, 43).[22]

How are we to understand these inconsistencies? I believe the Commission is seeking to walk a very fine line. Public demand creation in response to the erosion of supply control broke the ideological taboo against advertising. Law centres were doing it (8–33) and professional dignity was not undermined; indeed, the reputation of lawyers was actually being enhanced. Then why not allow private practitioners to advertise?[23] Furthermore, differential treatment gives some lawyers a competitive advantage. The Commission therefore supports liberalization of the rules about advertising partly to equalize the competitive positions of public and private sector lawyers (just as it proposed that law centres be required to charge legal aid contributions). This same attitude explains the willingness of the Commission to tolerate advertising by lawyers who are competing with other occupations that advertise, such as bankers (27–32).

The real difficulties arise when the Commission seeks to apply this principle to competition within the private profession. Here there seem to be three groups with distinct interests: young practitioners (the demographic source of oversupply) must engage in aggressive competition for clients if they are to survive; older practitioners in the lower strata of the profession are severely threatened by such competiton; and the élite wish to retain their influence within the profession while simultaneously enhancing its image. It is precisely along these lines that the struggle over advertising has been waged in the USA (cf. American Bar Association Journal 1977). The Commission seeks to give something to everyone. It acknowledges the appropriateness of advertising by 'the newly-established firm or the recently-qualified specialist' solicitor and by 'barristers who form a new set of chambers' or join a set (27–32–49). But it severely limits the scope of advertising and promotes the older practitioner: lawyers should be allowed to advertise the date of qualification and recognised specialisms; though the latter is elaborately disguised as an index of technical competence, it is actually a privilege of age (27–35b).[24] The Commission then seeks to balance these competitive advantages by recommending that no solicitor be qualified as a specialist in more than two areas and that the qualification be specific to the individual rather than the firm (27–21). Finally, the élite are offered an emphasis on institutional advertising and a proposal to locate the regulation of advertising in the Law Society (27–6–38), which they control (see *infra*).

The basic problem with this elaborate apparatus, as well as with the mechanisms for allocating publicly-created demand, is that it ignores everything we know about how the public find lawyers. The Users' Survey revealed that half of those who consulted a solicitor in the previous year were referred by acquaintances (family, friends, or workmates), and most of the rest were directed by someone involved in the particular transaction that gave rise to the need for legal services. Less than 10 per cent used the kind of universalistic mechanism – such as a CAB or telephone directory – through which the Commission proposes to spread work (II: 8–147–62 and table 8.23).[25] This is consistent with studies of the source of intake in law centres in the UK (Byles and Morris 1977, p. 75) and Australia (Redfern Legal Centre 1978, p. 10), choice of lawyer in open-panel prepaid legal service plans in the USA (Marks *et al.* 1974, pp. 67–71), and client choice of private lawyers in the UK (Cain 1979), Australia (Tomasic and Bullard 1978, pp. 68–9). and the USA (Curran 1977 pp. 200–302; see also Ladinsky 1976). When the profession switched to demand creation in response to its loss of supply control it created problems that it appears unable to solve. Some of the consequences of this dilemma will be explored in the next section.

The Transformation of Productive Relations

The changes described above reveal the heightened level of competition among lawyers, notwithstanding the profession's efforts to reduce or control it. If competition is not sufficient to drive prices down (see Zander 1980, note 20), it nevertheless limits the profession's ability to force prices up, as suggested by the failure of incomes to keep up with inflation.[26] This compels producers to turn their attention to reducing costs in order to avert a falling rate of profit. Because the production of legal services is labour intensive, the primary means of reducing costs is to alter the composition of the labour force.[27]

Whereas capitalists obtain the power to extract surplus value from their workers through ownership of the means of production, professionals extract surplus from their subordinates through market control. Because the profession controls production by producers, subordinates (other occupations and junior professionals) cannot sell their services directly to the consumer but must instead sell their labour to members of the profession (cf. Freidson 1970, Chap. 3, Larson 1977, pp. 214–15). The importance of subordinated labour to lawyers is most readily visible within the solicitors' branch. First, solicitors have suppressed any challenge to their dominance by occupations that had been successfully subordinated in the past, as illustrated by their continuing struggle with legal executives.[28] In 1949 and again in 1963, the managing clerks sought to professionalise by controlling supply through the requirement of a credential; each time the Law Society frustrated this ambition by refusing to treat the credential as mandatory (31–4–5). As a result, ILEX did not achieve the dominant position of the Law Society; its membership is presently only about 65 per cent of all legal executives and steadily declining (31–8–9–15). Solicitors have further ensured the continued subordination of legal executives by keeping them overspecialised (31–14) (cf. Larson 1977, pp. 204–205).[29] ILEX seems to have viewed the establishment of the Commission as another opportunity to achieve professionalisation; if so, it was sadly disappointed. The Report recommends that: legal executives should have no right of independent practice; their rights of audience should remain limited; membership in ILEX should not be compulsory nor should the credential mandate higher pay; legal executives should neither share in profits nor participate in the governance of the profession (31–20–26–31–34–38–42). The Commission is quite explicit about the value of subordinated professions to those who dominate: 'the proper use of the skill and expertise of legal executives will enable costs to be kept down' (31–25) – costs to the solicitor, not prices to the consumer!

If solicitors have preserved, and even strengthened, their domination of legal executives, there have also been significant changes in other categories of subordinated labour. The shift to graduate entry (38–27–32) has meant that the length of articles for most clerks has been cut in half, from four years to two, but the rapid rise in the number of entrants has more than compensated: new articles increased 39 per cent from 1970–3, and 71 per cent from 1970–8 (II: table 1–4). The net result is that the number of clerks increased 24 per cent from 1966–76 and 72 per cent from 1966–78 (II: 1–11 and table 16.9). But if the size of this category has increased, other indicia of subordination have declined: graduate clerks may inspire status anxiety in their employers, many (perhaps most) of whom did not attend university; and clerks have been able to command increasing salaries. It is the category of assistant solicitors, however, which displays the most dramatic growth – 120 per cent from 1968–78, during which period the number of principals increased only 25 per cent (II: table 1.7).[30] If we combine these demographic shifts to obtain a composite picture of changes in the labour force, we find that the ratio of assistant solicitors and articled clerks to principals dramatically increased between 1966–78, whereas the ratio of legal executives and administrative clerical staff to principals actually declined slightly (31–9–10; II: I–11 and tables 1.6, 16.9).

I believe that these changes represent an increase in the exploitation of subordinated labour by solicitors seeking to maintain or increase profits by reducing costs in an increasingly competitive market. I noted earlier that the production of legal services is highly labour intensive: average capital per person in solicitors' firms is little more than £2,000,[31] and there appears to be no consistent relationship between profitability and amount of capital invested (II: table 16.45). I have made a crude calculation of the rate at which surplus value is extracted from subordinated employees, using data on the median rates at which the smallest and largest firms bill the time of and pay those employees, and making the conservative assumption that employees are expected to bill 1,500 hours (30 hours/week) (II: tables 16.15.17.19.21).[32]

Employee Category	Hourly Rate (£)	Annual Income Generated (£)	Annual Salary (£)	Ratio of Income to Salary
Articled Clerk				
Sole practitioner	7	10,500	1,482	7.09
Largest firm	10	15,000	2,276	6.59
Legal Executive				
Sole practitioner	9	13,500	3,481	3.88
Largest firm	21	31,500	4,238	7.43
Assistant Solicitor				
Sole practitioner	12	18,000	3,990	4.51
Largest firm	24	36,000	5,262	6.84

The role of subordinated personnel in generating profits can be shown another way. Their numbers have not increased equally in all firms: large firms have more salaried employees per partner, and this ratio has been increasing more rapidly (II: tables 16.8.10). As we will see below, median net profit per principal also varies directly, and strongly, with size of firm (II: tables 16.34.85).[33]

The internal structure of the Bar and barristers' relations to subordinated occupations are very different. The ratio of principals to employees, ignoring pupils, (34–11) in a typical set of chambers is more than 4:1 (II: 14–52), compared with the more than 1:5 ratio in larger solicitors' firms. Nevertheless, there are tensions between barristers and their clerks that parallel those between solicitors and legal executives. The Commission makes a number of recommendations that would increase the subordination of senior clerks: urging that they be salaried rather than share in profits,[34] opposing the efforts of the Barristers' Clerks Association to achieve supply control through a mandatory credential, threatening even the existing level of demand by proposing to eliminate the rule requiring every set of chambers to have a clerk, and reprimanding clerks for exercising too much influence over their principals (34–7, 22–23–32–39). Yet if clerks are subordinated, their labour is not exploited: senior clerks are well-paid, averaging more than twice the income of legal executives (II: tables 14–22, 16.21, 22).

The age profile of the Bar has been transformed in the last decade by the loss of supply control: in 1977, 57 per cent had less than ten years experience (compared with 34 per cent in 1967) and 71 per cent less than 15 years; 38 per cent were under 30 and 73 per cent under 40 (II: tables 1.14, 18.16). This demographic shift must create problems for the intesely hierarchical relations among barristers. A set of chambers is a total gerontocracy. The head possesses exclusive political authority: he is the sole tenant and therefore unilaterally decides admission and expulsion; he monopolizes information – only he knows the earnings of the other members (33–16 and Annex 33–1). He also possesses considerable economic power: junior barristers frequently owe their briefs to the prestige of their head, a dependence that was institutionalized in the two-counsel rule and survives its formal repeal. Gerontocracy is reflected in income inequality: a barrister with less than four years of experience earned £2,769 in 1976–7; a QC who took silk before 1974 earned £22,168 (II: table 18.9). Compare this extraordinary 1:8 ratio with the approximately 1:3 ratio for solicitors, where the earning curve is much flatter (figure 36.2, table 36.6, II: table 18.9). Nor can young barristers rely on time to carry them to the top: many are forced to leave the Bar for economic reasons; QCs have been held to a fairly constant 10 per cent of the Bar by keeping the rate of successful applications at a steady 20–30 per cent a year (33–71).[35] It is not surprising, in light of these relationships, that the Commission rejects partnerships among barristers, which might require seniors to share power and income with their juniors (33–56–66).[36]

The extraordinary incomes of senior barristers seem to be attributable to two factors. First, there is still a high level of supply control at the top of the profession, sustained by the political and economic domination that seniors exercise over their juniors. Second, if barristers do not directly exploit their juniors and clerks, the entire solicitors' branch – principals as well as employees – might be considered the subordinated labour of senior barristers, engaged in the preparatory work whose profits the latter alone can reap.

Heightened competition as a result of loss of supply control not only transforms productive relations between superordinates and subordinates, it also leads to an increase in the size of the productive unit. This is clearly visible at the Bar. Deliberate restrictions on the creation of new sets of chambers – more pronounced in London than the provinces – have resulted in a growth in their average size from 8 barristers in 1965 to 14 in 1978 (tables 33.1.6).[37] Nearly half of all solicitors practise in firms of five or more, 17 per cent in firms of ten or more (table 17.1). Furthermore, the trend is toward greater concentration: between 1968 and 1978 firms of five or more increased 87 per cent whereas sole practitioners and two-person firms decreased 8 per cent (II: table 16.4). But different reasons, reflecting the divergence in productive relations between the two branches, explain these similar patterns. Within the Bar, concentration represents an effort to preserve gerontocracy. Among solicitors, on the other hand, concentration creates some unease, revealed in the Commission's opposition to fusion, to expansion of solicitors' rights of audience, and to partnerships between solicitors and other occupations (17–31–36, 18–54, 30–2–15). Yet these restrictions will not affect the underlying dynamic of intra-professional competition. Solicitors' firms are growing in size because increased use of subordinated employees is necessary to cut costs and enhance profitability and because the shift to a strategy of demand creation places a premium on the mass processing of clients. Concentration is inevitable for the same reasons that the efforts to spread public and private demand (described in the previous section) must fail.[38]

A third change in the structure of production is increasing heterogeneity among producers. One form of differentiation is specialisation in response to new and unequal market incentives[39] and in an effort to regain control over supply and resist competition by younger practitioners. The Commission's attitude is two-faced. It accepts the proliferation of élite specialties serving business interests as the by-product of inevitable growth in legal complexity (27–19), unwilling to see that it is lawyers who are largely responsible for this complexity. But when lawyers specialise in satisfying publicly created demand, and especially when they represent poor, politically oppressed, or deviant clients, the Commission turns censorious: encouraging all lawyers to learn welfare law (29–19), recommending rapid turnover in law centres (8–23), opposing salaried lawyers (5–7–8, 7–27), and criticizing specialisation in legal aid (4–30–33) or in criminal defence to the neglect of prosecution (18–45). Specialisation at the base is clearly more threatening to the image of a homogeneous profession than differentiation of an élite.

Another source of heterogeneity is even more directly a consequence of loss of control over entry: the profession can no longer exclude women or ethnic minorities through either formal rules or informal mores. Women, who constituted insignificant proportions of either branch until recently, now represent 8 per cent of the Bar and 6.5 per cent of solicitors, and these numbers can be expected to rise rapidly since women are 31 per cent of law graduates, 32 per cent of articled clerks, and 24 per cent of those called to the Bar in 1977–8 (35–9, 10). The ban on non-citizen solicitors (which effectively excluded racial minorities) was lifted in 1974; members of the non-white Commonwealth have qualified for the Bar for over a century, but a larger proportion have stayed in England to practise in recent years, for economic or political reasons, and there are now more than 200 (35–31).[40] But the same prejudices that once excluded women and minorities now keep them at the base of the professional hierarchy. At the Bar, a third of all chambers contain no women and another third only one; they are only 1 per cent of QCs; and their income is a great deal less than that of their male age-mates; three-quarters for those under 30, only a third for those over 50 (II: 15–17 and tables 15.10.11). They are channeled into less remunerative specialties – matrimonial and criminal practice – but even within those categories they make little more than half of men in the same fields (II: 15–21 and table 15.12). Women are also under-represented in the leading firms of solicitors (II: 15–15). Racial minorities are relegated to 'ghetto' sets of chambers (35–33). Thus racial and sexual discrimination compound the growth of low status specialities to create an increasingly explicit and rigid stratification within the profession.[41]

Professional loss of entry control has indirectly fostered heterogeneity in two other ways. First, the rise of graduate entry has meant the rapid growth of academic lawyers: the 71 educational institutions offering 80 degree courses employ many hundred teachers (39–18). The need of academics to differentiate themselves from practitioners inevitably produces tensions – for instance, over who will define the content of legal education (38–23–26, 39–18) – and these are certain to increase in the future.[42] Second, overproduction of lawyers has contributed to the rise of a salariate. Employed barristers almost equal the number of barristers in private practice (20–2, but see II: table 1.1). Solicitors employed outside private practice constitute only one-eighth of all solicitors (30–2), but if assistants and consultants employed within private practice are included in the category, salaried solicitors become 41 per cent of the number of principals (II: tables 1.1,y). The differences between the finances reflect the relative levels of overproduction combined with the lesser ability of barristers (who practise independently) to absorb this overproduction by employing subordinates. Employed barristers may thus be the equivalent of assistant solicitors. But even solicitors employed outside private practice are increasing more rapidly than principals (61 per cent compared with 25 per cent, 1968–78) (II: tables 1.7, 8, 16.3). Salaried lawyers have become so numerous, and the similarities between employed barristers and solicitors so small compared to the differences between each and the private practitioner, that some see the emergence of a 'third branch' of the profession, a view the Commission vehemently repudiates (20–24).

Each change in the composition of this labour force contributes to a transformation in the structure of professional control. The rationalization of administration, the growth of hierarchical, bureaucratic authority, is necessary: to maintain, and even increase, the subordination and exploitation of labour; to manage productive units of increasing size, administer them internally and co-ordinate them externally; and to govern an occupational category whose divisions are constantly growing in number and depth – two branches, proliferating substantive specialties, small firms and large, public and private sectors, academics and practitioners, salaried employees and independent producers, and differences of gender, race, and age. There is considerable evidence of the need for greater rationalization of control. In the private sector, the Commission recommends more accurate systems of billing (37–20–33),[43] formal contracts between barristers' clerks and heads of chambers, pension plans, etc. (34–12, 27). But it is in the public sector that the tendency toward central planning is most evident. The Commission recommends that hierarchy displace the egalitarian ethos of the law centres and that the autonomous centres, now loosely associated through the Law Centres Federation, be subordinated to a new central agency that will engage in detailed planning (Ch. 8, especially 8–25–27, 32b–d). The more than 100 duty solicitor schemes, which have developed in response to the circumstances of particular courts, should also be subjected to greater control by the Law Society (9–9). And the voluntary legal advice centres should be replaced altogether by centrally controlled CABx (7–29).

The twenty enquiries into the legal profession in the last 15 years (table 3.1), culminating in the present Report, are further evidence of the pressure for public oversight. Although the Commission expresses the hope that lawyers will now be left in peace (3–14–17), the prognosis, and its own urgings, point in exactly the opposite direction. For it notes and commends the ongoing work of the Royal Commission on Criminal Procedure, the suggestion of a similar commission on civil procedure (43–3), the Law Commission, and the Council on Tribunals (15–1); and it proposes a fees advisory commission (37–89–98), a Joint Committee on Legal Education (39–116), and committees to co-ordinate all aspects of legal service planning at the regional level (6–32–38). Most important, the Commission recommends the creation of a Council for Legal Services: 'somewhere, legal services as a whole have to be considered so that gaps can be identified, priorities tested, and proposals for change put in context' (6–21; see generally 6–14–26).

Once again, the shift in strategy from supply control to demand creation is a critical stimulus for this transformation in the structure of control. Acceptance of public money generates irresistible demands for subordination to state scrutiny, if not control.[44] The Commission explicitly invokes this rationale to justify the taxation of legal aid costs (37–25–75), the assertion of public control over the law centres (8–23), and the need to systematize and regulate the duty solicitor schemes (9–9). And we have already seen that demand creation requires mechanisms to distribute business. Thus every ingredient in the transformation of the market for legal services accentuates the tendency toward centralized, and increasingly state, control.

Legitimation

Lawyers, like all people, are constantly engaged in the process of legitimation, explaining and justifying themselves.[45] Legitimation may be an act of mutual reassurance, lawyers seeking to resolve for each other perceived inconsistencies between actions and values or between contradictory values, as well as an exercise in public relations. That legitimation is sought does not mean it is achieved: no-one may be listening or the audience, including the lawyers themselves, may remain unconvinced. Legitimation is probably more often whistling in the dark than effective demagoguery. What is felt to need legitimation, what is done to achieve it, and what succeeds are all historically specific. This section analyses the ways in which the changes in the market for legal services described above stimulated new efforts at legitimation and how those efforts impinged upon the market.

The first task for an occupation that wishes to become a profession is to justify supply control; the nature of the justification will also influence how control is exercised and how effective it is. The legal profession invoked a multiplicity of warrants in the course of its emergence in the nineteenth century, residues of which are still visible. First, it sought an aristocratic aura (Larson 1977, Chap. 7): lawyers were gentlemen (American lawyers still insist on being called 'Esquire'). Traces of this association can be seen in the Commission's justification of the conveyancing monopoly: 'by virtue of long-standing tradition, solicitors are able to exchange undertakings amongst themselves . . . knowing that they will be honoured' (21–25). If law is not trade but an aristocratic calling then lawyers can claim to be altruistic. Thus the Commission argues that the divided profession is actually inimical to the interests of both branches, whose 'members would find some advantages in a fused profession' (17–13).[46] An alternative strategy, if one that is fundamentally inconsistent, is to deny that the profession controls production and insist that the market itself governs through impersonal laws of supply and demand: 'in all occupations and walks of life there is an ebb and flow' (33–38).

Neither tactic is adequate to the present task. A market explanation cannot be maintained in the face of the abundant evidence of professional manipulation.[47] Aristocratic warrants have also been rendered obsolete. Though they may ground a claim to character, the rise of capitalism and the subsequent growth of the welfare state increasingly demand technical competence from lawyers. This, then, becomes and has remained the fundamental justification for supply control:

when a profession is fully developed it may be described as a body of men and women . . . recognised as having a special skill and learning in some field of activity in which the public needs protection against incompetence, the standards of skill and learning being prescribed by the profession itself. . . . (3–19, quoting the evidence of the Law Society to the Monopolies Commission in 1968; see also 3–18b).

Hence the introduction of professional instruction, examinations, and apprenticeship programmes. But in order to strengthen this image of professionals as the sole masters of the necessary technical complexity of law there is a tendency to assimilate it to the archetypical example of contemporary esoteric learning – the sciences – whose practical achievements have made them the paradigm, virtually the only model, of valued knowledge.

Because science is produced, and scientists reproduced, in the university, there is constant pressure to make it the *locus* of legal education. The profession successfully resisted this for nearly a century, but after the Second World War another social vector converged: the growing demand for equality. Apprenticeship appears to be (and is) a particularistic means of recruitment controlled by the profession itself; the university appears to be (if it is not) universalistic and outside professional control.[48] Consequently, the university has become virtually the sole mode of entry into the legal profession.

The Commission is concerned to strengthen the symbolic power of the credentialing process as a warrant of scientific competence by playing down sociability and the acquisition of useless knowledge (which speak to aristocratic values) and emphasizing academic scholarship. Thus it notes approvingly that examinations for the Bar 'ceased to be mainly tests of memory; in style and content, they became similar to university examination papers' (39–45). It recommends that 'the compulsory eating of dinners should be abolished' unless it can be shown that dining in hall actually involves the instruction of students by barristers and benchers (39–55). It is even more critical of the system of articles and urges that the vocational stage be placed under academic control unless it is promptly reformed (39–73–90). And it applauds the growth of continuing education, a trebling of courses and a doubling of places between 1972–6, and even suggests that this be made mandatory for both branches (39–82, 86–90).[49]

But if rigorous, extended academic education justifies entry control by symbolizing the acquisition of scientific skills, it offers a less satisfactory response to the demand for equality. For meritocracy contains an inherent contradiction. It proclaims that entry is open to all:

Anyone who is able to qualify is entitled to attempt to establish a practice (33–39).

What is required in the future is that a person of ability is not excluded from the opportunity of setting up in practice for want of wealth or connections (33–48; see also 36–26, 39–7).

The Commission thus implicitly suggests that there is equality of opportunity because 'ability' is distributed randomly and impersonal standards of competence rather than biased individuals determine who is admitted. Yet its own evidence falsifies this claim: the children of professional and managerial families are over-represented at the Bar by 3:1 (in comparison to their proportion of the population) and those of fathers in manual occupations are under-represented by 1:10 (II: table 2.1). Nevertheless, the Commission rejects the criticism that the present mode of qualification is class or race biased and places any blame for the situation (together with responsibility for its solution) upon the system of primary and secondary education (33–44, 39–5; but see Jencks 1972, 1980). This is not likely to satisfy those who find themselves disqualified.

The university, as the new gatekeeper of the profession, not only excludes certain segments of the population without adequate justification, it also lets in too many people. As we have seen, it is this erosion of professional supply control, leading to an overproduction of producers, that forced the profession to turn to demand creation as an additional strategy of market control. This shift brings with it new problems of legitimation, as well as new resources for the task. Instead of explaining why only some can produce legal services, the profession must now show why everyone *needs* legal services and why the state should help to satisfy those needs. For this purpose, the aristocratic warrant originally invoked to justify supply control is not just unhelpful but downright obstructive. The Commission appears to recognise this:

It must be accepted by the profession as a whole that, for reasons which are complex and often long-standing, its image is not satisfactory (3–27). It has been said that sections of the public find lawyers remote and unapproachable (3–36).

Furthermore, it acknowledges that the traditional relationship between the 'family solicitor' and the middle or upper class client has largely atrophied (2–20, II: 8–141). The reasons are clear: the strategy of demand creation requires a mass clientèle; this can only be drawn from working class and poor populations who are inevitably fearful and suspicious of professionals; furthermore, this group must be persuaded to accept a routinized service, not to seek a personal relationship with a solicitor.[50]

But the real problem is not convincing people that they need legal services: law centres and private practitioners specialising in legal aid have no shortage of clients.[51] It is rather to legitimate the expenditure of public funds to pay for such services. Two main arguments are advanced. The first is equality: 'all who receive legal services are entitled to expect the same standard of legal service irrespective of their personal circumstances' (5–5).[52] Starting from this principle, the Commission then cites the inequalities in lawyer use by age, gender, socio-economic status, and property ownership revealed by the User Survey (II: 8–33–36) in order to justify the growth of legal aid that has alredy occurred and the futher expansion it advocates. Furthermore, it proposes to eliminate the eligibility ceilings on income and wealth, thereby enrolling the middle class as beneficiaries, and presumably enlisting them as supporters, of the programme (12–29–32). The second argument is the increasing need to protect the individual against the state. Since state coercion is most obvious in criminal prosecutions, legal aid has first been granted there.[53] Only later is it extended to civil litigation[54] and finally to administrative hearings as the 'new property' they regulate increases in significance with the growth of the welfare state.

It is possible to trace the way in which these legitimations affect both the expansion of publicly subsidized demand that has occurred (or is proposed) and its limits. The Commission recommends extending legal aid as of right to those accused or convicted of crimes in virtually all circumstances – in custody before trial, when contemplating an appeal after conviction, or in prison following final judgment (9–11, 23–24, 14–9, 14–17) – and urges either eliminating contributions (in most cases) or making them discretionary (in the rest) (11–13, 14–31).[55] But it is far more tentative in endorsing legal aid before tribunals, proposing that it be discretionary and highly selective and require contributions; and it still feels the need to offer evidence that those without representation are disadvantaged (15–9–10, 28 and table 15.1, II: 4). For even if the importance of administrative hearings is acknowledged, law may not be the best protection against arbitrariness, and the public may not even want it (15–12).

Equality also has drawbacks as a legitimating principle. It can argue not only *for* expansion of legal aid but also *against* it once some minimum level of representation has been reached.[56] It can justify a formal equality that hides substantive inequality (cf. Abel 1979a).[57] It can inhibit affirmative efforts to redress inequality. Thus the Commission condemns law centres for representing tenants but not landlords (8–10–32d) and recommends that organisations like the TUC be denied public support because they only assist their own members before tribunals (15–21). Support for equality may be insufficient to overcome opposition to legal aid that is fundamentally political.[58]

The shift from a strategy of supply control to one of demand creation affects other legitimation tasks of the profession: assuring buyers of quality and justifying price and income. The profession has traditionally warranted quality by invoking the market:

a professional person, like any person conducting a business, is subject to the discipline that his livelihood is dependent upon the quality of his work. If he carries on his practice with competence, his reputation spreads and he attracts work and clients. If he does not produce the quality of work and service which is expected, his reputation suffers and he soon begins to lose clients and fails to attract new ones. A single lapse can be very damaging and one serious mistake may lead to an irretrievable loss of reputation . . . a single mistake can lead to bankruptcy (25–2, 3, see also 36–34).

This is a transparent rationalisation: if taken seriously, it would destroy the entire structure of control that professionals have constructed to protect themselves from the vagaries of the market. It is not only hyperbolic, lawyers make mistakes all the time and few go bankrupt. It is fundamentally dishonest. The profession denies the public the very information it would need to judge quality, and the Commission approves (27–36). Indeed, one of the foundations of professionalism is the assertion that the laity are incompetent to judge the quality of service. Consequently, as the Report shows, and other research confirms, client evaluation of professional performance is based on the *form* in which those services are rendered, the equivalent of the doctor's bedside manner, not their substance: client dissatisfaction correlates most strongly with inattention by solicitors, insufficient action, delay, and failure to communicate (II: 8–210–11, see also Curran 1977, pp. 210–14, Steele and Nimmer 1976, pp. 254–6).

This solution to the problem of assuring quality is rendered even less satisfactory by the shift to demand creation. The mass of new users have neither personal knowledge of, nor an ongoing relationship with, nor intermediaries who can vouch for the quality of, a solicitor (cf. Llewellyn 1938, pp. 115–16). At the same time, the fact that the state is now paying for those services intensifies the pressure for quality control (see Rosenthal 1976, Carlson 1976). The Commission therefore invokes another warrant we have encountered before – credentials for entry: because practitioners passed a difficult set of hurdles in their early twenties the services they render for the next forty years will be of high calibre (22–6a). Merely to state that legitimation is to reveal its flimsiness, and it would only marginally be strengthened if continuing education were made mandatory (22–6b). The Commission therefore proposes to supplement input controls with improved output controls. It urges the Law Society to promulgate written standards of professional conduct, use its powers of inspection to oversee the internal efficiency of solicitors' firms, and investigate public complaints of incompetence; and it recommends that local law societies establish panels of solicitors willing to represent clients asserting claims of malpractice (3–35, 22–51–52–58, 25–17–30–35). Yet its purpose is not to control quality but to *appear* to do so: 'we had evidence of a general feeling of unease about the Law Society's handling of complaints, a feeling that "lawyers look after their own". This is damaging to the profession and we make suggestions . . . we believe will be helpful in this respect' (25–34). The record of the profession in sanctioning serious misconduct (detailed below) does not encourage optimism about its commitment to, or efficacy in, correcting incompetence. This attempt at legitimation is likely to fail.

Public demand creation also aggravates two other closely-related perennial problems of the legal profession (and others): justifying the prices of services and the level of incomes. A frequent response is to dismiss them out of hand: the public are incompetent to judge –

'the amount and nature of the work involved in, and the benefit resulting from, a professional service are hard for a layman to assess'; and the complaints are baseless – 'the level of lawyers' earnings taken overall is not, in our view, excessive' (3–30, 31).[59] But this will not suffice. Public dissatisfaction with the cost of legal services is known to be widespread (e.g. Abel-Smith *et al*. 1973, pp. 249–50, Curran 1977, pp. 230–31). It was confirmed by the Commission's own research (II: 8–308 and table 8.48); and indeed criticism of the fees of barristers in legal aid matters was the immediate stimulus for establishing the Commission (Zander 1976, 1980). The first line of defence, as always, is the market.

One witness criticised the fact that counsel who specialise in certain classes of work are able to command high fees. . . . Provided that no artificial restrictions are imposed on the right to offer specialist professional services, we see no objection in principle to allowing such services to command their market value (36–35).

The fact that barristers work in a free and competitive market, in relation to fee-paying clients, results in the wide range of earnings at all levels of the Bar. The level of fees allowed on taxation are, even so, of considerable importance to barristers for two reasons: first, fees are directly controlled by taxation in all legally-aided work and secondly, the level of fees allowed by taxing masters sets an acknowledged market value for services (37–87).

These are hardly 'free markets,' quite apart from the fact that the Commission and the profession are on record as opposing price competition (27–36). In the first, the supply of services *is* 'artificially restricted' by professional control of the number of QCs – there are only about 10 barristers, and even fewer QCs, who specialise in defamation, the subject of that quotation. In the second, less than half the work of barristers is performed for fee-paying clients, and even the Commission concedes that the level of fees in such cases is virtually determined by what the taxing master allows in legally-aided work, which is fixed by the state (37–75).

The fall-back position, again, is meritocracy:

it is necessary to accept that the provision of legal services, which calls for the expenditure of time by skilled people, cannot be cheap (3–31).

There is nothing in the evidence before us to suggest that barristers or solicitors in private practice command a significantly higher return for their investment of training, professional skill and responsibility than others who provide services of a comparable character. . . . (36–29).[60]

Such a justification simply *assumes* what is to be proved – that income *should* be stratified by occupation; the Commission compares lawyers with physicians, architects, consulting engineers, and management in industry and commerce, not with manual workers or school teachers (II: 20). What little explanation it offers for this choice is buried within the phrase 'investment of opportunity'. But whereas the opportunity costs that a lawyer invests in qualifying, approximately five years of work foregone in a working life of nearly fifty, might possibly justify an income ten per cent higher than that of the school leaver, the actual difference is several hundred per cent. The argument is even weaker if investment is measured by out-of-pocket expenses. For one thing, the level of return (the income differential across a lifetime, surely more than £100,000) is many times greater than the individual's investment (surely less than £10,000). For another, most of the cost of training is paid by the state (39–91–112). The privileged incomes of lawyers, and of all professionals, are thus an extreme example of that fundamental characteristic of advanced capitalism: the costs of production, of producers, are socialised but the profits, from the sale of legal services, are privately appropriated.[61]

But perhaps the strongest pressure to justify lawyers' fees and incomes comes from the fact that they are increasingly paid by the state (as discussed at the end of the previous section). The result is an extraordinary apparatus for determining fees: the assessment of solicitors' non-contentious fees by the Law Society (21–89–90), the taxation of costs by taxing masters (37–8–10–33), the calculation of bills by independent specialist cost draftsmen (37–26), and the proposed Fees Advisory Council (21–87–95, 37–91–94). There are several reasons for interpreting this structure as a means of legitimation. Clients hardly ever use some of the procedures: for instance, they asked for taxation of solicitors' charges in only 0.2 per cent of all matters in 1978 (37–8). The Commission can therefore recommend that clients be informed about this option, and laypersons co-opted into it, confident that it will not be used (37–13, 14). In other processes clients rarely obtain a reduction in their fees (table 37.1). And the review frequently costs more than it saves (37–36). Hence none of the mechanisms for legitimating prices and incomes, market, meritocracy, or third-party review, is likely to succeed.

Thus far I have considered the problems of legitimation that derive from the professional project of controlling supply and creating demand. A third set of tasks is attributable to the effect of that project upon the structure of productive relations, espeically the

transformation of the labour force. I described above the growing
heterogeneity of the profession in terms of race, gender, and even
class. But if the elimination of explicit entry barriers may help to
blur the image of the profession as a white, male, upper-class
enclave, it simultaneously introduces a new problem that may be
more difficult to resolve – legitimating the allocation of entrants to
roles. We have already seen that ethnic minorities tend to be
ghetto-ized in a small number of chambers. The same is true of
women (70 per cent of women barristers are found in 30 per cent of
the sets of chambers, II: 15–17), who also tend to be restricted to
less remumerative specialties at the Bar, underpaid, and under-
represented among QCs and leading firms of solicitors.[62] The Commission responds with the usual excuses for prejudice, blaming the
victim – ethnic minorities like it that way and women are 'lost to the
demands of the family', and non-professionals – women, 'may be
less acceptable to clients', insisting that discrimination has
diminished, and denying that it exists (35–17–19–34). These various accounts are not only inconsistent, they are also contradicted by
the Commission's own evidence. Professional stratification is the
result of highly particularistic methods of placement. A pupillage is
found largely through personal contacts (39–65–66) and so are
articles. Most aspiring clerks had to make an average of 29 applications in order to obtain three interviews and one offer, but a
privileged one-third used personal contacts and required many
fewer applications in order to secure articles (II: 1–9). One-fourth
of women barristers experienced discrimination in seeking a pupillage and half in seeking a tenancy (II: table 15.7).

 The Commission therefore turns to proposals intended 'to prevent even the appearance of discrimination in legal practice' (35–
39). It would be more accurate to say that the Commission and the
profession are concerned to prevent *only* the appearance of discrimination, not the reality. They rely wholly on exhortation, the
formation of committees, publication of guidelines, and proclama-
tion of policies (35–20–30, 33, 39–45). Experience has shown that
such measures are largely futile. Yet the Commission and the
profession reject any form of coercive remedy as 'demeaning' to the
person who has suffered discrimination (35–29).[63] Ultimately, the
Commission falls back upon defences of discrimination that the US
Supreme Court condemned in *Brown* v. *Board of Education* (347
US 83. 1954) twenty-five years ago: people have a right to their

prejudices, you can't legislate morality: 'Associations between practitioners should be a matter for free choice' (33–39).

Heterogeneity also threatens the capacity of lawyers to govern themselves, an essential element of their claim to professional status. New categories of professionals are grossly underrepresented in the governing bodies. Women are 6.5 per cent of solicitors but have only one member on the Council of the Law Society (1.4 per cent) and no committee members; they are 8 per cent of the Bar but only 2 per cent of the Senate and smaller proportions of the benchers of each Inn (32–38, 35–9–10, 14); ethnic minorities apparently have no voice in the governance of either branch. Other changes in the labour force have also led to the emergence of large disenfranchised groups. Although half of all solicitors' firms have one or two principals, none of the 70 members of the Council of the Law Society is a sole practitioner and only three are from two-member firms (29–25, II: table 16.4). Provincial solicitors in small firms have responded by forming an alternative professional association which has grown to nearly 10 per cent of the size of the Law Society (29–9–11 and table 29.1).[64] At the Bar the salient division is not firm size but age. In the face of the enormously rapid increase in the proportion of junior barristers, authority is more gerontocratic than ever: the Inns are governed by a self-perpetuating group of some 350–400 benchers, only a third of whom are practising barristers (32–3, 60). All of these problems are likely to intensify in the future as the numbers of women and minority lawyers, and younger practitioners increase and solicitors' firms continue to grow in size.[65]

The Commission's response is threefold. First, it proposes that membership in the professional association be made compulsory, or virtually so, presumably to paper over these numerous divisions (29–29–32, 32–78h). Second, it recommends centralization and rationalization of administration to subordinate the regional organizations and the Inns that have been a focus of resistance to planning (29–43–47, 32–54, 69). Third, it urges the adoption of reified democratic forms to legitimate the authority of these strengthened organizations in the eyes of those who will have to become members but will have less protection from other mediating organizations. It counsels the profession that 'the different sizes and types of practice and the various specialisms . . . should be represented on [the governing body]. Control should not be vested in a single group or sector and there should not be an established governing clique' (29–16). Yet mere exhortation will not be enough if past experience is any guide. There has never been a contested election for President of the Council of the Law Society, the Vice-Presidency was last disputed in 1953, and there are hardly any serious fights over seats on the Council (table 29.2 and Annex 29–1–7). It recommends that only 60 of the 101 persons in the Senate of the Bar should be elected by barristers (32–70). And it opposes the reservation of seats on the governing body for women, not even mentioning ethnic minorities (35–29). It seems reasonable to predict that the oligarchy will remain intact even if these proposals are implemented and will continue to breed alienation.

If self-regulation is endangered by changes within the legal profession, it is also threatened from without. To the extent that the privilege rests on the claim that members of the profession are all of the highest character, it is undermined by the relative loss of supply control and the entry of people who have lower ascribed status in the eyes of the (prejudiced) public. To the extent that it rests on a claim of altruism, it is undermined by the conspicuous efforts of the profession to stimulate demand. But self-regulation is undermined most gravely by the increasing role of the state in subsidizing legal services: he who pays the piper calls the tune and is entitled to do so. The Commission and the profession seek to resist this powerful logic by repeatedly invoking the shibboleth of 'independence':[66] 'Legal services are required more and more by private individuals who are in dispute with authority in one of its many forms and to protect the interests of clients in such cases, the independence of the legal profession is of paramount importance' (5–7). Yet the dependence of the profession on the state is so blatant that even the Commission is forced to concede that the public are entitled to participate in governance. Its recommendations therefore strive to foster the appearance of participation while preserving the reality of professional autonomy. Thus it proposes: a Fees Advisory Committee (21–95, 37–89–98), a Council on Legal Services (6–17), consultation with the public in the development of standards of professional conduct (22–59, 25–21) and the selection of QCs (33–89), lay representation on the Law Society committees that issue remuneration certificates (37–14), and participation by lay persons in committees of the Law Society and the Senate, though not as members of those bodies themselves (29–40–41, 32–77). In each instance, however, the lay members are either a distinct minority of, if a bare majority, likely to defer to the professionals (cf. Arthurs, this volume).

The tenuous legitimacy of self-regulation can be seen most clearly in the failure of lawyers to discipline misconduct, an essential ingredient in their claim to professional status (3–18–19). Professional disciplinary processes, unlike most regulatory agencies, are completely reactive.

Clients, however, are virtually disabled from perceiving misconduct, not by accident, and professionals are not disposed to tattle on each other – they file less than a quarter of the small number complaints received from the public (Annex 22–1 and tables 22.9.11; cf. Steele and Nimmer 1976, p.973, Carlin 1966, p. 153). Even when clients feel aggrieved they do not mobilize the disciplinary apparatus: two-thirds do nothing, two-ninths speak only to the solicitor or his firm, and a mere 2 per cent complain to the Law Society (II: 8–350–51), perhaps because only 17 per cent of respondents in the Users' Survey knew about its disciplinary functions (22–13, cf. Steele and Nimmer 1976, pp. 962–3). Starting from this totally inadequate base of reported grievances, the Law Society appears extraordinarily lenient. Ninety out of 100 grievances are dismissed at the outset and 9 out of the remaining 10 are disposed without trial. In 1978, for instance, 5,006 complaints were filed: 4,958 (99 per cent) were dismissed without sanction; 23 solicitors (0.5 per cent) were reprimanded; 8 (0.2 per cent) had conditions imposed on their practice certificates the following year; and only 17 (0.3 per cent) were subjected to a trial that could lead to suspension or being struck from the rolls (25–31–33). Out of 47 cases in the last category during an eight-month period in 1978–9, 8 received a reprimand, 17 a fine of less than £750, 6 a suspension of less than five years, and 14 were struck from the rolls (25–48). If we combine these figures we can trace a pattern of systematic undersanctioning: 2 out of every 100 felt grievances reach the Law Society; 2 out of 1,000 are investigated; 2 out of 100,000 go to trial; and less than 1 out of 100,000 is penalized by suspension or more.[67]

The Commission recognizes that such a dismal record encourages mistrust and makes a number of recommendations designed to dispel suspicion: public assurances that the Law Society will fully investigate every complaint, differentiation of the prosecutorial and adjudicative functions, conciliation by local law societies, introduction of milder penalties, and co-optation of lay members onto investigative and adjudicatory bodies (25–24, 34, 36, 40, 45, 47, 50).

Yet none of these go to the root of undersanctioning, nor do they asset effective public control over discipline; at most they are likely to increase the number of penalties imposed at the cost of decreasing their severity (Steele and Nimmer 1976, pp. 935–46).[68]

The Commission has sought to enhance the legitimacy of the legal profession by offering justifications for, and proposing changes in, its control of supply, creation of demand, the quality and price of services rendered, its income, the allocation of professional roles, and the privilege of self-governance, including its responsibility for discipline. The Commission makes no bones about its objective:

> there have been a large number of inquiries of various kinds in recent years which have, directly or indirectly, affected the profession. . . . When the necessary decisions and action on our recommendations have been taken, a process of quiet and orderly consolidation will be needed to enable the profession to develop its service to the public without interruption and changes of course (3–16–17).

In other words – lay off! But the goal of legitimacy is never attained. The effort to legitimate is compelled by contradictions within the profession and in the larger society that cannot be resolved without radical change. Until that occurs, 'the temper of our times to subject all institutions and organisations to close scrutiny' will prevail (3–28).

The Future of the Market for Legal Services

Contemporary professions, including the legal profession, reached maturity during the latter half of the nineteenth century (Larson 1977). Although they arose in the context of triumphant capitalism and an increasingly intrusive bourgeois state, they claimed to be exempt from capitalist logic and state domination. Indeed, professions present themselves as a timeless, ahistorical ideal. But if 'professionalism' retains considerable power as an ideology (or aspiration) for many occupational categories, it is far more transitory as a functioning social institution. The latter half of the twentieth century may witness the demise of the professions. Let me elaborate this argument using the analysis of the legal profession presented in this paper.

The divided profession arose out of a number of competing

specialties: 'At first the practitioners in each sphere operated independently. Gradually they came to group together' not, as the Commission says, parroting the Law Society, 'with the object of extending their knowledge' (3–19), but in order to suppress competition among themselves and from outsiders. But the attempt to eliminate or at least reduce competition within a common market was always problematic. In recent years, the threat of increased competition has not only strengthened existing divisions between barristers and solicitors but has also inspired new categories of specialists to seek protection by carving out their own spheres in an increasingly segmented market: employed lawyers, solicitors' firms serving large commercial clients, lawyers who depend upon the public sector, and academic lawyers. The core relationship between the lawyer and an undifferentiated market for legal services, upon which rests the tenuous unity of the profession, has dissolved.

Professions justify their control of the market by claiming that they alone are qualified 'to give advice or service in a specialised field of knowledge' (3–18b). This boast of exclusive competence is substantiated by making 'admission to full membership . . . dependent upon a period of theoretical and practical training in the course of which it is necessary to pass examinations . . . (3–18c). But we have seen that the very foundation of contemporary professionalism significantly contributes to its downfall. First, it transfers control over entry from the profession to the college or university. Academic lawyers consequently assume major responsibility for the development of legal knowledge; because their frame of reference is higher education and scholarship, legal knowledge ceases to be autonomous and is strongly influenced by, or even subsumed within, other disciplines – economics being the fad of the moment. Second, the meritocratic foundation is itself fundamentally contradictory, since it is predicated on the value of equality but actually produces gross inequality. Third, just as the market for legal services has fractured, so many specialised sub-fields of knowledge have been constructed by sub-categories of lawyers seeking to re-establish their claim to exclusive cognitive competence, and thereby recapture control over supply. To the extent that these efforts are successful, and each one is highly problematic, the result will be proliferating categories of lawyers, each of which individually lacks the attributes of a profession but whose divergent interests make it as difficult for them to engage in unified action as a profession, as it is for the various branches of engineering or medicine to do so.

Giving colleges and universities significant control over professional entry was accompanied by a dramatic increase in the number of entrants. The legal profession responded to the threat of increased competition by seeking to create demand, both public and private. But this strategy, though providing temporary respite, has serious limitations. First, it can inflame, rather than appease, public hostility toward lawyers, who are seen as making work for themselves. Even if this does not occur, the public simply cannot be persuaded that they want legal services in the same way they can be convinced they need consumer goods. Law is not an attractive item even among services: contact with the law is almost invariably unpleasant, and the client, unlike the patient, rarely comes away feeling he is better off for having endured it. Second, there are limitations on what the state will subsidise, which are reached, and probably exceeded, by the Commission's recommendations; some are politicial, legal services can challenge the state's authority, but the more important limitations are fiscal (O'Connor 1973). Third, lawyers do not really want to satisfy the demand they are striving to create, especially not that subsidized by the state, for such work is relatively unprofitable and uninteresting and places the lawyer at the bottom of the status hierarchy. Furthermore, the services for which demand can be created tend to undermine the claim of the profession to exclusive cognitive competence: many are technically simple, e.g. representation at tribunal hearings. Indeed, the profession increasingly uses non-professionals to perform many tasks. But this strengthens the arguments of other occupations that seek to invade the professional monopoly.

Professionals are defined by the unique quality of their relationships with the persons for whom they perform services. 'In the case of lawyers this professional duty of maintaining the client's interests is paramount, subject only to their direct responsibility to the court' (3–18e). Lawyers claim to walk a tightrope, epitomized by the concept of independence, between fidelity to client and obligation to society; the lawyer's selfish interests are supposed to play no part (Simon 1978). Yet structural changes in the lawyer–client relationship have made it difficult, if not impossible, to maintain this balance. On the one hand, lawyers serve massive clients such as the state and large companies, which employ them or provide a significant portion of their income; self-interest, disguised as loyalty to client, is likely to outweigh obligation to society. On the other hand, lawyers serve individual one-off legally-aided clients; self-interest, disguised as obligation to society which, as state, is also the paymaster, is likely to outweigh loyalty to the client.

Related to this posture of independence is the lawyer's stance of autonomous individualism. Lawyers claim to be exempt from capitalist relations of production. They are neither bosses nor workers but pre-capitalist craftsmen. This image is best exemplified by the vanishing ethos of the nineteenth-century barrister who did not employ his clerk – an independent semi-professional, did not enter into partnership with other barristers, did not even have an enforceable contract with solicitor or client. Yet today virtually all solicitors are employees in their early years (articled clerks, assistant solicitors) and many lawyers remain employed throughout their careers. They also employ increasing numbers of subordinates. They do not practise alone but in firms with ever larger numbers of lawyers, some of which already contain more than 100 people. Those who preserve the ideal of the autonomous individual – the sole practitioner – are progressively marginalized.

Finally, a profession is differentiated from other occupations by the privilege of self-governance:

a profession is more than an aggregation of individuals. A governing body . . . represents a profession and is formally recognised as doing so; it has powers of control and discipline over its members.

A profession is given a measure of self-regulation so that it may require its members to observe higher standards than could be successfully imposed from without (3–18a, d).

The prerequisite for effective self-governance is homogeneity and community of interest among the governed. But lawyers today are divided by functional specialty, relationship to clients and especially to capital and state, social characteristics, age, gender, race, class, education, and structure of practice. Self-governance has visibly failed, whether the index is the level of membership and participation, the rise of competing professional associations, public respect, or the efficacy of the disciplinary process. Moreover, self-governance is increasingly challenged from without: employers expect to control their lawyer employees; large law firms are less easily subordinated to a professional association than are individual practitioners; but most important, the increasing role of the state in subsidising legal services entitles, and obligates, it to control quality, price, income, and discipline.

For little more than a century lawyers have enjoyed an unusual degree of immunity from capitalist relations of production. In the name of professionalism they have achieved considerable insulation from the market, dampening competition among themselves and restricting that by other occupations, taking pride in the quality of their work without being driven constantly to maximize profit, avoiding the dehumanization of either performing wage labour or exploiting the labour of others. They have also enjoyed an exemption from state intervention, a realisation of the laissez-faire ideals of liberalism. Yet these privileges are being drastically eroded. The lawyer today, and even more tomorrow, is an entrepreneur selling his services in an increasingly competitive market, an employee whose labour is exploited, an employer exploiting subordinates – all increasingly dependent upon state or capital for business and therefore increasingly subject to their control. Although the ideal of professionalism will undoubtedly linger on as an ever more anachronistic warrant of legitimacy the profession as an economic, social, and political institution is moribund.

Acknowledgements

I feel somewhat presumptuous, as an outsider, in offering this highly critical analysis, not from fear of seeming nationalistic – I am at least as critical of American lawyers (see Abel 1979a) – but because I am inevitably ignorant, and perhaps misinformed, about many aspects of the legal profession and society in the United Kingdom. I am therefore very grateful for the comments and criticism I received from the participants in the conference on 'Legal Services in the Eighties', and especially to Harry W. Arthurs, John Basten, Bryant Garth, Quintin Johnstone, Deborah Rhode, Robert Stevens, and Michael Zander.

Notes

1. Of those enrolled as students with the Law Society, three-quarters consistently pass the Solicitors' First Examination the following year (II: tables 1.3.4). Of those registered in articles, more than 90 per cent are enrolled as solicitors two

years later (II: tables 1.4.5). The number of students called to the Bar as a proportion of those admitted to the Inns of Court the preceding year rose from 35 per cent in 1967 and 26 per cent in 1968 to 79 per cent in 1977 and 110 per cent in 1978 (II: table 1.11).

2. Just as the demographic changes in the American and British legal professions are quite similar (cf. York and Hale 1973), so the elimination of the ban against price competition was almost simultaneous (see *Goldfarb v. Virginia State Bar*, 95 S.Ct. 2004, 1975).

3. This may be one aspect of the pervasive capitalist crisis, viewed as a problem of underconsumption (see Sherman 1979).

4. These efforts appear to be inspired by a mistaken analogy between the individual and the business enterprise. Although both, of necessity, use lawyers for contentious matters, those constitute a small (and often relatively unprofitable) fraction of lawyers' work. Most solicitors spend most of their time engaged in facilitative tasks. Aside from the sale of real property and inter-generational transfers of wealth, individuals do not invoke the law facilitatively, and they may be incapable of doing so for structural reasons (Abel 1979a).

5. I am concerned here only with the impact of demand creation on *lawyers*. I do not want to imply that because lawyers seek to generate demand for reasons of self-interest, the results are necessarily inconsistent with the interests of *society*, although I do have reservations about publicly-subsidized legal services (Abel 1979a).

6. Of course, the actual historical sequence in any particular state is more complex than this. For instance, labour relations are less fully legalised in the UK than in the USA, although the former may be changing. Many welfare rights are still 'proto-legal' – capable of being made the subject of administrative hearings and judicial review even though this has not yet occurred. Social relations can also be delegalized (see Abel 1979b): simplification of divorce procedures led to a withdrawal of legal aid for uncontested divorces in 1977 and a drop of 62,000 civil legal aid certificates, about one-third of the total (Annex 2–3). On the other hand, although land registration was promoted in part as a means of reducing the need for legal services to ensure effective transfer of title (21–6– 9), new bodies of regulatory law concerned with landlord and tenant, planning, taxation, and the matrimonial home have sufficiently muddied the waters once again so that continued demand for professional assistance in conveyancing is virtually guaranteed (21–11).

7. See generally Morris *et al.* (1973a). Other advanced capitalist states discovered and sought to document unmet legal need at about the same time, e.g. the USA (Curran 1977, cf. Marks 1976), the Netherlands (Schuyt *et al.* 1977, cf. Griffiths 1977), France (Baraquin 1975, Valétas 1976), Germany (Tiemann and Blankenburg 1979), and Australia (Cass and Sackville 1975); see generally Cappelletti (1978–9).

8. There may, however, be significant local variation within smaller units, e.g. urban areas, which the Survey failed to measure.

9. Perhaps to overcome this the Commission urges more education about law in the schools (4–25).

10. Consumer advice centres receive 700,000 enquiries a year; the approximately 120 legal advice centres, in which private practitioners volunteer, handled 200,000 cases a year until the central government withdrew funding; and trade unions and government offices service countless others (2–6–8).

11. American lawyers offer *pro bono* services for much the same reason (see Lochner 1975).

12. Legal aid in the UK is already at a level of *per capita* expenditure approximately three times as high as in the US, and about ten times as large a proportion of the total market for legal services.

13. Although four-fifths of the sampled population knew of the programme and three-fifths knew it was for lower income people (II: 8–402) there is other evidence suggesting widespread ignorance (Morris *et al.* 1973b, Byles and Morris 1977). Several American studies have shown that people consistently exaggerate the cost of legal services (e.g. Marks *et al.* 1974). The Commission also recommends that potential clients be told in advance the full extent of their contribution required if legal aid is rendered (12–34) – a degree of predictability it does not feel lawyers can give *paying* clients (37–16).

14. This may misconceive the real reasons for solicitor distaste: legal aid work is repetitive, insignificant, and confers low status (Katz 1978).

15. Even so, legal aid expenditures increased rapidly: from £9.4 million in 1967–8 to a projected £110 million in 1979–80 (Glasser 1979, p. 203), a 60 per cent increase (at constant prices) between 1973–4 and 1978–9, compared with the 10 per cent increase in total public expenditures; the legal aid budget was projected to increase another 20 per cent by 1982–3 even without the proposed reforms (Notes of Dissent 5–34).

16. The Royal Commission on Criminal Procedure recommends that solicitors be substituted for police prosecutors. This will undoubtedly create a comparable demand for more defence counsel (cf. *Argersinger v. Hamlin*, 407 US 25, 1972).

17. Of course, the biggest problem is persuading the state to spend the money, which the present government is very unlikely to do.

18. This is exemplified by distribution of government activities and business along geographic or regional lines and more recently to counteract inequalities of race and gender.

19. By contrast, the (US) Legal Services Corporation (1979, p. 29) only spent 2 per cent of its 1980 budget on management.

20. This admittedly crude estimate (100,000) was reached by averaging the August 1978 caseloads for the 28 schemes mentioned in the Report (9–4) and extrapolating over a year for the 107 extant schemes.

21. The Commission recommends a further parallel: courts and tribunals should alert parties to the availability of legal aid in much the way that the duty solicitor scheme introduces such information into prisons (27–8).

22. It is noteworthy that similar reversals occurred almost contemporaneously in the United States (*Bates v. State Bar of Arizona*, 97 S.Ct. 2691, 1977) and Australia (Law Society Journal, June 1980, pp. 309–10). In the USA professional restraints upon advertising have also been struck down in optometry (Los Angeles Times, 25 May 1978, Part I, p. 22; but see *Friedman v. Rogers*, 99 S.Ct. 887, 1979), architecture (Los Angeles Times, *loc. cit.*), and medicine (Los Angeles Times, 23 July 1980, Part I, p. 4). Yet the American experience displays just as many contradictions: some advertising is allowed but not all, (*Bates, supra*); advertising is allowed but not solicitation (*Ohralik v. Ohio State Bar Association*, 98 S.Ct. 1912, 1978); public interest lawyers can solicit but not those who practise for profit (*In re Primus*, 98 S.Ct. 1893, 1978).

23. A similar dynamic has operated in the United States, where poverty lawyers (ABA Code of Professional Responsibility, DR2–102(D)(i)) and public interest lawyers (Oregon Rules for Public Interest Law Firms) were allowed to advertise before private practitioners.

24. Certification of specialists in the United States has repeatedly been analysed, and criticised, as a means of restoring supply control to older practitioners (Pedrick 1970, Hochberg 1976).

25. Martin Partington (this volume) has noted the difficulty of persuading CAB clients to consult a solicitor. Universalistic mechanisms are also shunned in the United States; lawyer referral services, though actively promoted by the organised profession, (Berg 1979, ABA Code of Professional Responsibility DR 2–102(D)(3)), are barely used by the public because they fail to provide the information the public want in choosing a lawyer (Christensen 1970, Chap. 5).

26. Increased dependence upon the public sector has the same consequence, since it is virtually impossible to extract from the state annual increases equal to the rate of inflation.

27. The extraordinary success of the profession in exercising market control until recently is shown by the extent to which it has remained labour intensive, largely ignoring technological innovation. This is nicely illustrated by a passing remark in the Report. The Commission notes that all but one set of London chambers are located within the Inns, and explains

> it is important for the clerk to a set of chambers to have early and accurate information about future court hearings. . . . Until more modern methods of communication become established, such as a telex network or closed-circuit television, barristers practising at any distance from the Inns would be at a disadvantage in this respect (33–10).

> Communication across a few blocks within London is too difficult in 1979 – although instantaneous communication around the world is perfectly feasible!
>   For reasons that are historical, the English legal profession appears to rely more heavily on subordinated labour than the American (see Johnstone and Flood 1980) even though the former enjoyed more stringent supply control. What I am seeking to describe and explain *here* are contemporary changes in productive relations: both national professions appear to be experiencing an increase in subordinated labour in response to similar stimuli.

28. It is equally important to resist subordination to other occupations. Thus the Commission rejects the notion of partnerships between solicitors and non-lawyers (30–2–15). Its explicit arguments are unconvincing, since solicitors can employ and be employed by non-lawyers. The Commission's real fear is that 'it would be easier for large firms of estate agents to take in one or more solicitor partners than for firms of solicitors to recruit estate agents on level terms' (30–7).

29. This history may help to explain why legal executives did not challenge the solicitors' conveyancing monopoly (31–26). Large law firms in the United States maintain the subordination of their qualified 'associates' for a period of five to ten years through the same process of overspecialisation; the Law Society subordinates newly qualified solicitors for three years by means of a formal rule (38–33).

30. Another survey showed assistant solicitors increasing 72 per cent from 1966–76, while the number of solicitors grew 46 per cent (31–9–10) or 43 per cent (II: table 16.9). During the same period the number of legal executives grew only 16 per cent (31–9–10) or actually decreased 6 per cent (II: table 16.9), which may be related to the fact that their continued subordination to solicitors renders the career less attractive.

31. Average capital per principal in 1976 was £12,660 (36–79) and there were 5 staff per principal (II: table 16.10).

32. The fourth column, gross earnings per pound invested in labour, is not net profit, of course, since the principal must also pay office expenses and maintain a (small) capital investment. Even so, these figures are quite high, especially when compared with the so-called 'rule of thirds' in US law firms, where

associates are expected to generate gross earnings sufficient to provide equal shares for associate salary, overhead, and partner profit (cf. Hoffman 1973, p. 118; but see Liebowitz and Tollison 1978). If I am correct about this difference, it may help to explain why English principals have five to ten times as many subordinated employees as do American partners (Johnstone and Flood 1980, p. 30).

33. Yet the above table suggests that larger firms are also able to extract more surplus value from each employee.

34. The practice of taking a percentage of the barrister's fee is not only a symbol of professional status but also strongly correlated with the level of earnings (34–14). Clerks lost their right to collct a separate fee a decade ago, at the time of decimalisation (34–19).

35. The Commission, with false naivete, accepts these figures as purely fortuitous (33–91).

36. The Commission's justifications, conflict of interest and client choice, are not persuasive. The first is not a problem in the USA and though the Bar in England and Wales is much smaller, other changes could compensate for this, e.g. allowing the number of chambers to increase or, more radically, fusing the profession. The second is one of those arguments that is repeatedly invoked despite (or perhaps because of) its largely fictitious nature: clients often choose a set of chambers (as though they were a partnership) rather than an individual barrister, and it is the clerk who actually assigns the brief (34–32–37; see also Flood, n.d.).

37. 45 sets in London and 13 in the provinces have more than 20 barristers. Both the Senate and the Commission explicitly oppose an upper limit on the size of sets (32–55). I believe that a set should be viewed as the unit of production for the reasons detailed above, even though profits are not shared.

38. Concentration, like many of the other processes described in this paper, is more fully developed in the USA. In 1979 there were 89 firms with over 100 lawyers; the twenty largest firms ranged from 192 to 512 lawyers and had offices in an average of five different cities (National Law Journal 1979, see Galanter 1981). Legal clients for middle class individuals show the same tendency: Jacoby and Meyers, the largest, has offices in more than 35 cities in three states and has become one of the 100 largest law firms in the country in less than ten years.

39. Among solicitors, for instance, company law is far more remunerative than most contentious work (II: tables 16.58.64). Among barristers, London Chancery and specialist practice is generally fifty per cent more profitable than London criminal practice (II: table 18.15).

40. The exclusion of aliens from state Bars was struck down by the United States Supreme Court almost contemporaneously (*In re Griffiths*, 413 US 717, 1973). Women overcame the barriers to entry into the US legal profession at about the same time and in similar numbers as they did in the UK; token numbers of racial minorities entered earlier than they did in the UK, and the recent increase in the US has been much more substantial (see generally Auerbach 1976, Abel 1980, pp. 359–62).

41. Once again, there are antecedents in the ethnic and class stratification of the US legal profession (Ladinsky 1963, Carlin 1966).

42. For US parallels, see Auerbach (1971); see generally Larson (1977, pp. 44–5, 153–4). Academic lawyers are already among the most outspoken critics of the legal profession (e.g. Abel-Smith and Stevens 1967, Zander 1968), as participation in the Cardiff conference amply demonstrated.

43. Eighty per cent of all solicitors' firms have never calculated expense rates, but larger firms are more likely to do so, and firms are growing larger (II: table 16.13).

44. The eclipse of charitable legal aid by the federally funded Legal Services Program in the US in 1965 generated similar demands for public 'account-ability' — which in practice meant political conservatism (see e.g. Johnson 1974, Stumpf 1975).

45. 'Our contacts abroad have left us in no doubt that the standing of our legal profession is high in the eyes of the rest of the world' (3–14).

46. Like so many attempts at legitimation, this proves too much. If a divided profession serves public rather than selfish interests, then legal executives can seek recognition as a third branch in the name of altruism. The Commission is forced to backtrack:

    the greater the number of branches in the profession, the more likely it would be that a client would be forced to go from one practitioner to another in order to complete even a straightforward transaction . . . we consider that the creation of additional branches of the profession would be contrary to the public interest (31–32)

47. This does not mean that market justifications cease to be invoked; indeed, it is characteristic of legitimation to call upon anachronistic values. Thus when the Commission turns to demand creation it advances a fiction as an ideal: 'Advertising is inherent in any free or mixed economy and helps the consumer exercise the choice between competing products or services which characterises such economies' (27–31). In fact, advertising seeks to stimulate the public to consume legal services while denying them the information necessary to make rational choices (cf. Galbraith 1976).

48. Just as legitimation is enhanced by divesting the profession of control over the production *of* 'producers', so the Commission proposes to remove control over production *by* producers (i.e. responsibility for prosecuting breaches of the professional monopoly) since 'the Law Society . . . is bound to appear merely to be protecting the financial interests of its members . . . [and is] anxious to give up this function' (21–62).

49. Although continuing education and re-certification may initially be resisted by older practitioners, it will actually serve to strengthen their claim to superior competence, enhance their competitive position *vis-à-vis* more recent entrants, and may ultimately restore a degree of professional control over entry to specialised sub-markets (see note 24, *supra*).

50. The Commission sometimes appears incapable of appreciating the effect of social distance in inhibiting mass demand. Noting the criticism of the wigs and gowns worn by barristers, it responds: 'Uniform or ceremonial dress are regularly to be encountered in many walks of life (33–98). And it attempts to dismiss public resentment of professionals as hypercritical, 'ill-founded, or unjust', an expression of the pretty animus of poor losers (3–27–28). The latter explanation will not wash: the Commission's own evidence shows only a weak relationship between outcome and client satisfaction with lawyer performance (II: 8–187–91; see also Casper 1978, Curran 1977, pp. 237–9).

51. See, e.g. Law Centres Working Group (n.d. Section 3). An excess of demand over supply has consistently been experienced by all legal services programmes in the USA (e.g. Johnson 1974, pp. 127–8, Silver 1969).

52. The first Chairman of the (US) Legal Services Corporation similarly declared: 'the board intends . . . to ensure that the poor receive the same quality and range of service that is provided to the rich' (Crampton 1975, p. 1342).

53. Thus the Commission invokes Article 6(3) of the European Convention of Human Rights (5–6). Similarly, the Sixth Amendment to the US Constitution has been held to require legal representation in criminal cases (*Gideon v. Wainwright*, 372 US 335, 1963; *Argersinger v. Hamlin*, 407 US 25, 1972).

54. The US Supreme Court has repeatedly refused to recognise a constitutional right to counsel in civil matters, although some state supreme courts have granted such a right under special circumstances, as when a person is forced to assume the responsibilities, or deprived of the rights, of parenthood (*Sales v. Cortez*, 154 Cal. Rptr. 529, 1979; *In re Jacqueline H.*, 145 Cal. Rptr. 548, 1978) or a prisoner is a civil defendant. (*Payne v. Superior Court*, 553 P.2d 565, Cal. 1976).

55. It seems reasonable to interpret the original requirement of contributions in criminal legal aid as acknowledging the uncertain legitimacy of state subsidization by stigmatizing its recipients. The usual economic explanations are unpersuasive: overconsumption of legal services by those accused of crime is highly improbable, and contributions recovered only 3 per cent of the cost of criminal legal aid (11–13). By contract because the 'need' for medical services was more widely accepted, the National Health Service was never saddled with contributions although these were required for prescription medicines, whose consumption was seen as more discretionary. Whereas the Commission views criminal legal aid as having gained sufficient legitimacy to dispense with contributions, it assumes that they must be retained in civil matters, despite the fact that they recouped only 4 per cent of the cost of the 'green form' scheme and 7 per cent of the cost of civil legal aid, and the Supplementary Benefits Commission spent nearly as much (£3.3 million) as it collected (£3.65 million) (11–6–7, 10, 13–13). Still, the growing legitimacy of legal aid in general is indicated by the Commission's recommendations that it be extended to civil matters not presently covered (13–70–72) and that the ten per cent reduction in laywers' fees be eliminated (13–66).

56. Thus the (US) Legal Services Corporation expects this year to reach its stated target of 'minimum access': one lawyer for every 5,000 eligible clients. That goal helped to justify expanding the programme from a legal aid budget prior to its founding in 1964 of $5 million to about $30 million in its first year of operation, to $321 million in fiscal 1981 (Johnson 1974, pp. 127, 188; Legal Services Corporation News, July–August 1980). But the aspiration may now become a ceiling.

57. The quality of representation is inevitably going to be affected by the level of remuneration: successful private practitioners are not going to be attracted to legal aid work, and even those who are politically committed are not going to be able to do a thorough job, when the average amounts spent for criminal defence are £70 and £243 (in the magistrates' and Crown Courts respectively), £64 for civil matters in the magistrates' courts, and £21 under the green form scheme (11–7, 10–13; see also note 38, *supra*).

58. Thus the Commission recommends that law centres be prohibited from engaging in 'general community work' (8–19, 20) and that representation of groups should be severely limited (12–57–65). This, of course, totally violates the principle of equality championed earlier (see text accompanying note 52, *supra*) since the private profession is constantly engaged in 'attack[ing] the roots of problems' (8–19) on behalf of groups (i.e. companies).

59. This is an old refrain:

Let us put on one side laymen's complaints about greed and high fees, for such complaints have been the lot of any priesthood of mystery since man was man. Such complaints prove nothing because they are heard equally when the job of the profession is done well and when it is ill-done (Llewellyn 1938, p. 104).

60. Glasser (1980) has thrown considerable doubt on the methodology underlying this conclusion.

61. The invisibility of such public subsidisation of private consumption under capitalism is suggested by the failure of the Commission to see it when the Commission is clearly aware of, and uneasy about, other lesser subsidies – for instance, the reduced cost of meals and chambers in the Inns of Court by virtue of their charitable status (32–78c and table 32.1).

62. This may be part of the reason why the attrition rate for women barristers is greater (table 15.6), which in turn contributes to their under-representation in the more privileged (i.e. older) strata of the Bar.

63. The USA has made extensive use of affirmative action or reverse discrimination; if this has been only a mixed success in promoting equality I know of no evidence that the beneficiaries found it demeaning. I wonder why the punishment of criminals and the compensation of their victims is not seen as demeaning to the latter? Michael Zander tells me, however, that reverse discrimination has never been used in England; if so, bias is likely to be even more enduring than it has been in the USA.

64. The USA displays some interesting parallels. Lawyers in smaller firms and those outside the major cities are similarly under-represented in the governing elite of the ABA but they do control the state bar associations which, unlike local law societies in the UK, exercise real control over the profession. Nevertheless, those lawyers excluded from power in both kinds of profession bodies have formed their own associations: the National Bar Association, in response to the exclusion of Blacks by the ABA, and more recently the bar associations of other ethnic minorities; several associations of women lawyers; the National Lawyers Guild, in response to the political conservatism of the ABA in the 1930s and associations of younger and politically liberal lawyers in the 1960s.

65. In a sense the profession has already abandoned any pretence of unified self-government: repeated efforts to co-ordinate the governance of barristers and solicitors have consistently failed (Abel-Smith and Stevens 1967), and no one even suggests that those employed outside private practice, or academic lawyers, ought to be subject to the same governing body.

66. 'Independence', like so many of the values invoked to legitimate the legal profession, is a nostalgic appeal to a past that probably never existed and certainly has long since vanished. It is also hypocritical: a lawyer is seen as 'independent' when he serves the interests of capital but not when he serves the state. Has that half of the Bar which is employed lost its independence? Indeed, the Commission itself seeks to ensure that lawyers will not be 'independent' of the state by proposing that law centres be placed under the control of a central planning agency and limited in what they can do for their poor clients (8–19–21–24–25–32).

67. At the Bar, discipline is more stringent at every stage of the process (26–8–14–16–23).

68. The logical extension of these reforms, the transfer of discipline from the profession to the state, occurred in Illinois with the blessing of the Bar associations, which gained legitimacy by divesting themselves of responsibility, perhaps comforted by the notorious inefficacy of governmental regulation (Powell 1976).

References

Abel, R. L. (1979a), Socializing the legal profession: Can redistributing lawyers' services achieve social justice? *Law & Policy Quarterly* 1, pp. 5–51.

56   *Richard L. Abel*

Abel, R. L. (1979b), Delegalization: a critical review of its ideology, manifestations, and social consequences in E. Blankenburg, E. Klausa, and H. Rottleuthner (eds.) *Alternative Rechtsformen und Alternativen zum Recht*, Opladen, Westdeutscher Verlag, pp. 27–47 (*Jahrbuch für Rechtssoziologie und Rechtstheorie, Band 6*).

Abel, R. L. (1980), The sociology of American lawyers: a bibliographic guide, *Law & Policy Quarterly* 2, pp. 335–91.

Abel, R. L. (1981), Conservative Conflict and the Reproduction of Capitalism: The Role of Informal Justice, *International Journal of The Sociology of Law* 9 (August).

Abel-Smith, B. & Stevens, R. (1967), *Lawyers and the Courts: A Sociological Study of the English Legal System 1750–1965*, London, Heinemann.

Abel-Smith, B., Zander, M. and Brooke, R. (1973), *Legal Problems and the Citizen: A Study in Three London Boroughs*, London, Heinemann.

American Bar Association Journal (1977), Lawpoll, *American Bar Association Journal* 63, pp. 1541–3.

Auerbach, J. S. (1971), Enmity and amity: law teachers and practitioners, 1900–22, in D. Fleming and B. Bailyn (eds.) *Law in American History* (Perspectives in American History, Vol. 5).

Auerbach, J. S. (1976), *Unequal Justice: Lawyers and Social Change in Modern America*, New York, Oxford Univeristy Press.

Baraquin, Y. (1975), *Les Français et la justice civile: enquête psychosociologique auprès des justiciables*, Paris, La Documentation Française.

Belli, M. M. with Kaiser, R. B. (1976), *Melvin Belli: My Life in Trial: An Autobiography*, New York, Morrow.

Berg, C. E. (1979), Lawyer referral services in *Legal Services for the Middle Class*, Chicago, American Bar Association, pp. 1–13.

Bernstein, P. (1978), The Million-Dollar Men of the Inner Circle of Advocates, *Juris Doctor* 44–8 (February).

Bowles, R. & Phillips, J. (1977), Solicitors' remuneration: a critique of recent developments in conveyancing, *Modern Law Review* 40, pp. 639–50.

Brennan, W. J. (1968), The responsibilities of the legal profession, in A. E. Sutherland (ed.) *The Path of the Law from 1967*, Cambridge, Harvard University Press.

Burman, S. B., Genn, H. G. & Lyons, J. (1977), The use of legal services by victims of accidents in the home – a pilot study, *Modern Law Review* 40, pp. 47–57.

Byles, A. & Morris, P. (1977), *Unmet Need: The Case of the Neighbourhood Law Centre*, London, Routledge & Kegan Paul.

Cain, M. (1979), The general practice lawyer and the client: towards a radical conception, *International Journal of the Sociology of Law* 7, pp. 331–54.

Cappelletti, M. (gen. ed.) (1978–9), *Access to Justice* (4 vols.), Milan, Giuffrè and Sijthoff and Noordhoff, Alpen aan den Rijn.

Carlin, J. E. (1966), *Lawyers' Ethics: A Survey of the New York City Bar*, New York, Russell Sage.

Carlson, R. J. (1976), Measuring the quality of legal services: an idea whose time has not come, *Law & Society Review* 11, pp. 287–318.

Carr-Saunders, A. M. & Wilson, P. A. (1933), *The Professions*, Oxford, Clarendon Press.

Casper, J. D. (1978), Having their day in court: Defendant evaluations of the fairness of their treatment, *Law & Society Review* 12, pp. 237–52.

Cass, M. & Sackville, R. (1975), *Legal Needs of the Poor*, Canberra, Australian Government Publishing Service.

Christensen, B. F. (1970), *Lawyers for People of Moderate Means*, Chicago, American Bar Foundation.

Crampton, R. (1975), The task ahead in legal services, *American Bar Association Journal* 61, p. 1339.

Curran, B. A. (1977), *The Legal Needs of the Public: The Final Report of a National Survey*, Chicago, American Bar Foundation.

Deitch, L. & Weinstein, D. (1976), *Prepaid Legal Services: socioeconomic impacts*, Lexington, Mass., Lexington Books.

Flood, J. (n.d.), *Barristers' Clerks*, Coventry, University of Warwick School of Law (Working Paper No. 2).

Freidson, E. (1970), *Profession of Medicine: a study of the sociology of applied knowledge*, New York, Harper & Row.

Galanter, M. (1981), Larger than life: mega-law and mega-lawyering in the contemporary United States in R. Dingwall and P. S. C. Lewis (eds.) *The Sociology of the Professions: Lawyers, Doctors, and Others*, London, Macmillan (forthcoming).

Galbraith, J. K. (1976), *The Affluent Society* (3rd rev. ed.), Boston, Houghton Mifflin.

Glasser, C. (1979), The Royal Commission: the remuneration of the profession and legal aid, *Legal Action Group Bulletin*, September, pp. 201–05.

Glasser, C. (1980), After the Report–remuneration, *Legal Action Group Bulletin* February, pp. 29–32.

Goodman, J. T. (1979), Development of Prepaid Legal Service Plans in *Legal Services for the Middle Class*, Chicago, American Bar Association, pp. 15–26.

Griffiths, J. (1977), The Distribution of Legal Services in the Netherlands, *British Journal of Law and Society* 4, pp. 260–86.

Harris, D. R., Maclean, M., Glenn, H. and others (1981) *Compensation and Support for Illness and Injury*, London, Macmillan.

Hochberg, J. A. (1976), The drive to specialization in R. Nader and M. Green (eds.) *Verdicts on Lawyers*, New York, Crowell, pp. 118–26.

Hoffman, P. (1973), *Lions in the Street: The Inside Story of the Great Wall Street Law Firms*, New York, Signet.

Illich, I. and others (1977), *Disabling Professions*, London, Marion Boyars.

Jencks, C. (1972), *Inequality: A Reassessment of the Effect of Family and Schooling in America*, New York, Basic Books.

Jencks, C. and others (1980), *Who Gets Ahead? The Determinants of Economic Success in America*, New York, Basic Books.

Johnson, E. (1974), *Justice and Reform: The Formative Years of the OEO Legal Services Program*, New York, Russell Sage.

Johnstone, Q. & Flood, J. A. (1980), Unadmitted Personnel in England and American Law Offices, presented to the conference on Legal Services in the Eighties, Cardiff, 21–3 March.

Joseph, M. (1976), *The Conveyancing Fraud*, London, Michael Joseph.

Katz, J. (1978), Lawyers for the poor in transition: involvement, reform, and the turnover problem in the legal services program, *Law & Society Review* 12, pp. 275–300.

Ladinsky, J. (1963), The impact of social backgrounds of lawyers on law practice and the law, *Journal of Legal Education* 16, pp. 127–44.

Ladinsky, J. (1976), The traffic in legal services: lawyer-seeking behavior and the channeling of clients, *Law & Society Review* 11, pp. 207–24.

Larson, M. S. (1977), *The Rise of Professionalism: A Sociological Analysis*, Berkeley, University of California Press.

Law Centres Working Group (n.d.), *Evidence to the Royal Commission on Legal Services*, London, Law Centres Working Group.

Leat, D. (1975), The rise and role of the poor man's lawyer, *British Journal of Law and Society* 2, pp. 166–81.

Legal Services Corporation (1979), *Annual Report of the Legal Services Corporation Fiscal Year 1979*, Washington, D.C., Legal Services Corporation.

Liebowitz, A. & Tollison, R. (1978), Earning and learning in law firms, *Journal of Legal Studies* 7, pp. 65–81.

Llewellyn, K. N. (1938), The Bar's troubles, and poultices – and cures?' *Law and Contemporary Problems* 5, p. 104.

Lochner, P. R., Jr. (1975), The no fee and low fee legal practice of private attorneys, *Law & Society Review* 9, pp. 431–73.

Marks, F. R. (1976), Some research perspectives for looking at legal need and legal services delivery systems: old forms or new?, *Law & Society Review* 11, pp. 191–205.

Marks, F. R., Hallauer, R. P. & Clifton, R. R. (1974), *The Shreveport Plan: An Experiment in the Delivery of Legal Services*, Chicago, American Bar Foundation.

Millerson, G. (1964), *The Qualifying Associations: A Study in Professionalisation*, London, Humanities Press.

Morris, P., Cooper, J. & Byles, A. (1973a), Public attitudes to problem definition and problem solving: a pilot study, *British Journal of Social Work* 3, pp. 301–20.

Morris, P., White, R. & Lewis, P. (1973b), *Social Needs and Legal Action*, London, Martin Robertson.

Muris, T. J. & McChesney, F. S. (1979), Advertising and the price and quality of legal services: the case of legal clinics, *American Bar Foundation Research Journal* 1979, pp. 179–207.

National Law Journal (1979), National Law Firm Survey, *National Law Journal* 2(3), p. 28; 2(4), p. 30 (1, 8 October).

O'Connor, J. (1973), *The Fiscal Crisis of the State*, New York, St. Martin's Press.

Offer, A. (1977), The origins of the law of property acts 1910–25, *Modern Law Review* 40, pp. 505–22.

Pearson Commission (1978), *Report of the Royal Commission on Civil Liability and Compensation for Personal Injury*, London, HMSO (Cmnd. 7054).

Pedrick, W. (1970), Collapsible specialists, *DePaul Law Review* 19, p. 699.

Polanyi, K. (1957), *The Great Transformation: The Political and Economic Origins of our Time*, Boston, Beacon Press.

Powell, M. J. (1976), Professional Self-Regulation: The Transfer of Control from a Professional Association to an Independent Commission, presented to the annual meeting of the American Sociological Association, August, New York.

Reader, W. J. (1966), *Professional Men*, London, Weidenfeld and Nicholson.

Redfern Legal Centre (1978), *Second Annual Report*, Sydney, Redfern Legal Centre.

Reich, C. A. (1964), The New Property, *Yale Law Journal* 73, p. 733.

Rosenthal, D. E. (1976), Evaluating the Competence of Lawyers, *Law & Society Review* 11, pp. 257–86.

Schuyt, K., Groenendijk, K. & Sloot, B. (1977), Access to the legal system and legal services research, *European Yearbook of Law and Sociology* 1977, pp. 98–120.

Sherman, H. (1979), Inflation, unemployment, and the contemporary business cycle, *Socialist Review* 44, pp. 75–102 (March–April).

Silver, C. (1969), The imminent failure of legal services for the poor: why and how to limit caseload, *Journal of Urban Law* 46, p. 217.

Simon, W. H. (1978), The ideology of advocacy: procedural justice and professional ethics, *Wisconsin Law Review* 1978, pp. 29–144.

Spring, E. (1977), Landowners, lawyers, and land reform in nineteenth century England, *American Journal of Legal History* 21, pp. 40–96.

Steele, E. H. & Nimmer, R. T. (1976), Lawyers, clients, and professional regulation, *American Bar Foundation Research Journal* 1976, pp. 917–1019.

Stumpf, H. P. (1975), *Community Politics and Legal Services: The Other Side of the Law*, Beverly Hills, Sage.

Tiemann, F. & Blankenburg, E. (1979), *Working Paper on the Evaluation of a Legal Need Survey in West Berlin*, Berlin, Wissenschaftszentrum.

Tomasic, R. & Bullard, C. (1978), *Lawyers and Their Work in New South Wales: preliminary report*, Sydney, Law Foundation of New South Wales.

Valétas, M. F. (1976), *Aide Judiciare et Accès à la Justice*, Paris, Ministère de la Justice.

York, J. C. & Hale, R. D. (1973), Too many lawyers? the legal services industry: its structure and outlook, *Journal of Legal Education* 26, pp. 1–31.

Zander, M. (1968), *Lawyers and the Public Interest*, London, Weidenfeld and Nicholson.

Zander, M. (1976), Costs in Crown Courts – a study of lawyers' fees paid out of public funds, *Criminal Law Review* p. 5.

Zander, M. (1980), The Report of the Royal Commission on legal services, *Contemporary Legal Problems* 1980, pp. 33–35.

CHAPTER 2

The Report of the Commission: analysis and change in legal services

Philip Lewis

For both lawyers and sociologists, analysis and advocacy are closely related: for lawyers, even academic lawyers, the association is the result of an obvious occupational bias, while some sociologists are affected by a distinguished tradition, and others by a perceived theoretical necessity. Some, again sociologists and lawyers, make a deliberate political choice. The preferred combination of analysis and advocacy will differ by person, by topic and by time. People vary in their temperaments and abilities, topics are – or are treated as – more or less complex, arouse more or less emotion, and touch on more or fewer established interests, while at different times the social mood is calm or stormy, and responsive to reason or rhetoric. A Royal Commission is an occasion on which advocacy is emphasised and stimulated; it is even dignified by the name of evidence. If a Commission's Report is controversial, advocacy is even more urgent; the need to overcome inertia and push through long overdue changes, or to combat specious and fundamentally misguided proposals, becomes paramount.

Whether or not such urgency exists in relation to the Report of the Commission may be debated. This paper is in any case slanted towards analysis; the choice is not a matter of judgment but of personal preference, coupled perhaps with a sense of what is appropriate for academics, a point to which I shall return. There seems no lack of advocacy for causes with which I broadly sympathize, so that I feel no countervailing obligation to campaign for them on this occasion, and, if I did, I could take the view that these are causes to which analysis would be an ally.

This paper was written in response to a request to provide an overview of the Commission's Report. It is no such thing. It falls into three parts. The first two remain more or less as written for the Legal Services Conference in Cardiff: the first contains some reflections on the Commission as an object of socio-legal study, while the second discusses some of the more basic concepts adopted by the Commission, and relates them to its method of work. The third contains the beginnings of a discussion, stimulated by the Conference, of the course of change and reform in legal services and its relevance to academic study.

I have to accept that, while in the second part my distaste for the Commission's lack of any theoretical exploration or constructive use of principle will appear clearly, the first part is open to a corresponding criticism: it is sociologically speaking atheoretical. The paper falls in a middle ground. It certainly does not seek to engage in our current debate on legal services in the terms in which that is now formulated, but it is also not a thorough examination of the problems of characterizing and explaining the Report, let alone an application of any general sociological theory.

First, I consider in general terms how one might approach the task of characterizing and analyzing the Commission and its Report. If one sees the Report as a mere endorsement of the *status quo*, one will regard the need for explanations (if one does not already have them) for the apparent resistance to change of matters concerning the legal profession as urgent, whereas if one regards it as a thoughtful analysis of current problems and controversies, it will be more interesting to inquire how these problems and controversies come to be defined as such, and what obstacles there are to the emergence of other matters as problematic and controversial. Without wanting to disagree with the views of others on the comparative importance of possible inquiries, I try to choose some middle ground. Some of the difficulties that would arise in doing so are discussed later.

In the absence of any generally accepted theory, the first question to be answered in considering the Report is the viewpoint from which to begin. Are we interested in this Royal Commission, all Royal Commissions, all bodies set up to inquire and report on matters concerning the legal system and the legal profession, or some wider topic? These are not mutually exclusive. Once one starts to characterize the Commission and its Report, one will have to address questions of comparison and differentiation: asking what kind of Commission was this leads at once to a comparison with other 'similar' bodies, where similarity already imports some criteria of relevance, if no more than the commonsense criterion of sharing the basic political, organizational and institutional characteristics of being a Commission, or if one is more sceptical, of sharing the characteristics of being instituted and labelled as a Commission. Even if the initial viewpoint is wider, the setting up of a Commission – or what is involved in membership of such a body – are matters which themselves have a social context which cannot be ignored in any satisfactory characterization of what has happened.

Simply for purposes of orientation, I take as my initial viewpoint an interest in change and reform activities in the area of legal services and legal professions in the last fifteen to twenty years. What has caused or initiated such change, stimulated or restrained reform activities, and governed the attitudes and interests which, it seems likely, are responsible for what has and has not happened in different countries? Again, as a matter of personal preference, rather than as anything to be intellectually justified, I prefer to see what has happened as a story rather than as instances of underlying attitudes or the working out of general social forces, though I should be happy to see a convincing account in these terms. It is not a story I know how to tell, but the possibility of there being such a story underlies this paper.

An approach by way of story-telling will tend to underrate the importance of organizational and institutional approaches to the study of the Commission and its Report. But a full story would include these approaches. However, there is a problem for the moment with any kind of organizational analysis, in that little is publicly known of the Commission's method of work, other than can be inferred from initial questionnaires, the Interim Report, the Report itself, and information from those who had dealings with it. There are interesting questions to be asked; for instance, what in its operations were its links and contacts with other groups? What relationship did its pattern of links and contacts have with its acquisition of knowledge and the formation of its attitudes? Again, what did the members see as the role of a Royal Commission? Where did they acquire their role attitudes as Commission members? I do not know what organization theory would in fact make of such an organization with limited life. Much theoretical and empirical writing is devoted to the supremacy of survival amongst organizational goals, but unless one regards the recommendation for a Council for

Legal Services as an attempt at posthumous survival, this seems inapplicable.

If we view the Commission more institutionally, it presents some puzzling features: its terms of reference fell mainly within the sphere of one fairly specialized, concentrated and expert government department, and it had to deal with existing governing bodies with similar characteristics. As against this, it had limited expertise, and none of the authority of a Commission with a clear mandate from pressure groups or a government department. In addition, since it accepted the substance of the professional claim to autonomy, it was left with the difficult task of laying down what was to happen in relation to matters which in its view should be left to the profession to decide. It says (22–61) that it is not for it to write Professional Standards and it then appears (22–62, 63) to lay down what should be in them in some detail. It does not explicitly discuss its position as a Royal Commission, or the proper role of outside inquiry and influence in the affairs of a profession, so the ambiguity of its approach is unresolved. The minority of lawyers suggests the injection of a lay viewpoint and there was comparatively little other specific expertise. We should note that the concentration of attention on lawyers and legal services was not its own choice, but imposed by the terms of reference, and there might have been different results, if, say, conveyancing had been isolated as a subject for study. In this respect it has no clear predecessors; previous investigations have either been limited in their scope (legal aid, legal education or lawyers' incomes, for instance) or they have dealt with a topic which only partly concerns lawyers, such as the business of the criminal courts. It would be part of a complete story to tell why it was given such a task, or why there was no predecessor.

Whatever the story, the form of the institution is established enough for us to make a substantive distinction between those Commissions which do and do not have a clear agenda. There is no doubt that a Royal Commission's approach will be determined not just by the terms of reference formally laid down, but by the very visible agenda provided for it by the evidence and submissions it receives, and the rather more intangible agenda given by the circumstances of the Commission's establishment and by the pre-existing commitments and attitudes of its members. If some great controversy, such as the extent to which trade unions should be bound by the law, has provoked its establishment, it will have to tackle that controversy. If evidence is repeatedly directed towards particular issues, they will have to be confronted. If on the other hand, the circumstances of its establishment are no more than the outcome of some malaise accompanied by some particular criticisms, there will be a tendency to deal with the criticisms without necessarily going to the source of a malaise which may be ill-defined.

Similarly, without starting to write the background story, we can see the Commission as an event or incident in it. As such, there is an origin, a context and an outcome, as well as the Commission and its Report. I know little of the origin; the setting up of the Commission was not a political event thought by Mr. Wilson to be worth notice in his autobiography. In understanding the Commission I think the idea of a context is more useful. The immediate context was the flurry of criticism, or 'campaign', summarized by Michael Zander in *Legal Services for the Community* (1978 pp. 19–21). There was also (which he does not mention) a BBC programme in respect of which libel damages were later paid to a firm of solicitors. There was, of course, a long-term context in social feelings about lawyers and legal services and, as I would argue, about law as a social institution and technique.

There was also the context as perceived by the Commission, at least in the Report. It is said (5–27) that the news of the Commission was welcomed in Parliament in part

because it was expected that we would investigate abuses and inefficiencies and propose remedies. But we believe that the main hope was that we would be able to recommend an improved system of legal services which would bring them within reach of the great majority of the population.

A less bland view of the presumed context is given by Joe Haines in his Note of Dissent (ND4–1), in which he described the decision to recommend the continuation of the conveyancing monopoly as flying 'in the face of public opinion, public expectation and the public interest.' But on the whole the Report gives the appearance of being dictated more by the Commission's own sense of what it thought was required than by outside demands. (I shall return later to the question of its relations with the profession). My impression in reading the Report has been that evidence is used more to support the Commission's reluctance to be involved with certain questions, than to support stands.

But in fact, apart from those with whom the Commission came into contact during its work, there was little to affect them. Several months elapsed before its membership was announced and it held its first meeting, which was followed very quickly by the first of the massive questionnaires which appeared to be predetermining the lines on which it was to proceed. Again, as an event, it seems that it stimulated action by the Senate of the Inns of Court and the Law Society, especially by its preference for using these bodies for data-gathering, and its apparent reluctance to take responsibility for its own programme of research. There were also some who saw in the Commission, perhaps optimistically, the opportunity for substantial change, and at any rate a more receptive audience for suggestions of reform than the profession's governing bodies. Outside these groups, there does not seem to have been substantial concern for what was happening. This may be thought to be contrary to the very large amount of evidence received, but my impressionistic judgment is that much of the evidence from bodies outside the legal profession and those directly concerned with the legal system, was the obligatory response to the existence of a Commission rather than an expression of carefully thought out or deeply held views.

Once the Report was published, there was an immediate and on the whole unfavourable reaction in the press, and a friendly reaction from the professions, who have asserted that they will carry out the recommendations which are left to them to implement. But we have not yet heard from the government, and the Commission and its Report are no longer news. This does not seem a matter on which strong, defined views are widely held.

It does not then seem that the outcome will be dramatic. When the Report was initially published, there was a strong feeling expressed in the press and elsewhere that the Commission had not gone deeply enough into matters with which it should have been concerned.[1] I wondered whether it might not be one of the first Commissions to stimulate by the weakness of its arguments the real controversy which had not existed before it was set up. The second part of this paper argues, in effect, that that was an optimistic view, and that it is unlikely that any re-examination of the role of lawyers in our society will take place in the near future. The mere fact of a recent Commission makes it even less likely.

The other respect in which the Commission's Report was seen to be misplaced was that its proposals were for increases in public spending. In some sense, the Report is a building designed before the energy crisis to run on cheap oil; its cautious and uncosted indications on priorities for progress as extra expenditure becomes possible, now seem incongruous. There may be room, then, for new arguments based on cost-effectiveness. But even such arguments need a basis in social and legal principle.

What part will the Commission play in our story? It will lend support to further expressions of some of the more traditional forms of legal aid: the proposals on duty solicitors, legal services in prisons and representation in tribunals are good examples. It will also lend support to extensions of the authority of the governing bodies of the professions. I doubt myself whether we shall see citizens' law centres in the form and with the organisation proposed. At the most I think we may associate the Commission in the future with a change in mood, rather than a change in direction.

In the second part of the paper I look at the Report from a more analytic point of view, in order to relate some of what is contained in it to the evidence received by the Commission and to the Commission's methods of work. I do not intend to criticise the Report, though I would not wish to present myself as uncritical. Though some progress has been made, and there could be more if some of the Commission's approaches were exploited, there is a great deal which is disappointing. The nadir is the chapter on law centres, where the Commission's failure to consider what was involved in the giving of a legal service by professionals has led to a complete absence of any attempt to get to grips with a well-documented discussion of legal services for groups or the poor. There have been extreme reactions: it may be as appropriate tactics for the Legal Action Group (LAG) to write the Report off as totally useless, as for the governing bodies of the professions to take it (if indeed they do) as their new starting-point. As I have said, in this paper I am taking a self-consciously analytic point of view, from which it would be wrong to regard the Report either as orthodoxy or heresy, to be taken as self-evident or discarded as inconvenient, and retrogressive. In that spirit, I suggest as a hypothesis to consider that the Commission and its Report are to a considerable extent to be explained in terms of prevailing attitudes.

Comparatively late in its work, the Commission sought to commission studies on the principles to be adopted in the provision of legal services. I was one of the people asked to write such a paper and in fact the only one who did so. I was struck by the general lack of any attempt in the evidence submitted, to formulate and justify general principles, and by the comparatively small quantity of evidence which sought to argue from even dogmatically stated general principle to the recommendations made. On the whole, the evidence tended to make recommendations on the basis of implicitly assumed goals or principles. Very little of it addressed questions of legal services in terms other than the standard ones of protecting and enforcing rights, though it is true that LAG pointed out that rights might differ in importance, the TUC pointed out that one could approach the enforcement of rights without assuming that lawyers were the best way of achieving it, while the Scottish Legal Action Group (SCOLAG) questioned the whole social desirability of providing remedies in the courts, rather than providing cheaper and more informal and flexible means for solving disputes. Apart from these limited points, I would apply to the evidence what is said by Ole Hansen and Jenny Levin in an article about the Report: 'This is simply asserted: basic questions, such as the role of lawyers in society, the need for their services and how these services should be provided and financed, are barely mentioned.' (Legal Action Group 1979).

Some part of the failure to tackle general questions can be blamed on the Commission. It points to the conflict between the time required for basic research and 'the need to complete our work without undue delay' (1–10). Some part of this difficulty may have arisen from the failure of the academic community, with a few honourable exceptions, to have undertaken basic research previously. But one can make two comparisons with the Royal Commission on Trade Unions and Employers Associations, the Donovan Commission. The Donovan Commission was, if anything, rather quicker to report.[2] Yet it appointed a Research Director, and published research done under its auspices. It is true that the Commission on Legal Services also sponsored research, but it was not of relevance to any basic question it had to decide. Secondly, the Donovan Commission also sent out at an early stage a substantial questionnaire, but if one looks at its opening questions, there is a refreshing openness as to the functions and proper role of the institutions with which it was concerned; this Commission's questionnaire seemed uninterested in any such question and the

Report shows no change in attitude. It is also true that the Commission preferred to play its hand close to its chest (except for the dialogue with the profession's governing bodies, to which I shall return), and not to communicate its thinking or lines of approach. I think one can exaggerate the effect that a willingness to work more in the open might have had on the Commission, but nevertheless it is interesting that the Chairman of the Royal Commission on Criminal Procedure found it possible, while his Commission was still sitting, to give a published lecture on the extent to which evidence did or did not support propositions put to his Commission.[3]

Whatever may have been the faults of the Commission, its method of working or its Report, in my view it is a serious misjudgment to regard it as an aberration, an isolated unfortunate incident, something to be blamed on the membership, the chairman, the secretariat, the profession or the Lord Chancellor. It is nearer the truth to regard it as a reflection, in general terms, of the climate of criticism of lawyers and legal institutions which predated the establishment of the Commission, and which pervades the evidence. As a society, we do not have any coherent view of the role of law or legal institutions, let alone lawyers, nor is there any clearly defined battle-line between opposing views, where a Commission could have stepped in to arbitrate or give a lead. Thus, complaints have no context, are informed by no principle, and define too closely the form of an appropriate answer. The answer to a complaint that lawyers earn too much is 'no, they do not', not an analysis of the role of lawyers. The answer to a complaint that conveyancing costs too much is 'procedures should be simplified, but no other system would cost less.'

Similarly, if lawyers are distrusted and some are incompetent, a survey can show widespread satisfaction or dissatisfaction, while improving the image of the profession, and introducing 'professional standards' and treating incompetence as a disciplinary matter will improve things. If lawyers do not do sufficient social welfare work they should be adequately paid for doing it. If it is said to be self-evident that the aim of the legal system and legal services should be to improve the lot of the poor and disadvantaged, this is not a matter appropriate for a legal service (8–20: the relationship of this reasoning to the emphasis in 44–4 on the social aims of relieving that part of the population suffering permanent and multiple deprivation, is touched on later.)

We are fortunate in having many in this country who put forward and carry into practice imaginative and constructive suggestions for the improvement of legal services. But it is not their habit to argue the case for seeing them as justified by our current conceptions of legal services, or as justifiable extensions of existing conceptions. Thus, I think it unsurprising that the Commission similarly refrained. Again, since our national ambivalence about law and legal processes seems universal, it was not to be expected that the Commission would seek to tackle such a fraught topic as a means of deciding what lawyers should be and do. It was, to put it shortly, the Commission we deserved.

I now turn to the Commission's attitude to some fundamental matters which might on another approach have dominated the Report. The first is the legal system and its place in our society, the second is the role of lawyers and the nature of legal services, while the third is the nature of a profession. Only its attitude to the third is detailed, and the kind of inferences it sought to draw from it are limited.

Is it really necessary to decide the nature of our legal system and what its purposes are in order to make recommendations about the legal profession and legal services? In my view, one has at least to be aware of some current developments which make a simple rule of law and protection and enforcement of rights model inappropriate. The Commission took the view (4–10) that it was unnecessary for its purposes to decide whether the situation was accurately described as 'a flight from the law', since it was satisfied that there was a large demand for legal services which was inadequately met. The resolution of disputes inside courts of law is contrasted with methods apart from the use of legal procedures. It does not address the extent to which procedures may be formalised by legal means without the underlying dispute being brought before the courts. If one sees our legal system as exhibiting such a tendency, it is arguable that skilled professional help should be given so that individuals and groups may negotiate such procedures. If one reads the evidence of the City of London Solicitors' Company – the only evidence, so far as I know, describing in any detail the work of any group of lawyers – it is plain that they regarded their work as including all kinds of dealings with governmental and regulatory agencies, including informal city institutions such as those policing the conduct of take-overs, which do not apply legal rules. I would suggest that the existence and ever increasing importance of such alternative methods of regulating conduct and settling disputes has to be taken into account in considering the provision of legal services.

Although the Commission did not regard alternative characterizations of the legal system as relevant to its task, it did (4–24) assert one general principle on a kind of reciprocity basis which may have had some influence on the recommendations on CABx and education in schools:

The principle is always followed in our courts that no-one may plead ignorance of the law as a defence of answer, but the corresponding principle that a person should be entitled to know when the law is able to help him is not observed with any consistency.

Otherwise the most general argument based on the nature of the legal system is contained in: 'citizens will not have equal access to the courts nor enjoy the full benefit of rights and safeguards provided by the law without the provision of adequate legal services' (5–1).

The principle is never clearly worked out, as will be plain from the next section, discussing the concept of 'legal services', but one point is noteworthy. The general emphasis of the Report is on the protection and enforcement of rights, and it is thus a shock to read para. 44–4 which states that the first priority should go to measures which would make some contribution to the relief of that part of the population which suffers permanent and multiple deprivation. I am no doubt not the only person who finds this odd when set against the restrictive terms on which legal aid is to be made available to groups, and the various restrictions to be imposed on law centres, but my point here is that what is said in this paragraph injects an entirely different dimension into the rights-oriented approach of the rest of the Report; it is a purpose-oriented approach.Compared to this departure, I do not know whether it is of importance to notice that it does not say what evidence it has for saying that the proper use of the law will solve certain problems or even which problems are contemplated. This is particularly important when one comes to arguments for public funding.

There is one last point which rests on a view of the proper form and function of the legal system. In more than one place (e.g. 18–45 and 35–38) the Commission comes out against segmentation of the profession, as opposed to specialisation, which it favours. It takes the position that it is undesirable for any group of lawyers to be

acting always in one interest (though it does not ⟨
solicitors under this head), particularly for prosecution
This is put forward as a reason against ethnic segreg⟨
profession (others are deployed). This argument rests partly on a
view that the legal system should be protected from too direct an
impact of lay concerns, and that it will develop best if advocates are
not too closely committed to the interests and outlooks of their
clients. Other views are held, particularly by some of those who
favour lay representation, and it is important that this should not be
seen as a rather technical question about career opportunities.

I turn now to the general concept of legal services. The Commission disclaims any intention of defining legal services, which would
probably have been wise if there had been careful analysis of the
policy questions which tend to be answered by use of the concept. In
fact it flirts with some inconsistent definitions, and seems in practice
to use a somewhat restrictive one. There is a very mysterious
passage (5–23) distinguishing between preventive services and legal
services. 'It is better', they say, 'to prevent a problem arising than to
provide a legal remedy for it after it has arisen.' If one is to take the
distinction as drawn literally, one would be ruling out of legal
services a whole class of activities which lawyers emphasize as
valuable: it seems better to assume that they really only had in mind
marriage guidance and accident prevention, which they mention,
and that they recognise that legal services can be preventive.

In 2–2 the Report says that legal services are regarded: 'as being
concerned with advice assistance and representation which is
required by a person in connection with rights, duties and liabilities
of a legal character,' and apparently rejects any suggestion that it
should include what at least some lawyers do and are prepared to
accept professional responsibility for doing. This would neatly side-
step any possible argument for saying that because some lawyers
give certain services society should subsidise such services for all.
But it apparently accepts what was earlier rejected: 'A legal service
may be described as any service which a lawyer performs for his
client and for which professional responsibility rests on him' (4–16).
'No precise definition has been put to us,' it is said, 'and none is
needed for our purposes.' I think the Commissioners delude
themselves. It is not that anyone will examine the Report to see
whether it conforms or not to the Commission's terms of reference,
but there are some problems for which some kind of principle, if not

certainty, is necessary. There have to be criteria by which people are thought worthy of the specially expensive kind of help which is given by lawyers: something about the knowledge or experience needed, or the nature of the situation will surely be part of the criteria, even if they are not conclusive. Arguments, both for professional autonomy and client confidentiality are based on the nature of the services performed for the client. Nor is the position helped by the use of the phrase 'of legal character' (see for instance, 4–18). I do not know what that means, just as I do not know what is meant by the phrase 'in respect of legal rights, duties and liabilities' to which I have referred, or 'not directly connected with legal rights, duties and liabilities' (8–9). The Commission actually distinguishes 'legal advice, assistance and representation' and carrying out general community work which in 8–20 (a) is apparently categorised as not 'legal advice and assistance.' At this point attempted analysis seems an inappropriate and clumsy tool. We seem to be faced with assertion, rather than argument. To be fair, they are not the only ones. Academics interested in this topic tend to prefer a wider definition which will include the activities of law centres, which they support. But there is little discussion of why such a definition should be accepted by those who are as doubtful whether those activities should have the protection and support which go along, in our society, with the characterization as 'legal services', as I am about the activities of those who advise on artificial tax avoidance schemes.

As I said earlier, my aim is not to criticize the Commission's Report, but to characterize it. It is no rarity in English public life to distrust serious argument, or argument from principle; the oddity is perhaps the legal context where practitioners' style of argument is to connect principle and practice. I think the style of non-argument is at least partly to be explained by the Commission's emphasis on the concept of a profession, rather than on the concept of legal services. Perhaps it is in the nature of such bodies to adopt a theme, and no more than one theme. If one feels that both the concept and content of legal services are inadequately dealt with – and I should repeat that there is very little, except in the conveyancing section, on what lawyers actually do, and practically nothing on the contribution or otherwise that they make to social life in general by what they do – it will be that the Commission started with a profession and looked to improve it, rather than looking to legal services, and seeing how they could be improved. In this sense, it adopts an institutionally-based approach, building on concepts which in its view were sound and well-supported, rather than attempting to construct new concepts or develop old ones as a guide to whatever institutions may arise in the future.

The last general matter is the attitude of the Commission to lawyers as a profession. It returns repeatedly to the characteristics of a profession, its responsibilities and rights. Much of what is said, however, would apply equally to any occupation giving services. To take a trivial example, the Report states (33–85) that in any profession it is in the public interest that a practitioner should not undertake work which is below his level, and which should be done at a lower charge. Whatever the validity of this point it cannot be restricted to professions. The possible contrast is made clear in the chapter on conveyancing (21–21 ff.): it is the nature of the transaction which imposes the need for various protections, even though professional rules add further safeguards. There is, too, a tendency in the Report to throw in many additional requirements as 'necessarily imposed on a profession for the protection of the public.' It refers (21–50) to indemnity insurance, contributions to a compensation fund, and maintaining a proper accounting system. None of these necessarily has anything to do with membership of a profession, though they are very proper features to introduce for people whose activities involve handling the money of others, or who risk loss to the public through negligence or dishonesty.

There is one preliminary point, though an important one. Among the five main features of a profession set out by the Commission (3–18) independence is not explicitly included except in relation to self-regulation. Nevertheless, the need for independence is constantly stressed and forms the foundation of a number of the Commission's recommendations and preferences. There is, however, very little discussion if any, of the topic, and of the extent to which the case for independence of the legal profession rests – on the one hand – on considerations general to all professions, and – on the other – on the interests and relationships with which the legal profession is specially concerned: the Report does not go into the issues debated by Zander and others in the *Law Society Gazette* in 1977.

Those engaged in socio-legal studies may have come to see the concept of profession as one aspect of an historical process in which occupations have achieved for themselves a degree of autonomy and independence from external regulation by putting forward claims to special knowledge, expertise and ethicality and by claiming to have undertaken special responsibilities to the public in return for the power and privilege of policing their own members' conduct and controlling their relationships with their clients. We should be ill-advised to assume that such an analysis is widely accepted in our society, still less that the claims are treated as problematic and the bargain as one-sided or illusory. Though the weight put on the professional character of lawyers may have been unexpected, it should not have been expected that there would be doubts as to professional status. There is, it is fair to point out, one concession to relativism (30–15), where the Commission, in deciding that partnerships between solicitors and other professions should not at present be permitted, concedes that: 'divisions of function between different professions and callings are the result of historical development and are not fixed for all time.' The insight is not used.

Three points stand out in the Commission's treatment of lawyers as a profession: the emphasis on hierarchy and self-regulation, the emphasis on competence and efficiency and the suggested use of 'professional standards.'

First for its views on hierarchy. Classic definitions of a profession have not given such weight as the Commission to the idea (3–18 (a)) that a 'governing body (or bodies) represents a profession and is formally recognised as doing so; it has powers of control and discipline over its members.' Sociologists have, in fact, pointed out that the prevailing norms of a profession may represent a view imposed by one part of a segmented profession on the rest and the governing body may be a means of effectuating such control. The Commission seems untroubled by such suggestions, though in the case of the Law Society it does regret the absence of sole practitioners from the Council and considers that others have a responsibility to take part in the government of the profession. This leads to the majority proposal that any solicitor who holds a practising certificate and pays dues should be entitled to vote in elections and hold office in the governing body (29–32). The dissent on this point highlights the tension between the associational and regulatory functions of a modern profession.

This theme of representative government comes out in the recommendations both for the Law Society, where it seeks to achieve implementation by district organizations of the Council's policies, and in the case of the Bar, where it seeks to strengthen the position of the Senate at the expense of the Inns (see 32–64 ff.). The emphasis is, I think, novel, and comes from a combination of a concern for effective regulation and efficiency generally, with an attempt to take seriously the idea of self-regulation. We are accustomed to thinking of the latter as absence of outside regulation, but their use of terms such as 'democratic,' 'constitutional' and 'representative' gives 'self' added force. (I am not here discussing the extent to which these ideals are likely to be realised, only their nature and source.) The Commission obviously has no confidence in a process which seeks to build a professional consensus, and probably feels that such a process, even if possible, would take too long. Its picture is of an active governing body formulating coherent policies and standards of conduct within the profession, and taking charge of and responsibility for their implementation. As others have commented, this is a general preference on the part of the Commission, which proposes a hierarchical structure for and within law centres. The theme of not dividing responsibilities, and thus concentrating accountability, is recurrent.

The Commission's concern with competence and efficiency has, I think, been underrated by those who disagree with its specific proposals for improvement. A number of the Commission's recommendations relate to efficiency and good business practice; while the Commission showed no general concern with the cost-effectiveness of legal services or of different forms of legal services delivery, it did regard it as an obligation of the professions to ensure that those practising in it did so efficiently, not just in order to ensure quality of service and to avoid delay, but so that services should be available as economically as possible. There may also have been a feeling that the profession could not legitimately ask for higher fees out of public funds, unless it could show that it was efficient. In any case this too is an extra dimension to the requirements of professional status.

The reluctance of professions to concern themselves with incompetence or bad work, in spite of their assertions that only professionals have the expertise to judge the quality of professional work, is well-documented; and the Commission has made a number of suggestions with a view to the legal profession's making good these assertions. The two main ones concern the commitment to treat such work as a disciplinary matter, and the suggested introduction of professional standards.

To take the second first, while many professions formulate and publish rules and rulings, what is suggested is the introduction of written rules covering not so much 'ethical' requirements and obligations towards colleagues, as the way in which work is to be carried out and obligations towards clients. There is an interesting contrast with current proposals in the USA, which emphasize the obligations of the lawyer to legal institutions and the public.

As I have said, the Commission expressed ambivalence at laying down rules for an independent profession, which led it to specify the proposed standards in some apparent detail without claiming actually to write them (see 22–57 ff.). The argument is that changes in the work of lawyers, the growth of the profession, and increased public expectations have made it 'more difficult to maintain a uniformly high quality of service by traditional methods alone.' I do not know what other professional bodies do in fact use this method; the best known standards are those put out by accountants, which actually deal with quite controversial matters of principle in accounting and relate to an accountant's obligations to those who are going to use the accounts, and not to the client.

In relation to competence and the quality of work, there has been substantial disagreement as to whether or not the Report was critical of lawyers, and whether or not it has made any useful recommendations for improvement. Again, I am more concerned here with form and explanation than substance. There is no doubt that the Commission went out of its way (3–27 ff.) to express support for the profession as against its critics, and to characterize the criticisms as problems of the public image of the profession. Nevertheless, that public image is characterized as indifferent and the legal profession is exhorted to change it; reading 3–40 suggests that the change being required is one of substance. When one comes to Chapter 22 on 'Quality of Service', it may be that one is faced with a choice of interpretations: should one take more seriously the pats on the back in 22–16, or the criticism in 22–17? Myself, bearing in mind the fact that both governing bodies are invited to enter into the field of formulating written standards for professional work and to undertake disciplinary action for bad professional work, I think that the criticism was seriously meant. Why does the Commission speak so indirectly?

I think that this Commission – because of the existence of the governing bodies of the profession, and because it was unwilling to override what it saw as the prime importance of the independence of the profession, perhaps too, because much of what needed to be done would have been difficult otherwise – decided to proceed at least part of the way by persuasion. Not all by any means of the list of actions taken by these bodies since 1976 contained in Annex 44–1 was taken as a result of the Commission's urging or existence, but there were some. The clearest example was in fact the question of disciplinary action for bad professional work, where the Commission persuaded the Law Society Council and the Senate to adopt the view that they should accept the responsibility of disciplining bad work, which, in spite of protestations, had scarcely been the case before. The Commission obviously took the view that persuasion was better than recommendation, and this, if anything, is the justification of the close relations between the Commission and the profession's governing bodies. It obviously saw itself as able to adopt an active role, rather than as making recommendations which it was for others to adopt or not, and to some extent in so doing it imposed self-limitations.

In siding with the governing bodies of the professions, both against outside pressures and as against elements within the profession which are reluctant to accept direction and change, it maximised its chances of achieving a short-term response, at the expense of staying within the limits of attitudes acceptable to those bodies. Increasing the powers and responsibilities of these bodies was an aspect of this process, and it is worth remarking that the Senate, which is probably closer to the majority of the Bar, was less reluctant to follow the Commission in the path it was charting, than the Law Society Council, which has much greater difficulties in formulating and implementing policies acceptable to its much larger and more diverse constituency.

Such a process involves a form a co-option: one does not speak harshly of the friend who, as one feels, has just been persuaded to reform. There is little excuse for the extent to which the Commission failed to come to grips with the issues involved in publicly-funded and salaried legal services; at the same time, it is widely accepted that the majority of legal services will be given in the private sector, and without a radical reorganisation of that sector – not, as far as I know, suggested by anybody – this technique for

achieving improvement seems defensible. Even if fusion or the
extension of rights of audience had the impact on the efficiency of
the legal process, and lawyers' acceptance of total responsibility for
their work which some have prophesied, some further involvement
by the profession in the competence and quality of service of the
private sector would have been necessary. Speaking with my moderately reformist hat on, I hope that the profession will be strongly
encouraged to accept what the Commission regards as criticism
which should be met: I suggest that those who see the Report as a
whitewash, or are disappointed (justifiably, in my view) at its limitations, may undercut what good effects it might have by rejecting it
totally. That is a tactical choice, though, which cannot be made for
them by others.

The last general topic which I discuss is the attitude of the Commission to knowledge and research. There is a range of relevant
knowledge, from the success rates of different forms of representation to the techniques of successful emergency injunctions and
tax-avoidance schemes. Within this range, some are more relevant
to policy and some to practice, but I doubt whether any very clear
distinction is possible. I have mentioned the Commission's reluctance to do research, and the reliance on it was qualified, sometimes
rightly, as in 4–34 it points out that, although the Users Survey
showed that most people know how to set about finding a solicitor,
it was less certain 'that in all cases they would quickly find a solicitor
willing and able to provide the legal services they required.' The
work done on duty solicitors also received a qualified acceptance:
the Commission exhibited one of its odder characteristics in the face
of the evidence of misconduct, making no clear finding but recommending a method of avoiding the difficulty (see 9–10 ff. and
especially 9–17: the disputed matter of the basis of competence and
experience on which the duty solicitor rota should operate is tacitly
left for Law Society standards). Findings on the effects of representation are presented as relevant to the Commission's views on legal
aid for tribunal matters (15–9–11). The proposed Council for Legal
Services should have a research capacity, though how this fits in
with the recommendation that the professions should be left alone
for a time (3–17) is unclear. Plainly the Commission's Report will
not directly be a contribution to discussions of the relations of
research to public policy, but it probably represents the mixture of
reluctant fascination with and doubt about research in policy mat-

ters which marks our society. The failure of the Commission to come to grips with policy matters before identifying its lines of inquiry has led to an absence of information about possible choices and priorities.

I think the Commission's attitude to practice-oriented knowledge is of interest. It does not take it lightly, and one of the points on which it differs from the Senate is over its policy for post-qualification education and training, which in the Commission's view did not go far enough (39–85 ff.). But I think the subject-matter of professional knowledge is treated as if it were entirely affected by changes from outside, in the form of new legislation or cases. An important deficiency is the failure to identify the kinds of knowledge involved, and their source. It is not surprising that we do not see a Freidsonian analysis of the kinds of knowledge which do and do not support the profession's claim to regulate itself and its relations with its clients. But a failure to identify the processes where by legal techniques are constructed and disseminated does weaken the approach, for they fail to identify a substitute in welfare fields, say, for the market forces which generate new tax-avoidance schemes or unit trusts, or Eurodollar loans. I think this leads to important points being missed about the contribution of law centres, and the extent to which an approach to legal services on the basis of individual rights, deprives even middle-class clients of benefits which they might have received, if there were better mechanisms for aggregating claims, and lawyers had thus an incentive to develop new forms of assertion and protection of rights. In this context too, the Commission's continued preference for examining the organization of the profession rather than the contribution it makes to society has led to omission. This, too, I am willing to suggest, results from the narrowness of the complaints which led to the establishment of the Commission, the consequences of which may be with us for a generation.

I turn to the third part of the paper, which consists of a different kind of speculation. Time taken from the discussion of particular issues and spent characterizing and explaining the form and outcome of the Commission is unlikely to be productive, unless it leads to some general understanding of the processes of debate, reform and change or to some particular lessons for the future. As I have said, it is too early to write a complete story but I should like to use the occasion of beginning it, to raise some questions about the role of academics in the discussion of legal services.

Let me develop remarks made at the beginning of the paper. Whatever may be the case in other academic communities (though sociologists seem to have the same characteristics), those engaged with the law have always regarded it as at least legitimate, if not obligatory, to be concerned with its improvement, though the rationalisation of doctrine has, to the relief of some of us, given way to a concern with the way in which legal rules and institutions operate in practice to achieve certain ends. Insofar as these ends are implicit in legal rules or institutions, or their acceptability is assumed or imposed, no problem arises. Two things logically separate – but practically associated – can alter the situation. The first is substantial disagreement about ends, and the second is disagreement about methods of achieving change, where change no longer results from a mere demonstration of the non-correspondence of intention and reality. Both of these hold in the field of legal services, and raise problems for at least some academics, of whom I am one.

The existence of a Commission and speculation about the outcome of its Report concentrates our attention on the processes of change, and it seems worth reflecting on some of the ways in which change in the legal profession or the delivery of legal services is seen as coming about. I have picked out seven ideas from papers or discussion at the Conference.

1. Some part is played by argument. There are a number of concepts which are associated, and they turn on the acceptance in the world of purpose, rationality, consistency, justification and even hypocrisy as real constraints on, or guides to, action rather than as cloaks over what is really happening or as mere illusions. The fact that a Commission purports to proceed in this way may be thought by some to over-emphasize the attention paid to this form of change at this time and disappointment may have a similar effect: if people are persuaded by the force of our arguments, it does not follow that it is their weakness which has been ineffectual. But calls for more accountability (as opposed to control) tend to emphasize the importance of argument, for it is suggested than an extending audience or possible criticism will improve the quality and alter the content of arguments, and so have consequences for action.

2. At the other extreme it may be differences in the environment which result in changes – for instance, the increase in home-ownership, which has made domestic conveyancing more important

for the profession, or the competition of other occupations for work.

3. As Abel suggests in his paper, some such changes are not really external to the profession, but quasi – purposeful: the actors are not always clear in what they are doing, but they are working towards a self-seeking ideal. On this view it may be the profession and the state in alliance which are creating a demand for particular kinds of services, rather than there being a pressure from outside.

4. Some changes come from bargaining, as when law centres bargained with the Lord Chancellor's Office for support in return for the provision of valued services.

5. Some changes, it is plain, come only through alliances, obstruction and countervailing power: it is not the strength of the argument, but of those who put it forward which carries the day.

6. Some people apparently assume that institutional reform can bring about change, that outside control will bring about changes in the legal profession.

7. Finally, mere changes of mood and sentiment may be seen as influential; the decline in respect for professionals, or the backlash against professionalism has led to the growth of new institutions and the involvement of new sections of society, in what has been for some time a narrow preserve.

There were substantial differences in the discussion at the Conference about how much change had taken place in the delivery of legal services in England and Wales, and why, so that disagreement on how change is to be achieved is also to be expected. What in this context is the responsibility of the academic? In this context, the role of the academic is likely to be as controversial as that of the lawyer, but I would assert, rather than argue, that it involves some kind of commitment to argument rather than assertion, and to a style of discourse which gives some weight to argument and evidence, without necessarily being committed to the view that argument and evidence are primary in achieving change. Even if academic lawyers cannot but be actors, still they should in my view, contribute what others plainly do not.

Many of those at the conference came as actors, not as academics: nevertheless, in such a context, even for the detached academic there is a problem. Different styles of argument will anpeal to different academics, so that a choice of style is a choice of audience, and an implicit judgment of the relevant audience; that is, the one with the right or ability to make a judgment or decision. The relevant audience may legitimately not be an academic one. Similarly, evidence is evidence for a proposition, and collecting evidence is itself a decision as to what propositions are worth debate. This decision may itself be based on some judgment as to how relevant such a proposition should be to a rational conclusion, but it may not irrationally be based on a judgment that those who have the power in some way or other to bring about change, treat that proposition as relevant. Since it is debated and debateable who has that power, the scope is large, nor will anyone making a case or bringing forward evidence wish to limit the number of possible audiences.

Is anything, then, permissible? Let me conclude by putting forward one consideration which may counsel caution. It seems at least arguable that academics have as a group won for themselves special privileges in return for undertaking special obligations, just as much as have lawyers. Their formal arrangements for self-discipline in the performance of those obligations are, for good reason, derisory, and this fact itself may make the force of the obligations, if they are recognized at all, still greater. The promotion of understanding, irrespective of the forwarding of personal preferences, is, I think, seen as one of those obligations. Our record in its performance, in the field covered by these papers, is spotty. It was a cause for comment that the Royal Commission contained no academic known for work in the field. But at a meeting of the Society of Public Teachers of Law held soon after the membership of the Commission was announced, discussion of the Commission turned almost entirely on issues of legal education; there was nothing on the nature of our legal system or the place of lawyers. The teaching of Legal System courses has not, as far as I know, produced any published analysis of the purposes for which we maintain systems of civil adjudication and provide machinery for the enforcement of private rights. Such areas, as well as the topics of the course of change which I have mentioned, provide tasks for academics which are socially important, and will not be performed by others.

Notes

1. See *The Economist*, 6–12 October 1979, pp. 30–32.

2. Donovan, Lord (1968) *Royal Commission on Trade Unions and Employers Association*, London, HMSO.
3. Sir Cyril Philips, *James Smart Lecture*, (1979), London.

References

Legal Action Group (1979), *LAG Bulletin*, November, p. 251.
Zander, M. (1978), *Legal Services for the Community*, London, Temple Smith.

CHAPTER 3

Legal Services in Scotland

Ian Willock

To many Scots the establishment of a separate Royal Commission on Legal Services in Scotland was a welcome indication of the government's recognition that their legal system differs in significant respects from that of England and Wales. Yet its creation was not a foregone conclusion. Two and a half weeks elapsed between Mr. Harold Wilson's announcement of a Royal Commission for England, Wales and Northern Ireland and the statement, as if by an afterthought, in a written parliamentary answer that Scotland too was to have its own Commission and whatever blessings might flow from it. When, after further delay, the membership of the Scottish Commission was eventually announced on 25 October 1976 there was a different Prime Minister, James Callaghan. Why was Scotland given this belated favour? The distinctive character of legal services in Northern Ireland did not warrant separate examination. There was in 1976 a total absence of law centres in Scotland on the English model to expose the deficiencies of the orthodox organisation of the legal profession and demonstrate what could be achieved to remedy them. A Scottish Legal Action Group (SLAG) had been formed in the summer of 1975. Its founders shared the concern of the London-based Legal Action Group about various inadequacies in legal services which were to be found throughout the UK, while regretting LAG's understandable inability or unwillingness to apply its critique to Scottish conditions. But although the SLAG wrote to the Prime Minister calling for the setting up of a Scottish Royal Commission shortly before its creation was announced, it was a small and little-known society at that time and can scarcely claim to have directed the Prime Minister's thinking. The Scottish Commission's Report noted that 'we found no evidence of strong disenchantment with the legal profession' (1–4). It seems likely therefore that it was the generalised pressure of Scottish Nationalism (then

represented by 11 Scottish National Party members in a House of
Commons where the government party did not have a clear majority) which induced the Prime Minister to give Scotland its Commission and thus deny the SNP a further chance to depict Scotland as a
deprived area.[1]

When the composition of the Scottish Commission was
announced it was found to differ in a significant respect from that
headed by Sir Henry Benson. Lord Hughes, the chairman, was not
a member of a profession closely associated with that of law, but a
full-time politician, once a master builder in Dundee, who had
become Lord Provost (Mayor) of that city, and had later become
the chairman of a New Town Development Corporation and the
Labour spokesman on Scottish affairs in the House of Lords. The
corridors of power he had walked were those of government, local
and central. He was familiar with the practice of the delegation of
governmental functions to agencies (the now maligned quangos)
and might be expected to be receptive to the notion of co-opting
members of the legal profession to supply a service for which the
activities of the state created a need. His English counterpart, on
the other hand, wielded influence as the confidential adviser of
moneyed individuals and large corporate bodies in commerce and
industry, whose posture is usually one of hostility or defensiveness
towards all but the most basic activities of the state. He was a leader
of his profession of accountancy, an organisation which parallels in
many respects that of the legal profession. His appointment may
well reflect the government's initial intention to have a Royal
Commission on the Legal Profession.

The Scottish Commission was smaller than its English
counterpart, for no very apparent reason, since their remits were
almost identical; and indeed that of the Scottish Commission was
subsequently widened in that it was permitted to examine the
structure of the courts in so far as it had a bearing on the terms of
reference. Its membership exemplifies the cult of balance among
acceptable interests and the careful carpentry of construction to be
found in such bodies: a businessman, the managing director of
Scottish Television; a trade union official, who was also a law
graduate; a leader in local government who was also a minister;[2] a
champion of consumers and advice agencies; a retired director of
education; a university professor of economics, a discipline adjacent to law. From the legal profession came a judge, an advocate

and two solicitors – one from Edinburgh, one from Glasgow, one male, one female.

It was perhaps a blessing in disguise that the Benson Commission commenced briskly on 2 July 1976, sixteen weeks before the Hughes Commission met. It had formulated its questionnaires, placed advertisements in the press inviting responses and sought out research before Hughes had begun to get organised. With this headstart there could be no question of Hughes keeping strictly in step with Benson, at a pace set by the latter. Hughes did follow Benson in issuing detailed and lengthy questionnaires to both branches of the legal profession in Scotland (Appendix 2–1 and 2–2). It also commissioned research on legal problems and legal services from its research staff, and on the organisation and financing of solicitors' firms, the buying and selling of residential property, the education and training of solicitors and other subjects from outside organisations. The Benson Commission had also arranged for research, but Hughes did not follow its range of topics. It had legal education thoroughly investigated, which Benson did not, but Benson showed greater curiosity over the remuneration of the legal profession and it found it worthwhile to do a much more thorough survey of law centres and legal advice centres. So while doing the same sort of job as Benson, the Hughes Commission did it in its own way and surveyed a legal scene that differed in significant respects from that examined by Benson. Their separateness is reflected in the substantial difference in conclusions arrived at by the two Commissions.

From the outset the Reports of the two Commissions manifest a difference of approach to their remits, one which becomes sharper as they examine different facets of their subjects, although it does not lead them to disagree throughout. The distinction is, however, a radical one. By 2–3 Benson has already identified legal services as services provided by lawyers, both in private practice, and in a variety of forms of employment. It is noted that lawyers may also give advice on matters which have no close connection with law; equally members of other professions often give advice about legal problems (2–5). Advice agencies are regarded as giving a general service of advice and helping inquirers who need legal services to gain access to those services. Thus Benson will not concern itself with helping such organisations to improve their methods (2–11), but rather with examining how the legal profession can help them in their work. So in effect legal services are defined as what the legal profession does, even though initial contact may be made with them through a number of agencies, and the task of the Commission becomes to examine how the profession is performing its function and what changes, if any, are necessary.

For Hughes, by contrast, the emphasis is on the recipients rather than on the providers of legal services. Its starting point was people as users of the law, which confers on them rights and imposes on them obligations, both on an increasing scale. The legal profession and its health and efficiency was of concern as the principal supplier of legal services to the populace. But not the only one – lay or voluntary legal advisers could meet the initial needs of many people. Recourse to professional lawyers should be limited to the occasions when it is really necessary (1–38). Hughes took seriously its title and remit as a Commission on legal services and thus, as we shall see, has a restricted understanding of the meaning of law.

Hughes' Recommendations

Having described in Chapters 3 and 4 how needs for legal services are presently met by the legal profession and by other agencies such as citizens advice bureaux, the Hughes Commission, following its people-centred approach, grapples with the thorny question of whether there exists an unmet legal need and if so what its extent is. It had the results of its own enquiries to guide it (Appendix 4). The investigators were well aware of the criticisms levelled at research into unmet legal need which assumed that what the researcher posits as a problem calling for legal solution, is perceived in the same way by the respondent. They tried to minimise the force of this criticism in two ways. They invited the respondents in open-ended questions to talk about any of a pre-selected list of problems with a legal content in which they had been involved, and about any others which, though not on the list, they had experienced. Less than 20 per cent had received legal advice from a lawyer or para-legal body, the figure being as low as 10 per cent in landlord–tenant, 13 per cent in consumer and 14 per cent in employment cases. The number relying on their own resources, that is to say, consulting no-one or only friends, ranged from 22 per cent in consumer cases to 67 per cent in matters of debt. Those who did consult solicitors seemed pleased with their choice. 82 per cent were satisfied or very satisfied. Large majorities reported that their solicitor was easy to contact and talk to and he kept them informed. Predictably the use of solicitors declined in step with the socio-economic status of the head of the household, and non-manual workers had a more favourable view of the legal profession than manual ones. The Commission concludes that when people make contact with a solicitor over a legal problem they are unlikely to be disappointed, but that there are three barriers which may prevent them from making that contact. They must know enough about the law to recognise that they may have a legal problem, they must have access to the intended legal service and they must not be deterred by considerations of cost.

The Commission treats the supply and co-ordination of information about the law as one of the functions of the Legal Services Commission for which it later argues. It also urges that all pupils in the third year of their secondary course should receive some instruction on law and legal services, using radio and television. The Law Society (i.e. of Scotland) is criticised for its restrictive attitude to advertising by solicitors and it is urged to adopt the proposals of the Monopolies and Mergers Commission and allow advertising by solicitors of their services and prices, so long as they do not claim superiority to others, maintain accuracy and do not bring their profession into disrepute.

The Commission enthusiastically espouses the model of the non-specialist free advice agency manned by volunteers with a stiffening of paid organisers, and access – on or off the premises – to professional legal advice. In other words, it recommends the service already provided by the better-equipped citizens advice bureaux. Legal advice given by solicitors is not rejected, and indeed it is considered that that model provides the best means of making an initial service available. Law centres are treated more hesitantly, being seen as a subject for experimentation – perhaps understandably so, in view of the very limited and not very encouraging experience provided so far in Scotland by such centres. Law centres are regarded as filling gaps in the provision of legal services by solicitors, both in supplying a generally free service of initial legal advice and in providing further services (such as representation) on the same basis as solicitors, by payment of fees or under legal aid. The Commission recommends that they should be set up first where the unmet need is greatest. Yet with apparent inconsistency it stresses that law centres should not be seen as a service for particular groups in the community. But in so far as a particular locality is regarded as a 'deprived area', the provision of the legal service which it lacks and other places enjoy would seem to be a form of compensation for the real thing. Like Benson, Hughes reprobates law centres becoming bases for political campaigns. They 'should help to conciliate and resolve local differences, not harden them on partisan lines' (7–16).

After considering whether the funding of such public legal services should be entrusted to central government, local authorities or the Law Society, the Commission comes to the conclusion that only a national agency, independent of government, albeit in receipt of public funds, could operate with the desired degree of detachment. It would provide grants to local groups, who would run the services, in the same way as citizens advice bureaux management committees do at present. This organisation is given the name of the Legal Services Commission (LSC). As well as distributing grants, it would conduct research, experiment with other ways of providing legal setvices and set standards for the recipients of its largesse. Exceptionally these might include firms of solicitors proposing to set up branch offices in under-provided areas.

In these ways Hughes hopes to lower the second barrier impeding access to legal services. In so far as the services offered would be free, financial obstacles would also be removed at the stage of determining whether a problem would benefit by legal remedy.

The Commission then addresses itself to the question of paying for specialist legal services provided by trained lawyers. Unlike Benson, it makes the bold recommendation that the Law Society should no longer be entrusted with the administration of the legal aid schemes, because of the inescapable conflict of interests arising. While it is careful not to blame the Law Society, there are hints of dissatisfaction with the complexity of the legal aid system and the lack of independent control over the setting of fees to be paid for by the legal aid fund. It is also suggested that the financial assessment of applicants for civil legal aid should be removed from the Supplementary Benefits Commission, which is said to perform it in an unnecessarily complex way. Instead, in a bold proposal, it suggests that solicitors should be responsible for means testing their own clients seeking representation in civil cases, as they do at present in a simple way when legal advice and assistance is being sought. Indeed it is recommended that the two present schemes should be merged. Under a new eligibility scheme, solicitors would be encouraged to collect any contribution due, but where no such arrangement was made the contribution, if need be in instalments, would have to be collected by the central administration, the LSC. The determination of probable cause and reasonableness in civil litigation would also be entrusted to the solicitor, to the extent that he should be permitted to take an affirmative decision himself, referring to a committee only such cases as he proposed to reject or thought doubtful.

When it turns to consider legal aid for accused persons, the Commission appears to borrow from the proposal of the Scottish LAG, which it had earlier been at pains to reject (8–17), namely that legal aid, depending on the gravity of the case, should either be free, subject to a flat rate charge, or given no financial support. It proposes that, as at present, the services of a duty solicitor should be available free to anyone held in custody and awaiting a first appearance in court. But in addition all those not in custody should be given the services of a solicitor to advise them how to plead. For this a flat rate charge would be imposed on all except those who would be entitled to free civil legal aid. (The Commission does not seem to have been aware of how much use is already made of the legal advice and assistance scheme for this purpose.) As to the granting of legal aid for representation at a trial, the Commission recommends that as at present this should be a duty of judges, but they should be entitled to delegate to sheriffs, and clerks the power to grant aid, though not to withhold it. To assist sheriff-clerks and promote uniformity, it is proposed that criteria should be laid down in statute. These would be based on the list prepared by the Widgery Committee, but the Commission considers it necessary to specify which offences carry little or no risk of imprisonment and so would not qualify. As at present, any person prosecuted under solemn procedure and thus for a serious offence, should be entitled to legal aid.

In concluding this stage of their Report, the Commission makes three novel suggestions. The first is that solicitors should be available in prisons to help both convicted and untried prisoners on a continuing basis, not as Benson proposed, drawn from duty solicitors of the district (Benson 9–24). In a more hesitant manner it is suggested that public defenders – salaried lawyers acting solely on behalf of accused persons, as found in the USA – should be appointed experimentally to offer an alternative to a solicitor chosen by the accused, but only when resources permit of a longterm experiment. Even more tentatively it is suggested that consideration be given to the awarding of legal aid to either party or both in order to make appeals so as to facilitate the development of the law.

The Hughes Commission then turns its attention to the improvement of particular forms of legal service. Conveyancing was one such subject which the Commissioners could not avoid, for the monopolies attached to it were specifically mentioned in their remit and they directed one of their surveys to testing the satisfaction of house purchasers and sellers with the service provided. Differing sharply from Benson, Hughes regards the present monopoly of solicitors over the preparation of writs relating to domestic heritable property, when done for reward, as not demonstrably in the public interest. He is therefore not prepared to follow Benson in recommending its extension to the preparation of missives, or the contract of sale. Other professional bodies and organisations would be permitted to engage in domestic conveyancing, provided there were safeguards for clients' funds, indemnity insurance, rules of conduct and a complaints procedure, and their members were competent at the job – requirements which might perhaps be met only by the legal profession. The Commission found considerable public dissatisfaction with the expenses incurred by intending house-purchasers in paying for surveyors' reports commissioned by building societies whom they approach for loans. They suggest that the societies should set up a common agency which would supply a single valuation when a house was offered for sale. The similar problem of the need for multiple valuations might be overcome by requiring all sellers of house property to provide potential purchasers with a standard report prepared by a surveyor.

On divorce the Commission gives backing to the demands of several Scottish organisations, including the Law Society of Scotland itself, that jurisdiction should be transferred from the Court of Session – the Supreme Court of Scotland – to certain designated local sheriff courts. Venturing beyond their remit they urge Parliament that separation for a period no longer than two years, with no requirement of consent, should be the sole evidence of matrimonial breakdown resting on the lapse of a period of time. Concern is expressed at the ineffectiveness of the Court of Session in performing its duty to consider the arrangements proposed for children of the marriage before granting a divorce. Instead it is suggested that the Reporter to the Children's Panel – who in Scotland brings before a Children's Hearing of lay persons children appearing to be in need of compulsory measures of care – that Reporter should be required to prepare for the court a report on the arrangements for custody of every child under 16 affected by a divorce. Parties should be able to conduct their own undefended divorces by completing forms, a signed declaration on which would be sufficient evidence of the facts stated.

A similar concern is shown by the Commission that people should be enabled to operate legal services for themselves in the proposals that there should be an informal small claims procedure within the sheriff courts up to a limit of £500 in value, which litigants could use without legal representation. In replacing the present summary cause procedure, which has 94 rules, it would also have to serve as a debt enforcement mechanism. In the winding up of the estates of the deceased, the call is again for things to be made simpler. Sheriff-clerks are urged to help executors to obtain confirmation (probate) where the value of the estate is up to 80 per cent of the threshold of capital transfer tax. A Small Estates procedure enabling estates under a value of £10,000 to be wound up without the intervention of a solicitor should be implemented and this has in fact happened.

Only in Chapter 15 do the Commissioners turn their attention to the main providers of legal services, the legal profession. First they examine the Law Society of Scotland, a statutory body to which all solicitors practising in Scotland must belong. It has as its objects 'the promotion of the interests of the profession of solicitors in Scotland and the interests of the public in relation to that profession' (a formula then hidden away in a schedule to one of the many Acts affecting solicitors in Scotland, but now brought into prominence in Section 2 of a consolidating measure, the Solicitors (Scotland) Act 1980). This dual role is noted to be fraught with potential conflicts, but the Commission concludes that although at times the conflicts may become real, the Council of the Society does strive to reconcile the two. Various reforms recommended in the Report would further strengthen the position of the client and the public interest.

The Commissioners conclude that there is benefit to the public in having their interests protected by the same body which safeguards the interests of solicitors and the present dual responsibility of the Law Society should remain. But it is not immune to criticism. Its knowledge of the organisation of the firms in which its members work was found to be inadequate, making impossible any full appreciation of how the profession was working.

Turning to the other branch of the legal profession in Scotland, the Commission readily adopts the Faculty of Advocate's view of itself and its arguments against fusion with solicitors or any form of relationship other than the present one. In this members of a small Bar concentrated in Edinburgh, about 140 in current practice, can be instructed to appear in court only by a solicitor, partnerships among them are forbidden, and they have a monopoly in the representation of clients in the High Court, Court of Session and courts of equivalent rank. One minor addendum which is offered tentatively is that professional persons, other than solicitors (for example, patent agents and chartered accountants) should be entitled to obtain the opinion of an advocate on a point of law or to instruct him to appear at a tribunal or inquiry, without the intervention of a solicitor.

The Hughes Commission devotes considerable attention to legal education for the practice of law. Several surveys were conducted, in which the views were sought of law students, apprentices (the Scots equivalent of the articled clerk), teachers of law, recently qualified solicitors, senior partners of firms, and graduates in law who were not known to the Law Society. The justification was the argument that the quality of service provided by a lawyer depends in large measure on training and education, both before and after qualification. Some pointed criticisms and recommendations emerge from this examination. It regrets the reliance of the university law faculties on academic attainments at school in selecting applicants for admission, and suggests that more account should be taken of aptitude for the study of law, for which an aptitude test might be devised, and that in selecting among those who satisfy the minimum educational requirement, an attempt should be made to create a student population with a more varied age and socio-economic background (though a quota system is rejected). The LL.B. or first degree in law is seen as being too short and, in satisfying the requirements of the legal profession, too narrow. The

Commission's preferred solution is that the three year, non-specialised, ordinary LL.B. degree should be extended to four years in duration, the same as the present honours degree. The additional time should be used to encourage students to study a foreign language, a social science and more 'social law'.

Teaching methods should also be updated with less use of the lecture and more small group instruction and use of audio-visual aids. There should be more opportunity for law students to meet people with genuine legal problems. Examination methods are criticised as placing too much stress on the memory and more use of legislative texts is recommended, coupled with a higher standard of attainment. The Commission give a cautious welcome to the Diploma in Legal Practice, a one year course provided from 1980 by the five Scottish law schools in certain branches of the practice of law and to be obligatory for all entrants to the legal profession in Scotland. While recognising the difficulties the Commission express a preference for some form of block release system and urge that the Diploma scheme should be reviewed after five years. After obtaining the Diploma, intending solicitors are to spend a further two years as trainees in offices.

As checks on the quality of their training Hughes recommends that each trainee should keep a record of experiences; the solicitors responsible for the training should have to report to the Law Society on the trainee's performance; the trainee should have to report to the Law Society on the quality of training, firms found unsatisfactory should be black-listed from taking further trainees and the standard of training in designated areas of the law should be laid down by the Law Society. These multiple checks reflect the volume of criticism from organisations making submissions to the Commission and by respondents to their surveys on the variable quality of apprenticeships, as they have been hitherto known, and of the lack of effective means of raising the standard.

On the education of lawyers, the Commission stresses the need to keep abreast of changes in the law and while acknowledging that the Law Society has provided short courses, usually at weekends, it notes that they are basic in character and proposes that they should be supplemented by progressive courses studied over a period of time. The Commission considered the signification of specialist knowledge by certificates of competence, but confined its encouragement of specialisation to the formation of more groups of lawyers with interests in particular areas of the law, such as already exist in european community law and in industrial law. The Commission deplores the low level of involvement of advocates in such courses. The Commission's discussion of legal education concludes with some very broad observations on the training of judges, of tribunal chairmen and members, of citizens advice bureaux staff (their courses should be shared with the staff of other advice agencies), and the employees of law firms, who do work of the level of English legal executives, without being accorded their status (progressive certificate courses on a day release basis should be provided by the Scottish Business Education Council).

When it turned to consider professional conduct, complaints and discipline, the Commission was struck by the absence of any official statement by the Law Society (or the Faculty of Advocates) of the standard of professional conduct which a lawyer is expected to maintain. The one publication of this nature was stated by the Law Society to convey the author's own views and was in no way binding on its Council. The Law Society's line was that its members lived by principles, not detailed rules, but it was difficult to ascertain what the principles were and the practice was admitted to be constantly changing. Hughes therefore recommends that the Law Society should publish an authoritative guide to the professional conduct of solicitors, in terms which laymen can understand. A similar guide should be promulgated by the Faculty of Advocates. Some fairly substantial changes are proposed in the Law Society's handling of complaints against its members. The separate complaints schemes for legal aid and non-legal aid cases should be merged into one. There should be participation of non-lawyers at the stage of consideration whether a complaint discloses conduct justifying prosecution before the Scottish Solicitors Discipline Tribunal. The Tribunal itself should be reconstituted with a larger lay element, enabling equal number of lawyers and laymen, with a legally qualified chairman, to sit in judgment on every case. The Tribunal should have powers to impose a higher fine than the then maximum of £250 which seemed 'totally inadequate.' (The maximum fine was raised to £2,500 in the Law Reform (Miscellaneous Provisions) (Scotland) Act 1980, Sec. 24).

The Law Society should not delay taking action in respect of evidence of incompetence, simply because the complainer may have a remedy for negligence in the civil courts. The Discipline

Tribunal should have power to make an award of compensation up to a maximum figure to a complainer who renounces his remedies in the courts. The Lay Observer, who as in England and Wales, is appointed to examine allegations about the Society's handling of complaints, should be retained but given powers to bring cases before the Discipline Tribunal. It should have the power to override the solicitors' lien over property belonging to a client to enforce payment of sums due to them. Complaints against advocates should be investigated by the Dean of the Faculty and if required an *ad hoc* Discipline Tribunal chaired by a judge should be set up by the Lord President at the request of the Dean. Both complaints procedures should be publicised in a joint leaflet and decisions of Tribunals should be communicated to the press.

The Commission then examines the remuneration of the legal profession. It suggests that its explicit mention in the remit reflects complaints from the public that lawyers' fees are too high and from lawyers that they are held too low. The fact that some fees are based on monopolies and some fees are paid by the legal aid fund also prompted this part of its remit, the Commission thought. The coyness of members of both branches of the legal profession about their incomes, despite elaborate precautions to ensure anonymity, almost thwarted the Commission in this endeavour. Some of the most senior advocates, and presumably the highest-earning, were reticent about disclosing income. The overall response rate of the advocates was at 75 per cent much better than that achieved by the solicitors. The overall response rate from firms was just over 50 per cent and as low as 38 per cent in Glasgow and 43 per cent in Edinburgh. The researchers conclude optimistically that although the replies were too few to produce statistically satisfactory results, the indications were that the response was not significantly different from firms of different sizes, and thus some broad conclusions could be drawn.

More disturbing to the Commission was the revelation that many firms were quite ignorant of the relative profitability of the different branches of their work and unable to specialise in the areas in which they were most at an advantage. The Commission deplores this dearth of information which enables it to conclude only tentatively that 'the solicitor profession offers attractive net lifetime income prospects (19–39) and that the remuneration available 'is adequate to maintain and if necessary increase the size of the profession'

(19–40). The scale fee basis of charging for conveyancing (and domestic conveyancing is shown to provide 34 per cent of the income of firms) is criticised as imposing cross-subsidisation from high price to low price property transactions. There is a suspicion that the more profitable forms of the legal practice of solicitors subsidise the less profitable, a surmise which the lack of cost and income analysis made it impossible to prove or disprove.

The Commissioners are critical of the number of persons and bodies involved in the fixing of fees and of the lack of information as to what basis fees were originally calculated on. Recent up-rating of fees appeared to have been done on a percentage basis, perhaps because the fee fixers lacked the resources to investigate the cost of the various services. A simple means of assessing fees is proposed: a base factor consisting of an hourly time rate, reflecting the cost of doing the type of work in a particular case with reasonable efficiency, subject to variation reflecting skill, knowledge, responsibility and special attention. This, it is claimed, would encourage competition and improve efficiency. For pre-fixed fees a statutory independent body should be set up by the Secretary of State for Scotland, with appropriately qualified professional members. To adjudicate on disputed fees, there should be a Department of the Auditor of Court staffed by experienced solicitors, replacing the present unco-ordinated system in which sheriff-clerks throughout Scotland perform this duty as a sideline, while full-time auditors are attached to the Court of Session.

This financial section of the Report concludes with a bold proposal concerning interest on the money of clients held temporarily by solicitors. After the exposure of the practice of solicitors in retaining the interest (*Brown v. Commissioners of Inland Revenue* (1964) 3 All E. R. 119 and Benson 23–16), the Law Society made rules that where such funds are in excess of £500 and are likely to be held for more than two months, interest must be paid to the client. But otherwise it may still be retained. Hughes estimates that about £3.5 million was earned by Scottish solicitors' firms in this way in 1977. The Commission urges that 'if at all possible' interest should be paid to the client whose money provides it (though it does not say what obstacles would suffice to make it impossible). Any other interest should be paid to a Scottish Law Foundation which would have among its functions financial involvement in the production of text books, establishment of a computerised law retrieval system, the provision of scholarships and the support of socio-legal research. Before such a scheme was set up there should be a levy on principal solicitors likely to benefit from such interest, the proceeds being used to give the Foundation a start. It is one proposal which is not likely to endear the Commission to Scottish solicitors but it has precedents in Canada and Australia.

The Commission turns finally to the administrative structure necessary to sustain the changes it advocates. After noting the division of responsibilities in matters of Scottish law and legal services among various departments and personages, it recommends that 'all Scottish legal affairs' should be entrusted to a new Department of Legal Affairs under a senior minister (except for the Lord Advocate, who would retain his present responsibility for prosecutions and for providing legal advice to the government). They also call for the setting up of a Legal Services Advisory Committee to parallel the Lord Chancellor's Advisory Committee on Legal Aid. But the keystone of the edifice is one rejected by Benson – a Legal Services Commission which would administer legal aid, allocate public funds to advice agencies and inform the public about the law and advice services. All three bodies should have access to research services. Information on how the Scottish legal system works was found by Hughes to be woefully inadequate and the absence of personnel forecasting was particularly noted. Other bodies proposed include court advisory committees, area advice services management committees, a standing committee on the Land Register, and a committee to review the structure and procedure of civil courts.

The Commission was not without its dissenters. In fact there are as many as 15 Notes of Dissent. They are by the judge, the advocate and the two solicitors, singly or in various combinations. All four urge that the conveyancing monopoly should be extended to cover missives for the sale and purchase of property. They also stand together in opposing the proposal that the revised legal aid scheme should be administered by the LSC. Yet on a wide range of issues the Hughes Commission is united. In particular the members subscribe to the proposals on the extension of legal services outside the legal profession and on changes in legal education at every level from school pupils to sheriffs.

Weighing-up the Report

The Hughes Report is not, like some Royal Commission Reports, wholly devoid of theory. Nor does one have to deduce the authors' assumptions. In a few paragraphs headed 'The Main Issues' and 'Our Approach' the Commissioners reveal what they thought they were about and why they recommended as they did. Their primary concern is with people as users or potential users of the legal system. So they attach great importance to access to and delivery of legal services (1–35). That leads them to consider the needs and preferences of those who supply the services, especially the lawyers, for a satisfactory system of legal services must depend on a viable and adequate profession. It is one that supplies services to commercial as well as to individual clients (1–36). The need for legal services has greatly increased because of governmental activity since the Second World War. It behoves the government which created a plethora of rights and obligations to ensure that they are known and understood (1–37). Though the law is complex, there is a role for the non-lawyer, including volunteers, in analysing whether a problem is susceptible of legal resolution (1–38). The state should sustain and supplement such efforts (1–39), while preserving the independence of the legal profession (1–40). At this point theory peters out, as the Report proceeds in pragmatic fashion to justify the stances to be taken later on particular issues in the remit, such as the training and remuneration of the legal profession and their monopoly in conveyancing.

One must not blame the Commission for putting at the centre of its argument the concept of legal services, for that was the topic handed to it by the Queen. But any competent student assigned an essay by a professor on the topic: 'there is an unmet need for legal services. Discuss.' would begin by teasing out the idea of legal services (as well as of need) and coming up with a working definition. One can fault the Commission for not beginning to probe the complexities of its subject, for it leads it to slide past difficulties unnoticed and ultimately to produce a broken-backed Report. Let us try, in a fashionable term, to unpack the notion of legal services – or should it be unpick, as of a lock? It is well-embedded in our consciousnesses, yet it is a comparatively new idea. Hobbes or Austin seem to be unfamiliar with it. Jeremy Bentham, patron saint of the determined do-gooder, did not associate service with judges and lawyers.

The truth is that it verges on an oxymoron, a contradiction in terms, like bitter-sweet. Service or servility is not the first thing one associates with law. Rather it pushes people around, telling what they must do and must not do. Even when it does dole out benefits, it hedges them about with conditions and obligations which must be complied with on pain of forfeiture, as any social security claimant will testify. But the Commission seems to have an image of law as a cornucopia of blessings of which some people are not getting their fair share, though only because of their short-sightedness or the imperfections of the administrative arrangements for distributing the largesse. But such people may be quite sensible in pursuing their own interests, not just because, in Philip Lewis's vivid image, when a tenant's roof is leaking, it may be wiser to get a ladder rather than a lawyer.[3] The opportunities presented by law may be so fenced around with hassle or expense, that people simply say no thank you.

So an accused person may prefer to conduct his own defence, rather than entrust it to an advocate to play as he thinks fit. Couples will start living together, rather than plunge into marriage with its pre-determined legal scheme of rights and duties. Married couples will drift apart, rather than face up to the expense and recriminations of divorce, unless and until one of them wishes to re-marry and has to comply with the law's condition. Commercial enterprises which are mutually dependent on one another will smooth over their differences, though one may have committed a breach of contract, rather than resort to law and imperil their relationship. True the supplementary benefit claimant will toe the legal line (unless a loop-hole can be found), but that is because by definition the claimant is one whom necessity compels to comply. It is rather like a black, legal economy. People opt out of the law, just as they opt out of the visible labour market, but yet do jobs for one another, free of its various restrictions.

If law is something that is openly coercive, as is the criminal law or taxation, or makes benefits available only on its own terms, then there is something odd about the expression 'legal service.' Either it is a part of that coercive apparatus, making sure people know what the terms are, but masquerading behind the word service, which carries favourable associations. Or it is better called a contra-legal service. A hint of this dilemma is to be found in the passage where the Commission observes that 'the government and government agencies have done a certain amount to bring new law, new rights and new obligations to public notice, but the evidence presented to us suggested that nevertheless there was a wide gap between the needs of large sections of the population for legal services and their ability to satisfy these needs' (1.37). The coupling together of rights and obligations is confusing. But as to rights it is not surprising that any government committed to reducing public expenditure and taxation should be slow to publicise benefits which will cost it more. Obligations are another matter. The government is not conspicuously slow to publicise and enforce new obligations. A new obligation to maintain sufficient tread on tyres is first advertised, then upheld through the MOT test, the police and ultimately prosecution.

The vaunted independence of the legal profession, which the Commission takes on trust (1–40, 18–29) presents another puzzle. The lawyer is presented as a Mr. Valiant-for-Law, warding off abuses of law with his only weapon – law. If the only function is to check that the rules have been applied correctly, then independence is something of a sham. The lawyer is still part of the legal apparatus ensuring that people toe the line, the right line. If truly independent, then he must be acting outside the law and against the law, though perhaps under the ideal of some higher law.

To express these reservations is not to scoff at the whole idea of legal services or the Commission's uncritical acceptance of it. There is a case for making what the law has to offer, snags and all, accessible to everyone who contemplates using it. This is particularly so where two persons are in an adversarial situation and only one has access to legal knowledge. For example, an electricity board possesses its terms and conditions of supply and its customer does not. But the consumer's eye view of the law which the Commission shares does assume that it is an unmitigated good from which some are unjustly excluded. Some may prefer to run their lives without resort to what the law offers. They will certainly do so if they regard the rules of law as rigged against them in the first place.

What might a contra-legal service have to offer? Being truly independent from the operators of the legal system, it would not try to sell legal services, but rather describe options open to people in difficulties, their costs and consequences. There is always at least the option to do nothing. It is not beyond the bounds of possibility that the 'generalist advice centres' sketched out by the Commission might fulfill this specification. It stresses that problems do not arise already labelled 'legal', that trained volunteers, as used by the citizens advice bureaux, should form the bulk of the staff, that solicitors should only be a supporting resource (7–5, 7–10). The centres should be run by 'independent local management committees much as Citizens Advice Bureaux are at present' (7–28). Area advice centre committees should inform the LSC of local needs for advice services and make bids for financial support. But at that point this non-specialist localised provision would dovetail into the official provision of 'legal services', for the LSC would also be running the present legal aid schemes, albeit reconstituted and with their financial conditions changed, but still with an open-ended commitment to pay the legal profession for its services and on its terms. Law centres, as envisaged by Hughes, seem to be confined to filling gaps left by private solicitors, to whom they should refer those with 'traditional problems' (7–15). Though advising groups, they should not become bases for 'political campaigning.' But a contra-legal centre would advise groups on how to change the law – for example, a local authority's housing allocation scheme, or standard lease, or securing parking restrictions, or the exclusion of through traffic from residential streets. Hughes would give to law centres 'an active educational role in the Community, ensuring that groups and individuals know the legal resources available to them' (7–15). But it will be an inadequate education if it does include how to change the rules, 'political' though that may be.

Assuming, reasonably enough, that some people, when fully informed of the choices before them, will wish to utilise legal services of the kinds now provided solely or mainly by lawyers, the question arises of the fitness of the legal profession to provide these services. In para. 1–36 the Commissioners stated that 'a satisfactory system of legal services must depend on its ability to maintain a viable and adequate profession' (falling already into the legal profession's habit of calling itself *the* profession). They dismissed in 8–15 the notion of a national legal service without fully exploring what that might mean, and they rejected any change in the mutually exclusive relationship between advocates and solicitors (15–50). The Commission was aware from its own researches, that a substantial slice of the income of lawyers, exactly how large they could not tell, derived from commercial clients. But because there were few complaints from that quarter, it felt excused from looking for scope for improvement there. It does not seem to have occurred to the Commission that absence of dissatisfaction with the 'quality of the legal services' (1–36) shown by commercial clients might be a sign that they were getting too great a share of the quality, leaving the scrag-end to legal aid clients. It is quite permissible for apprentices to provide legal advice and assistance under a solicitor's supervision which may be quite nominal.[4] Duty solicitors are generally recruited from recently-qualified and hence inexperienced solicitors and the Commission criticises the low standard of pleading in the district and sheriff courts (16–36). Advocates tend to reduce or give up legal aid work as they attain seniority (Appendix 8.33). The Commission noted that legal aid work 'tended to have a depressing effect on profits' (19–50). Of course it is priced on the same scale as non-legal aid work, less a deduction in civil legal aid of 10 per cent which it is proposed should be abolished (8–49).

But elsewhere, and particularly in advocacy, the price of the service is whatever the market will bear. Money talks, and those who have it will use it to buy up specialised assistance when they are in a tight corner. In medical services only massive public expenditure and financial arrangements, by which most of the time of most doctors is bought by the state for National Health Service patients, has kept private practice at bay. In the hospital sector it is making inroads, with the encouragement of the Tory government. Analogies drawn between medical and legal services are always imperfect and may be misleading. But at least one can place them on a scale and say that one is *a fortiori* of the other. Money talks with a louder voice in calling for legal services than medical services for two reasons. Corporate bodies of unlimited wealth, as well as individuals can purchase legal talent. Corporate bodies and individuals can use that talent to maximise their profits, as well as to ward off adversities. On the other hand, individuals, regardless of their wealth, are nearly always ready to pay a higher price for the preservation of health than for any possible benefits flowing from the use of law.

The Hughes Commission delimits two small zones from which the pressures of the market would be held at bay; the network of generalist advice centres and the scattered and experimental law centres. Otherwise legal services would be supplied by the private legal profession essentially in the present manner, though rather more individuals would qualify for financial help. There would be more external scrutiny of the setting of fee levels and in the determination of particular fees. But feeing rests on such open-ended terms as 'a reasonable salary' or 'a fair return on capital' to which, like x and y, one can assign any value. The Commission shows a surprisingly ambivalent attitude to the legal profession on whom it relies so heavily for attaining its objectives. On the one hand the virtues of competition are praised. The conveyancing monopoly, so far from being extended as the Law Society urged, is to be abolished. Competition in prices is to be encouraged. Solicitors should be allowed to advertise the services they offer, with the price attached, so long as permitted maxima are not exceeded. All this is done in the interests of the consumer and of efficiency. But also in the interests of the consumer, the legal profession must 'meet the highest standards of probity and professional performance' and must have 'adequate machinery to maintain rigorous standards of professional care and conduct' (18–1).

So the institutions of the Law Society's Professional Complaints sub-committee, the Lay Observer and the Scottish Solicitors Discipline Tribunal are approved, subject to some changes. What are these high standards? The Commission could find no authoritative statement, neither for solicitors nor advocates. The Commission calls for a guide on ethics and practice for solicitors. It recommends that it should show a new attitude to advertising and that a solicitor, when approached by a client, should be under an obligation to give an estimate of the cost of the work requested. That apart, its content is left to the Law Society (18–5). But what kind of rules will be appropriate to legal entrepreneurs who are encouraged to compete with one another in their prices? And why is the Commission so critical of firms which cannot say what the profitability of each branch of their business is, if it is not to enable them to concentrate on the most profitable? (19–42, 19–51) The Commission seems to have been uncertain whether to espouse a professional ethic of service and moderation or a commercial ethic of competition. Both are to be found among solicitors today. But the Commission has failed to reconcile the two. Rather by proposing the intensification of competition, it has made it more difficult for a self-regulating profession to curb its more unruly members.

The Prospects for Implementation

In the current atmosphere of retrenchment in spending and disenchantment with affirmative state action, the prospects for implementing the more constructive proposals of the Hughes Commission, such as law centres and the LSC are gloomy. Legal services, even if they could be disentangled in the public mind from the restrictive and unappealing side of law, are a much less popular cause than health, housing, some forms of social security – such as pensions – or even perhaps education. Anything that could be depicted, however inaccurately, as putting more money in the pockets of lawyers, is unlikely to win many votes.

Even where savings can be made in legal aid expenditure, it is by no means clear that the current drive for cuts in public expenditure would permit them to be used elsewhere on legal services. There is considerable scope for such savings in divorce. Hughes notes that 'actions for dissolution of marriage in the Court of Session cost the legal aid fund some £2.9 million in the year ending 31 March 1979. This was more than three-quarters of the total paid from the legal aid fund in respect of civil actions' (10–3). It recommends that, as in England and Wales, legal advice and assistance should be available in divorces only where no matter was in dispute (10–47). This is coupled with the recommendation that the local sheriff courts rather than the Court of Session should have exclusive jurisdiction in divorce actions, defended or undefended, at first instance. (10–18). That transfer is unlikely to come about in the immediate future, involving, as it would, additional expenditure. But the Report of a Working Party set up by the Lord President under the Chairmanship of Lord Cowie, a judge, has recently recommended that in divorces based on two or five years' separation, where there is no dispute on custody or financial provisions, a procedure should be devised enabling parties to conduct their divorces by correspondence and without legal representation. About 25 per cent of divorce cases would be covered by such a procedure. If the funds amounting to about £750,000 a year were released and diverted to improving and extending the citizens advice bureau network in Scotland, something approaching the Commission's vision of 100 generalist advice centres throughout Scotland could be achieved cheaply and speedily. The use of volunteers (though more highly trained than the average CAB worker at present) would be in line with the views of the Commission in 7–4 and 7–7, as well as with the philosophy of the present Conservative government.

Apart from that major development, there are many recommendations which could be carried out without extra expenditure or at slight extra cost to the two branches of the legal profession. They were told by the Secretary of State for Scotland in the House of Commons on 3 November 1980 that he expects them to give consideration to the recommendations which it is within their power to implement.

Notes

1. Mr. Gordon Wilson, SNP member of Parliament for Dundee East, has mentioned to the writer that after expressing concern in the Commons at the delay in announcing a corresponding Royal Commission for Scotland, and pleasure that the Scottish legal profession was not to be included in the remit of the Commission announced for England and Wales (H. C. Debs. Vol. 905, col. 621), he was asked by the Lord Advocate what he thought the reactions of the Scottish legal profession would be to such an inquiry. (At that stage the inquiry had not been widened out to embrace legal services.) He made it his business to sound out opinion among individual lawyers and groups of lawyers, including the Law Society, and was able to report a favourable reaction.
2. Geoffrey Shaw, who died in April 1978 and to whom tribute is paid in the Report. He was replaced by Sir George Sharp, a former County and Regional Convener and like Mr. Shaw a member of the Labour Party.
3. Morris P., White R. and Lewis P. S. (1973), *Social Needs and Legal Action* Oxford, Martin Robertson, p. 79.
4. Legal Advice and Assistance (Scotland) Regulations 1973, Reg. 5(3). ('Nothing in these regulations shall prevent a solicitor from entrusting any function under these regulations to a partner of his or to a competent and responsible employee of his employed in his office').

CHAPTER 4

Law Centres and Citizenship: The Way Forward

Mike Stephens

The Report of the Royal Commission on Legal Services was an opportunity to restructure legal services in Britain so that they might better meet the needs of a variety of consumers. That opportunity was largely spurned in favour of the misguided and somewhat unseemly desire on the part of the Commission to protect the interests, not of the consumer, but of the legal profession. Nowhere is this more clear then in the Commission's recommendations relating to law centres. Within the space of a mere thirteen pages a series of ill-conceived and misinformed proposals are trotted out which, if ever implemented in full, would lead to the emasculation of the current law centre movement. Fortunately for the movement it appears that the proposals are highly unlikely to be implemented, but the thinking behind these recommendations still bears some scrutiny and offers important lessons for the future operation of law centres.

Taken as a whole, the Commission's proposals (8–17, 32) for Citizens' Law Centres (CLCs) do very little to enhance actual citizenship; to promote and extend what Marshall (1963) referred to as the civil, political and social elements of citizenship. Marshall felt that the most important of these elements of citizenship was the civil element, especially the right to justice (Marshall 1963, p. 74) 'because it is the right to defend and assert all one's rights on terms of equality with others and by due process of law.' As I argue later, simply opening up access to the law for individuals previously denied its services, is insufficient to secure the rights and interests of the poor, or even of the mainly working-class clientèle of existing law centres. All that CLCs would appear to offer citizens seeking to assert their rights in an effective manner, is routine legal advice and assistance under the somewhat restrictive régime of the legal aid scheme. These same citizens visiting their CLCs would be made subject to a traditional lawyer – client relationship in which the professional is the most dominant and active partner, and the client passive and generally accepting of whatever narrowly legal strategy has been decided on his behalf. Legal strategies and remedies are by no means always adequate. However, the attempt to improve the adequacy of remedies available to clients at law centres, through the adoption of group and project work and community campaigns, is looked upon with extreme disfavour by the Commission which felt that it is (8–21) 'inappropriate for a law centre to devote its resources to taking part in political or community activities . . .' Moreover, in keeping with the Commission's general concern to stimulate demand for private legal practitioners, the proposed CLCs would find it necessary to refer an even higher proportion of clients to private solicitors than is currently the case in many existing centres. This should come as no suprise, for the intention of the Commission's recommendations is both to control the unacceptable elements in current law centre practice, and to safeguard the interests of the private profession. CLCs were to be the vehicles for simultaneously extending the traditional or reactive model of delivering services to today's 'deserving poor', while also making those services supplemental to private practitioners. They, in turn, were expected to take clients referred from CLCs and generally to take more interest in social welfare law. Through its ignorance of the aspirations of the law centre movement, and its dislike of the combination of legal and non-legal strategies in law centres, the Commission fails even to consider the merits of a proactive approach to legal services.

Reactivity and proactivity may be viewed as opposite ends of a continuum, and individual law centres may be identified as exhibiting an operational philosphy tending towards one pole or the other. A reactive tendency or orientation within a law centre is based largely on a system of self-referral by clients of referrals from outside agencies. Once the client has decided to seek advice at the law centre the relationship with the lawyer is likely to be passive, the lawyer typically taking important decisions about the legal viability, processing, and eventual disposition of the case. Informed consent is low and many problems are handled or referred routinely, thus not allowing clients to develop their own legal and civil competences. The emphasis in such centres is on law and legal strategies, with few resources effectively devoted towards group work and educational projects in the community etc. CLCs are extremely reactive in their design, being no more, in the main, than institutional holes into which would pour a stream of individual clients whose problems would be processed in isolation from one another, with no attempt made to attack the structural causes of those problems.

A more proactive approach seeks ways to transcend the individualizing process of the traditional lawyer–client relationship. It demands that law centres reach out into their respective communities in order to encourage collective and concerted action by neighbourhood groups. This requires that law centres act as a resource for such groups and that lawyers and non-lawyers within the centres co-operate to promote legal and non-legal solutions to commonly experienced problems. Expertise is shared with local people under a proactive orientation, and clients are encouraged to take an active role in the disposition of their case. The attempt is made to develop competence and to strengthen the capacity of clients to realize their rights through group formation. Despite difficulties in overcoming some of the problems caused by the adoption of an overly reactive approach, in the majority of British law centres the operational trend is towards proactivity.

For its part the Commission acknowledges (8–11) that law centres have made an important contribution to the delivery of legal services and have produced an impact out of all proportion to their size. Law centres also enjoy certain advantages over the private profession, not all of which the Commission relates, but which include *inter alia*: an informal atmosphere coupled with a free, non means-tested service; the development of expertise and experience in specialist areas of law and of social problems of relevance to working class clients; the development of skills in project and group work and in community development and education. These advantages have allowed law centres to provide a flexible, innovative and, to some extent, proactive service to clients. The Commission, however, while kindly asserting that it has no wish to put a stop to further experimentation (provided, it seems that this was done outside the CLC format) decides that the time has come:

to move forward from a period of experiment to one of consolidation, characterized by continuity, orderly development, adequate resources and proper administrative and financial control. The purpose of our recommendations is to combine the achievement of these objectives with the preservation of the special qualities which have marked the formative years of law centres, their dedication, imagination and commitment to meeting local needs and to ensuring that the rights of citizens are upheld (8–13).

Consolidation, continuity, orderly development, proper administrative and financial control – these are the words of a Commission hell-bent on administrative tidiness; on controlling a 'problem' that has got out of hand, and doing all of this at the cost of undermining the best features and advantages of existing law centres. Moreover, whatever citizens' rights had been upheld in the past, under the proposed CLC format they could not count on the 'right' to a free service. Means-testing is proposed and the Commission see no reason why clients of CLCs should not 'pay for the services they receive on the same basis as legally-aided clients of private practitioners' (8–22). So much for one of the advantages enjoyed by law centres. It is true that the Commission endorsed the giving of advice to local groups and the carrying out of educational work, but the whole issue was so clumsily made subject to ill-conceived eligibility criteria under the legal aid scheme, that its operation would be almost unworkable.[1]

The pattern of reactivity in the Commission's recommendations is already evident and may be seen as reflecting to some extent the preferences of the Law Society for a reactive law centre style of operation. The Commission conceived of CLCs as extensions of and, more importantly, supplementary to traditional private practice. In short 'the efforts of private practitioners will need to be supplemented in certain areas by salaried lawyers, deployed in law centres' (8–17). In its evidence to the Commission, the Law Society recommended the creation of Area Legal Services Committees which would primarily be responsible for the co-ordination and provision of legal services in the fourteen areas in which the country is divided for the purposes of the administration of the existing legal aid scheme. An Area Legal Services Committee according to the Law Society (1977, para. xx. 18.3, p. 217) 'would be in an ideal position to decide where legal services needed supplementing, and by what means.' These means were to include establishing new private solicitors' firms, duty solicitors schemes, CAB rota schemes, referral of clients to solicitors from advice centres, and the setting up of legal aid law centres with slight modifications from those which the Law Society was empowered to set up under

Section 16 of the Legal Aid Act 1974.[2] Where the emphasis is not on the actual direct role of private solicitors themselves in making the best use of existing legal resources, then it focuses on the ways in which clients may be referred from other agencies to private practitioners. With regard to existing provision, the Law Society (1977, para. xx. 18.4, p. 217) 'rejects the view that law centres are the only or, in many places, the best way of providing legal services in deprived areas.' Whereas the Law Society (1977, para. xx. 18.6, p. 217) envisaged that existing law centres would continue to operate, so far as any future development was concerned, the Society preferred a highly reactive structure: its view was that some law centres should be set up under the wing of the CAB organisation and there should also be legal aid centres set up by the Law Society itself.

Running throughout these proposals in the evidence of the Law Society is an overriding concern to avoid the duplication of services between law centres and the private profession. A laudable goal which also has an element of financial self-interest; namely, law centres should not do remunerative work that can be done by private practitioners and, moreover, all law centres – either existing or proposed – should continue to refer wherever appropriate fee-generating cases to the private profession. In effect, law centres already refer substantial numbers of cases to the private profession and to other agencies, a matter which the Law Society itself has acknowledged (1977, para. xx. 16.3, p. 216). The cases the private profession receive on referral would be further expanded through the Law Society's proposal to strengthen the role of CABx and to appoint resource lawyers to work in the larger bureaux. Clients requiring (Law Society, 1977, para. xx. 18.5, p. 217) 'legal action will be referred to solicitors working locally either in private practice firms or in law centres.' Given the ability to control the type of law centre existing in local areas that the Law Society seeks for itself, CABx referrals would be much more likely to be of benefit to the private practitioner than the law centre.

The Commission, while not favouring exactly the same reactive structure for law centres preferred by the Law Society, nonetheless recommended (8–32) that wherever possible CLCs 'should be sited adjacent to a CAB.' Whatever else CABx may do for their clients they certainly generate work for the private profession. Linking CLCs with CABx could only compound the reactivity of the deliv-

ery of legal services. CABx, and those law centres that are required
to refer a substantial proportion of their cases to private practitioners, are acting as filters for the profession – they filter appropriate
cases but do not challenge the private profession's services or
methods of working, and they leave intact, indeed they enhance,
the traditional lawyer – client relationship which results in further
individual client and general public dependence upon private
practitioners. Moreover, CABx tend to individualize the social
problems that clients take to them, which results in treating those
problems in isolation from one another.

One method of overcoming the individualization of client problems and of exploring more radical solutions is through group and
project work, and through the institutionalization of consumer
control of law centres' general policies. The idea that the consumers
of law centre services should participate in the management of the
centre was given short shrift. The Commission argued (8–26) that it
did 'not think it right for people who have no knowledge of the law
or the handling of legal problems and possibly little experience of
managing an office, to be expected to assume direct responsibility
for the professional work of a CLC.' But law centres have never
expected local people to manage the *professional* work of centres:
local consumers have been expected to discuss and set the priorities
and policies which centres would follow, in order to meet more
effectively the particular needs of varying local conditions.
Possibly, the Commission did not wish to endorse the concept of
consumer control of law centres, for fear that it might set a prece-
dent in other areas of legal services. Group work and campaigns,
what the Commission calls general community work, is also dismissed since it undermines the 'independence' of law centre services
(8–20). Individual casework is imputed both to be professionally
acceptable (i.e. ethical) and politically neutral and, if only by association therefore, group work is both unacceptable and 'political' – a
view which conveniently ignores the varied activities of private
lawyers servicing the needs of corporate clients.

These implicit attacks on the non-individual casework activities
in law centres, and the involvement of local people in actively
seeking legal and non-legal solutions to their problems, are redolent
of similar attacks in the USA on the legal services programme.
While many individual legal services programmes in the USA were
essentially reactive and were no more than extensions of traditional

legal aid societies run by local Bar associations, nonetheless there were some radical law centres devoted to community action and the 'maximum feasible participation' of the poor. Centres such as the San Francisco National Legal Assistance Foundation and the California Rural Legal Assistance programme established themselves as aggressive, law reform and community action-orientated agencies dedicated to social change. There were sufficient of these sorts of law centres fighting in the 'War on Poverty' for them to have aroused political and professional hostility. Though the process leading to the emasculation of the radical activities (and potential) of law centres was a long and complex one, it reached its culmination during the Nixon administration. As Auerbach in his study of the Office of Economic Opportunity (OEO) has noted (1976, p. 298):

representing a silent majority that had little tolerance for equal justice, and capitalizing upon opposition within the legal profession to OEO, the administration accused OEO lawyers of placing 'causes ahead of cases' and using clients 'as mere vehicles to promote sweeping social and political change.' Once again traditional professional values were applied in defense of the political status quo – and to perpetuate the maldistribution of legal services.

In 1974 the passage into law of the Legal Services Corporation Act eradicated the potential of legal services programmes to pursue politically effective strategies, by forbidding law centres either to carry out general law reform activities, or to encourage or help local people to form organised groups.

The Commission's recommendations on law centres may be seen as one aspect of an attempt in England and Wales to control the more proactive side of their operations and to stimulate the reactive elements.[3] In due course, I shall outline further what I consider to be the merits of the proactive approach, but first I detail the disadvantages of an overly reactive orientation.

Wherever law centres have initially chosen, or have been forced through circumstances (such as a lack of resources etc) to adopt a largely reactive approach, they have been invariably inundated with individual cases and, consequently, their 'impact' has not been extensive. That is to say, an overly reactive approach has generated problems for law centres in respect of the realization of proactive goals that the majority of law centres formally and ideologically espouse, and which are to be found in a variety of law centres' annual reports and in important documents of the Law Centres' Federation (LCF), such as *Towards Equal Justice* (1974) and *Evidence to the Royal Commission on Legal Services* (1977).

Rather than over-concentrate on the provision of legal services to individual clients, the LCF has stated that it is (LCF, 1974, pp. 7–8):

the duty of those who seek to provide legal services in poor and working class communities to concentrate their resources on helping people of those communities to create organisations capable of helping their members with their collective difficulties. Further, once these organisations exist, it is the duty of lawyers to use their skills in helping the organisations in their relations with outsiders. Not only is this a service which the established legal profession has failed to provide, and for financial and ideological reasons is incapable of providing, but it is also a means whereby scarce resources of qualified legal manpower available in the deprived communities can be put to the best use on behalf of the greatest number of people.

Moreover, the LCF's attachment to proactive goals is strongly reiterated (1977, p. 3):

law centres are heavily committed to developing community involvement, community initiative, responsiveness and control. These we say are the answers to the tension, frustration and apathy which are the results of the deprivation under discussion. Groupwork then is the development of communal self-help facilities: it is the exploitation of test cases (in a wide sense); it is work which links the general with the particular – the community with the individual; work which encourages communal responsibility and discourages dependency.

The realization of such proactive goals has not, of course, been complete; law centres, in moving towards the proactive end of the continuum, have not done so without encountering difficulties. The most serious difficulties have been found in open-door reactive law centres where there had been a continuing need to control high individual caseloads if sufficient resources were to be freed in order to pursue more proactive activities. North Kensington law centre (1972, p. 3) reported a 'flood of cases' and of the pressure of work never having diminished, with the consequence that the centre was unable (1972, p. 3) 'to look beyond the immediate problems and crises of the clients. The Centre has tended to operate as a normal solicitor's office, giving advice and trying to find remedies to the problems of individuals on a case by case basis . . .' Balham law centre reported that it was (June 1974–March 1975, p. 5) 'one of many agencies that is in danger of being swamped by housing casework. The staff agreed unanimously that it must attempt to educate the public about the waste of time and money involved in taking case after case, instead of trying to find a real solution to the housing situation.' The attempt to pursue this aim however was tempered by the fact that the centre (Balham Neighbourhood Law Centre, April 1975–March 1976, p. 3) 'could only just cope with the number of people needing legal advice and assistance.' In the following year the staff reported that their work in educating local residents about the law and its operation had been somewhat curtailed (p. 7) 'because of the greater immediacy of the needs of individual cases.'

Faced with pressures such as these, overly reactive law centres have sought ways to limit caseloads. These have included resetting of priorities for acceptance of cases, increasing the numbers of referrals to private solicitors and other agencies, restricting the size of the catchment area, internal reorganization of staff into specialist units, and limiting the number of hours or days when centres are open to members of the public. That such measures have proved necessary is evidenced not only by the experiences of Balham and North Kensington law centres. For instance, Hackney law centre – the type directly linked to a CAB – reported that its staff continued (Hackney Advice Bureau and Law Centre, May 1976–March 1977, p. 7):

to discuss the balance between the case work and the other work of the centre. The demands, particularly from individuals, upon all sections of the centre makes this difficult, as . . . the volume of work dealt with by the centre is considerable. There is a danger of the workers being swamped by case work so that there is no opportunity to stand back and look at the broader issues of the centre's work and direction.

Staff under pressure in this way may well find that they handle in a routine manner not only cases requiring simple advice and/or referral elsewhere, but also that the quality of service devoted to cases requiring further attention is also suffering. There is some American evidence suggesting the onset of routinization in reactive agencies by Katz (1976 and 1978) and by Bellow (1977). Indeed, Katz (1976, p. 199) has suggested that where a law centre undertakes what he calls project work, that is to say, extending the centre's boundaries of operation, elaborating its structure and increasing the resourcefulness of the staff – the law centre activities cease to be routine and the organisational character of the centre is developed. In England and Wales evidence on this point is much more impressionistic, but Small Heath Community Law Centre reported that (1978–79, p. 4) 'the staff were becoming swamped by the amount of work coming through the door and this meant that there was a real risk of deterioration in the standard of work carried out for individual clients.'

Overconcentration on individual cases also runs the real risk of limiting law centres' services to legal tactics and remedies which are too often inadequate. The LCF itself has recognized this danger and pointed out in oral evidence to the Commission that (RCLS 1979, para. 8–8, p. 80) 'with limited resources, it is more effective to concentrate on the source of a problem rather than to attempt to alleviate its effect by legal action in individual cases.' In the light of the problems caused by an overly reactive approach and the desirability of attempting to concentrate on the source of a problem, the LCF stated that it was (LCF (1977), p. 46):

now quite common to find that Centres begin life with a fully open-door policy but quickly move towards more limited opening hours or limit the areas in which they do casework, partly in order to handle the immediate influx of work which any Centre encounters and to be able to work to elected priorities and policies, but more importantly in order to safeguard time to perform groupwork and educational work.

Despite the preferences of the Commission, the trend within law centres has been away from reactivity, for the reasons outlined, and towards proactivity. What then are the advantages of a more proactive approach; how does it allow law centres to enjoy a greater 'impact' on the communities and clients they serve; and what role can we expect law centres to play in the 1980s?

Processing individual grievances in reactive law centres is unlikely to make any impact on the wider problems of poor housing standards, meagre welfare entitlements or rising unemployment. While it is true that proactive law centre policies will not provide 'ultimate' solutions, nonetheless more significant inroads can be made in respect of local solutions to such problems with the adoption of a proactive approach. The adoption of particular examples of groupwork and community campaigns in pursuit of solutions to commonly experienced local problems is the expression of community needs and demands; it is not the result of decisions unilaterally taken by law centre staff and imposed on the community. Adamsdown law centre, Cardiff, in an empirical evaluation of the work of the centre found that the key to successful intervention in local problems was held by the locally-based management committee and by non-legal law centre personnel, who between them ensured that the nature and form of involvement was acceptable to local people. The centre stated that in deprived communities (Adamsdown Community Trust (1978), p. 61) 'there are so many issues potentially to take up that only those which touch a nerve of genuine concern can have any hope of a successful candidature for Law Centre resources.' The process described here is (Adamsdown Community Trust (1978), p. 63) 'one of helping people express already held grievances – the Law Centre is not a mechanism for creating grievances, but a vehicle for their articulation.'

Locally-based management committees, composed of the actual or potential consumers of a law centre's services, are an important aspect of the trend towards proactivity and of the future direction of the law centre movement. No one would argue that law centres have not encountered difficulties in seeking to make a reality of the movement's faith in 'consumer control'; and equally, one should not ignore the progress that has been achieved. Adamsdown Law Centre which, along with Brent for example, has enjoyed some important successes in developing the concept of consumer control, has reported that (Adamsdown Community and Advice Centre (June 1975), p. 7)

when people are given the opportunity to play a constructive role, and so long as they are given support in terms of having the information necessary to make informed decisions, they will make good use of that opportunity. Local people can manage community facilities successfully, and they can participate in the formation of alternative policies, ones which reflect their views and needs directly.

Such a management structure facilitates the vital interchange of information between various community interests and law centre staff. Moreover, a locally-based management committee serves (LCF (1977), p. 47)

as a constant check that the Law Centre is remaining responsive to local need and not getting bogged down in rigid work-structures as professionals left to their own devices have an inclination to do. By imposing upon the lawyers a demand for constant explanation in terms that are comprehensible by a lay Management Committee, they fulfill the additional valuable function of preventing the lawyer from drifting back into a professional distance from the community and hiding in the shadows of professional or technical language and ideas.

Thus, such committees may act as a safeguard against the re-emergence of reactivity and the professionalist domination of the lawyer-client relation, in which the professional and not the client (Johnson (1972), p. 45) 'defines the needs of the consumer and the manner in which these needs are catered for.'

The ability of local consumers through management committees 'to reflect their views and needs directly', or in Johnson's terms (1972, p. 46) 'where a community as a whole or a community organisation imposes upon producers [of law centre services in this instance] communal definitions of needs and practice', may also turn out to be another important safeguard for the law centre movement. As Elliott (1980, p. 11) has already noted, many of the recommendations of the Commission had a corporatist flavour and constituted one possible method of the 'co-option of legal services to the state apparatus . . .' The hallmark of corporatism according to Winkler (1975) is that there is a definite preference for indirect forms of administration through, for instance, quangos which avoid the appearance that the state is directly involved in the regulation of policies. If, in the future, central government funding for law centres becomes either an attempt to 'co-opt' legal services in a corporatist manner – so that the centres become highly responsive to state interests – or to emasculate the more radical aspects of their work as happened in the USA, then the institutionalization of a system of consumer control may provide an important avenue of resistance. Mindful of the need to ensure that management committees should be composed of a majority of consumer interests and not subject to domination by lawyers, other professionals or local councillors, the LCF has been working steadily to develop the effectiveness of local management committees. It states that (Law Centres' News 1979, p. 2):

the practice (as opposed to theory) of local consumer control is developing strongly. For instance, two years ago the Federation started organising annual management conferences. These have been well attended and have fulfilled the role of experience sharing between management committee members in ways of turning the concept of local control into a working reality.

In particular, the role of the LCF's full-time secretariat (Law Centres' News 1980, p. 3)

is to bring more efficiency to the Federation in its work of disseminating information and providing support to existing members; and, perhaps more crucially in this context, of fostering and providing substantial assistance to community initiatives for locally controlled and publicly accountable legal services throughout the UK.

There is, then, a body of experience in respect of consumer control on which the law centre movement is, and should be, looking to build in the 1980s. As for other areas in the development towards the realization of a more proactive approach, there is a much larger body of experience and achievement. For instance, Newham Rights Centre (1974–75, p. 42) has argued that devoting resources towards the formation and subsequent servicing of local groups 'reduces the need and dependence on lawyers . . . it provides a wider range of possible solutions to problems than the purely legal . . . Indeed, it often happens that collective pressure on a particular issue can achieve more than the threat of legal action.' In essence, proactivity is a process through which one hopes that citizens will be able to pursue effectively as wide a range of civil and political rights as is possible.

Faced with increasingly complex legislation but all too often inadequate traditional legal remedies for the effective realization of rights embodied in that legislation, and encountering an economic and political climate in which seeking to pursue the rights of the poor, the underprivileged and the oppressed meets with little sympathy, law centres cannot rely on a reactive approach. In order to maximise opportunities to develop the claims of their clients to fuller citizenship, law centres must seek to operationalize more effectively the concepts of informed consent, party upgrading, and client competence. It is the operationalization of these factors, coupled with the institutionalization of consumer control that holds out the best potential for law centre clients to enjoy the distributive benefits of 'legality' in its wider sense.

The concept of informed consent requires that the lawyer – client relationship be more egalitarian and participatory than is the case with the more traditional professional – client relationship. Informed consent is a dialogue therefore between the lawyer and client in which the lawyer draws on his expertise to suggest possible ways to proceed towards a solution to the problem in hand. These possibilities are explored and discussed, and it is the client who ultimately makes an informed decision about the preferred course of action. Rosenthal has argued that the process of informed consent is an essential part of competent performance (Rosenthal 1976,

p. 272), 'not only because it enhances the dignity of the client, but because there is evidence it can actually increase the efficiency, the productiveness of the representation.' In law centres, informed consent is given meaning not only through management committees composed of local consumers, but in the manner in which lawyers and non-lawyers supply information to the local groups with which they work. The continuing exchange of information between law centre staff and group members may also serve to prevent any deterioration in service towards the routine processing of cases.[4]

Party upgrading is a concept introduced by Galanter and closely associated with notions of party capability and competence to realize the benefits of legality. Legality refers collectively to those distributive benefits which stem from access to law and, one presumes, from access to certain other dispute-resolving or decision-making processes. These benefits include (Galanter 1976, p. 226): protection, security, remedies for a variety of grievances and claims, securing accountability of officials, participation in decision-making, employment of facilitive rules to acomplish specific purposes, provision of framework for reliance, feelings of justice and fairness. However, access to legality is not equally enjoyed by everyone; party capability is variable. Galanter (1974, pp. 97–104) points to the advantages in capability typically enjoyed by organizations (the 'repeat-players' in the legal system) compared with individuals (usually 'one-shotters') whenever the two are parties to legal or other dispute-resolving processes. Because of the disparity in resources between organizational repeat-players and individual one-shotters, it is often the case that (Galanter 1976, p. 235) 'parties differ in their capacity to utilize legal services. What is routine and rational for an organization is monstrous for an individual.' In order to minimize barriers to legality, Galanter argues that individuals should seek the advantages enjoyed by organizational repeat-players: namely, the aggregation of claims and grievances, development of expertise, economies of scale, greater credibility in the eyes of others of significance, ability to deploy longer-run strategies and to share possible risks, etc. In short, individuals with common problems or grievances should form into organised groups and, thus, 'upgrade' their party capability to realize collective solutions. These solutions need not depend entirely on the pursuit of legal strategies alone, for in the case of proactive law centres they are able to advise local groups about legal and non-legal courses of action. Whatever course is chosen depends for its success not only on factors external to the group, but also on the strength of the group's competence. In the final analysis (Galanter 1976, pp. 230–31):

upgrading of party capacity holds the greatest promise for promoting access to legality. Party capability includes a range of personal capacities which can be summed up in the term 'competence': ability to perceive grievance, information about availability of remedies, psychic readiness to utilize them, ability to manage claims competently, seek and utilize appropriate help, etc.

Here then is perhaps the most important role for law centres in the 1980s, for as Nonet (1969, p. 9) has argued:

The organised group can be the agency for building effective constituencies and lending individuals the moral support and political skills needed for competent advocacy. Indeed, the greater the role of groups in sponsoring legal action, the more likely it is that advocacy will serve social interests and be a political instrument.

Encouraging and helping clients to develop their own competences, providing high levels of informed consent, facilitating group formation and acting as a legal and non-legal resource to such groups are all interconnected ways in which proactive law centres can help clients to locate their problems in a wider context of relevant help and community action. Non-legal staff within law centres are particularly important in this respect, for it is they who primarily can act as catalysts or as 'people-workers' in group formation and subsequent group action. Bennett and Hokenstad (1973, p. 23) have described 'people-workers' as catalysts who

through the communication of information and sharing of insights, attempt to help the client help himself. They can be differentiated from those professions who use knowledge to help the client but do not share it with them . . . Because the people workers are concerned with the client's relationship to his environment and communicate knowledge about this relationship, this type of professional frequently finds his performance related to economic or social goals of clients. Such a situation gives political meaning to his work.

For its part the LCF has pointed out that (LCF 1980, p. 6)

in delivering legal services effectively to poor communities the traditional methods of work have to be supplemented by methods which enable the service to make and maintain contact directly with potential clients and with the people that those potential clients may turn to in seeking advice.

Flexibility of approach and combinations of skills are what is needed to create the kind of relationship and confidence between a salaried service and its community that private practice has enjoyed with those particular sections of the public that it usually works for. Lawyers' background and training makes them the least likely candidates to make these contacts and develop these relationships, and whilst it is their legal skills which are the core of the law centre they must recognise their own inadequacies when it comes to putting those skills most effectively to work in deprived communities.

People-working skills, such as those deployed by community workers within law centres, are not simply a mechanism for delivering legal expertise more efficently. While legal skills are naturally of great importance, the work and role of community workers is to prevent an over-reliance on narrow legal strategies. My own conception of proactivity probably stresses the role of non-legal strategies as a necessary counterbalance to the purely legal, more than does the law centre movement itself. I do so because I feel that the movement has the potential to do more than open up access to legal expertise, as important as this is. It can serve also to develop the political as well as the legal competence of clients; that is to say, it can provide them with a range of services and areas of expertise which, taken together, can develop the capacities of clients and client groups to pursue the realization of their rights and of solutions to their problems in a more effective and innovative manner than reliance on legal remedies alone. This potential, if fulfilled, avoids what Scheingold has called the myth of rights, and is more likely to make advocacy (in its widest sense) the effective political instrument which Nonet sees as stemming only from legal action sponsored by organized groups. To Scheingold: (1974, p. 5, original italics)

Legal frames of reference tunnel the vision of both activists and analysts leading to an oversimplified approach to complex social processes – an approach that grossly exaggerates the role that lawyers and litigation can play in a strategy for change. The assumption is that litigation can evoke a declaration of rights from courts; that it can, further, be used to assure the realization of those rights; and, finally, that realization is tantamount to meaningful change. The *myth of rights* is, in other words, premised on a direct linking of litigation, rights, and remedies with social change.

Such a view does not by any means do away with the option of litigation or other legal avenues, it simply stresses the need for proactive law centres to *mobilize* support among clients and to seek a *combination* of legal and non-legal strategies if the rights of citizenship are to be more effectively pursued.

There are, of course, those law centres that have enjoyed considerable success in putting into operation some of the essentially proactive concepts that I have been discussing; but, there are also difficulties still to be faced. Chief among these will be funding. It remains to be seen whether any expansion of the law centre movement and any steps towards a more rigorous adoption of proactive policies will founder because of the reluctance of central and/or local government to provide funds for what they might see as unacceptably radical policies. In any event, in the short term central government funding on a large scale appears very unlikely, and here the importance of the LCF to maintain the current diversity of funding becomes apparent. The diversity of sources from which the law centres currently receive their funds may well prove advantageous to the movement and allow some, if not all, law centres to develop more proactive orientations. Moreover, any local authorities reverting to Labour Party control would be a development likely to do no harm to the movement, and may well be beneficial from the funding point of view. However, in the longer term the LCF and its full-time secretariat will have to continue the work of consolidating the advances and gains that have been made. Some issues, such as the standardisation of accounting and case-recording procedures may well be introduced relatively easily; and issues such as law centre staff training and the development of locally-based management committees are naturally matters for the continuing attention of the movement as a whole. The LCF has been quick to promote the work of law centres, and to offer detailed and practical assistance to new law centre steering groups which continue to emerge around the country. The fact that they continue to do so is surely an optimistic note for the future, so far as interest in law centres by local communities and professionals alike is concerned.

There is one issue, however, that deserves special attention. While the LCF has for some time wanted to commission a detailed empirical study to evaluate the work and role of law centres, funds have never been made available for such a purpose. I have sketched out one proactive alternative to the reactive service favoured by the Commission, and it is an alternative that finds similarities in the work of some existing law centres. An evaluative study of the work of the movement as a whole would, I believe, serve to strengthen the arguments in favour of a proactive alternative to the delivery of law centre services. In any event, it would surely provide valuable information relevant to solutions for some of the problems which many centres are still experiencing.

The position that law centres should fill in the future in the delivery of legal services will continue to be a focus of debate. Questions relevant to that debate should not simply concern themselves with different technical means of delivery, but should also ask: 'What is it we want law centres to achieve?' Put in its crudest form, but which nonetheless suggests the choice of *direction* in which events may move, do we want law centres to supply 'band-aid' legal advice and assistance or to protect and extend the rights of active, competent citizens?

Acknowledgements

I am grateful to Rick Abel in particular for his helpful comments on the original conference version of this paper, and also to Richard de Friend and Bob Martin for other information kindly supplied. Naturally, the views expressed in the paper are my own and do not necessarily reflect those of any of the above mentioned.

Notes

1. See (12–57, 65) for proposed legal aid regulations governing legal services for groups. For a critique of these recommendations see Lefevre (1979).
2. These modifications are contained in Law Society (1977) para. xx. 2. 2, p. 205.
3. Newham Rights Centre, one of Britain's more proactive law centres, in its publication *Two Years Work 1975–77* (p. 14) reproduced in part the following letter received from the Lord Chancellor's Office and dated 6 August 1976:

   What we do expect is that a substantial proportion of the work of your full-time staff should consist of work for individuals. You tell me that this is so and it would, therefore, be helpful to me if you could tell me that it is your policy that this should continue.

   To the extent that it is possible we should like to see an expansion of this individual work, and we welcome the establishment of your advice centres. At the same time we hope that the staff of the centre will continue to be closely associated with the advice centre, and be able to take individual cases referred from them.

4. White's *et al.* (1975) research on private law firms in Birmingham which handled a large amount of legally-aided cases in reactive manner, highlighted the absence of any significant level of informed consent. He noted that (1975, p. 247) those lawyers who do legally-aided cases in bulk 'find that the nature of the work leads to their dealing with clients by standard processes. The relationship may then become an etiolated one in which the client has a reduced capacity to instruct.'

References

Adamsdown Community and Advice Centre, Cardiff (1975), *Annual Report to Members 1974–75*, June.

Adamsdown Community Trust, Cardiff (1978), *Community Need and Law Centre Practice. An Empirical Assessment.*

Auerbach, J. S. (1976), *Unequal Justice*, New York, Oxford University Press.

Balham Neighbourhood Law Centre, London (June 1974–March 1975), *Annual Report.*

Balham Neighbourhood Law Centre, London (April 1975–March 1976), *Annual Report.*

Balham Neighbourhood Law Centre, London (April 1976–March 1977), *Annual Report.*

Bellow, G. (1977), The legal aid puzzle: turning solutions into problems, 5 *Working Papers for a New Society*, pp. 52–60.

Bennett, Jr., W. S. & Hokenstad, Jr., M. C. (1973), Full-time people workers and conceptions of the 'professional' in P. Halmos (Ed.) *Professionalisation and Social Change*, The Sociological Rev. Monograph, No. 20, Keele University, pp. 21–45.

Elliott, M. (1980), The Royal Commission on Legal Services: the theoretical background, *The Journal of Social Welfare Law*, pp. 1–12.

Galanter, M. (1974), Why the 'haves' come out ahead: speculations on the limits of legal change 9 *Law and Society Rev.*, pp. 95–160.

Galanter, M. (1976), Delivering legality: some proposals for the direction of research 11 *Law and Society Rev.* pp. 225–46.

Hackney Advice Bureau and Law Centre, London (May 1976–March 1977), *Annual Report of the Law Centre.*

Johnson, T. J. (1972), *Professions and Power*, London, Macmillan.

Katz, J. (1976), *Routine and Reform: A Study of Personal and Collective Careers in Legal Aid*, Doctoral Thesis, Northwestern University.

Katz, J. (1978), Lawyers for the poor in transition: involvement, reform and the turnover problem in the legal services program, 12 *Law and Society Rev.* pp. 275–300.

Law Centres' Federation (1974), *Towards Equal Justice.*

Law Centres' Federation (1977), *Evidence to the Royal Commission on Legal Services.*

Law Centres' Federation (1980), *A Response to the Royal Commission on Legal Services.*

Law Centres' News (1979), A Quarterly Bulletin from the LCF, Autumn, Issue No. 4.

Law Centres' News (1980), A Quarterly Bulletin from the LCF, Spring, Issue No. 5.

Law Society (1977), *Memorandum No. 3*, Replies by the Council of the Law Society to the Request for Evidence from the Law Society by the Royal Commission, Part I, April 1977, pp. 1–233.

Lefevre, P. (1979), Why didn't the Commission ask for more? *New Law Journal*, pp. 1223–4.

Marshall, T. H. (1963), Citizenship and social class in T. H. Marshall (Ed.) *Sociology at the Crossroads*, London, Heinemann, pp. 67–127.

Newham Rights Centre (1974–1975), *Report and Analysis of a Community Law Centre.*

Nonet, P. (1969), *Administrative Justice: Advocacy and Change in a Government Agency*, New York, Russell Sage Foundation.

North Kensington Neighbourhood Law Centre, London (February 1972), *Annual Report.*

Rosenthal, D. E. (1976), Evaluating the competence of lawyers, 11 *Law and Society Rev.* pp. 257–85.

Royal Commission on Legal Services (1979), *Final Report*, Volume One, Cmnd, 7648, London, HMSO.

Scheingold, S. A. (1974), *The Politics of Rights*, New Haven and London, Yale University Press.

Small Heath Community Law Centre (1978–9), *Third Annual Report*.

White, R. (1975), The distasteful character of litigation for poor persons, *The Juridical Review*, Part 3, December, pp. 233–51.

Winkler, J. (1975), Law, state and economy: the Industry Act 1975 in context, 2 *British Journal of Law and Society*, pp. 103–28.

CHAPTER 5

Problems of Principle*

Martin Partington

The Report of the Royal Commission on Legal Services[1] was extensively criticized on its publication and it is now widely assumed to be dead, in the sense that it is unlikely that its recommendations will result in any major changes in the nature of the legal profession, or modes of delivery of legal services (LAG 1980 cf. Zander 1980). Nevertheless, I would suggest that the Report has been of considerable value in at least one important respect. It has brought into sharp focus the question of what the principles are on which legal services should be developed in the foreseeable future. In the first part of this paper I offer a summary of the main features of the Commission's report in relation to legal services; in the second part, observations are made on two sets of additional questions and alternative approaches which I argue should be borne in mind in discussions of the development of legal services; in the third part, brief conclusions are drawn.

The Royal Commission's Views on Legal Services

The Commissioners defined legal services, apparently broadly, as 'services which should be available to any person or organisation requiring advice or assistance of a legal character, whether payment for the service is made from public or private funds . . . [We] regard legal services as being concerned with advice, assistance and representation which is required by a person in connection with rights, duties and liabilities of a legal character.' (2–1, 2). Having offered this definition, however, they made no systematic inquiry into the current provision of legal services. (Only the Users' Survey

---

* I should like to thank particularly Philip Lewis, Rick Abel, and Philip Thomas for their comments.

(II section 8) and the earnings survey (II sections 16–20) throw any light on the matter.) Instead, apparently relying on existing studies (none is cited) and other impressionistic evidence, they noted that legal services, as defined, were provided both by lay advisers,[2] and by the legal profession.

Solicitors and barristers were found to engage in litigation,[3] and non-contentious business. As the Commission rather casually put it: 'advice is given, negotiations are conducted and documents are prepared in relation to property, matrimonial and family matters, trusts, probate, consumer problems, company and commercial matters, taxation, planning applications, industrial property rights, shipping and other matters too numerous to mention' (2–18).[4] In addition, law centres were noted to have come into being, and dealt largely with cases relating to 'social welfare law':[5] and lawyers employed by companies and the government also performed legal services. The Commission made only passing reference to legal services provided on a 'do-it-yourself' basis (4–17).

The inadequacies of legal services provision, in the view of the Commission, were those that stemmed from limitations in the provision of legal aid;[6] and inadequacies of a more general nature 'to be found in particular among the poorer part of the population'.[7]

To remedy these defects it proposed four main developments:

(i) the creation and development of generalist advice services, principally by strengthening and extending the citizens' advice bureaux network. Such a service should be publicly funded and act, in effect, as the gate-keepers to other legal services provision.

(ii) The improvement of legal services in defined areas. To achieve this it recommended that the concept of the neighbourhood law centre be developed (albeit in a highly modified form) by the establishment of a (small) number of 'Citizens' Law Centres' (CLCs) in a number of areas.[8] Secondly, and most important for the Commission, it sought massive improvements in the levels of remuneration to private practitioners through the legal aid scheme. In addition, lawyers were to be encouraged to move to such areas by the provision of interest-free loans (16–23, 29). Thirdly, the CABx should have advisory solicitors attached to them to assist in referrals to CLCs or to private practitioners. Some CABx might employ a salaried solicitor if that seemed necessary.

(iii) The Commission recommended an extension of legal aid to tribunals, particularly to those dealing with welfare benefits, immigration and mental health. A role for lay agencies in the provision of representation was also envisaged.

(iv) An essential means of encouraging the use of legal services and the law would be to develop a programme of legal education in schools.

Principles Underlying the Royal Commission's Recommendations

It is not easy to discern the philosophy of the Commission which underlined these recommendations. However the following statements, from different chapters, provide some assistance in explaining the nature of its proposals.

(i) the past 100 years have seen a change from a *laisser faire* society to one in which it is regarded as right for the state to take a large and active continuous responsibility for maintaining individual welfare. This has reflected changing attitudes about morality and social relationships, in particular the view that a person who needs help should receive it as a matter of legal right, rather than an act of charity. One outward sign of this change is the enormous increase in legislation which is intended to improve the life and welfare of the population . . . (4–3).

(ii) A society in which all human and social problems were regarded as apt for a legal remedy or susceptible to legal procedures would not be one in which we would find it agreeable to live. But at present there are too many people whose rights, for want of legal advice and assistance, go by default. The improvements we propose are intended to remedy this, without creating an over-litigious society (2–28).

(iii) The legal profession should bear the primary responsibility for developments in legal services. 'It will . . . be necessary for the profession to make the best possible regular estimates of future requirements in order to form *its* policies' (3–13). The profession must be given the chance 'to develop *its* service to the public without interruption and changes of course' (3–17). '[The] solicitors' branch of the profession is of particular importance in meeting changing needs for legal services and in acquiring the necessary knowledge and expertise to do so' (4–11) (my emphases).

Thus the Commission seemed to recognize that society has changed in 100 years. This changed context had generated new demands for legal services, or made the provision of legal services more socially important. There were, however, ill-defined limits beyond which such trends should not be allowed to go: possibly the unspoken assumption is that the UK should not be turned into another highly litigious country like the USA, or West Germany.

Insofar as developments in legal services were to be encouraged, it was the private legal profession that should have primary responsibility for deciding the needs of society. Even though some lay participation was recommended to assist in the overall administration and management of legal services, (see eg. on the proposed Council for Legal Services, 6–17), it would be unrealistic to suppose that it would not be the professional lawyers who dominated the work of such a body.

From this position, the Commission advanced five main principles as the foundation for legal service provision:

(i) financial assistance should be available for each person who needs it, who would otherwise suffer 'undue financial burden in *properly* pursuing or defending his legal rights' (5–3, my emphasis);

(ii) all who get legal services should be entitled to receive the same standard of service (5–5);

(iii) the client should have freedom of choice. They rejected the idea of a system of lawyers assigned by the state (even though this satisfied the European Commission on Human Rights) (5–6);

(iv) the lawyers should receive a 'reasonable rate of remuneration' (5–5);

(v) the private practitioner should be the primary provider of legal services since only he is truly 'independent' (3–24). The discussion of the development of duty solicitor schemes (Ch. 9) is a specific example of what the Commission would like to see.

They recognized that an extension of the neighbourhood law centre concept may be desirable, but in the significantly changed form of the 'Citizens' Law Centre'.[8] Furthermore, it was clearly envisaged that any extension of law centres should be in a limited number of places.

The idea of alternative models for the provision of legal services was given short shrift. Indeed the primary benefit of the existing law centres was perceived by the Commission *not* as suggesting new models for the delivery of legal services, but rather as emphasizing 'the need for training in [social welfare] law, both for newcomers to the profession and established practitioners' (2–22). Thus, in particular, the notion of a national legal service is rejected. The principal reason is said to be the fear that its lawyers would not be 'independent' (5–7, 8). Further, since the proposal 'had scarcely any support in the evidence submitted to us and the majority of witnesses, including all the main political parties, are strongly opposed to the concept', it is illogically implied that these too were good reasons for not considering the proposal in any more detail.

An Alternative View

It can be seen from the foregoing summary, that the proposals the Commission made relating to the development of legal services were almost exclusively geared to those which it was thought the existing private legal profession would support.[9] But I suggest that any serious discussion of the development of legal services should move beyond the question of what legal services private practitioners can provide, to ask: (i) what do consumers of legal services want from their legal service provision? and (ii) what is the relationship between government and the provision of legal services?

A Consumer's view of Legal Services

It is clearly no easy matter to determine what consumers want in the way of provision of legal services. It has frequently been pointed out that the concept of 'the unmet need for legal services' is as much the product of lawyers arguing that they should be paid for doing more, or different kinds of work, than the result of any objective analysis of consumer demand, actual or potential. However it is very striking that the approach of the Scottish Royal Commission on Legal Services,[10] published shortly after the English report, did attempt consistently to bring consumer preferences to the foreground.

In addition, one of the most important lessons of the *Access to Justice* project (Cappelletti 1978–9) is that experiments with a range of models of legal services provision are likely to be most productive for socially desirable developments into the 1980s, and would afford the opportunity for consumers to express their views. The concentration of the Commission on the private profession blocked off this kind of broader, more flexible, approach. Instead, the strongest of the Commission's recommendations in relation to the development of legal services was that there should be a massive injection of money into the legal aid scheme (Cottrell 1980).

In so doing, the Commission made no attempt to calculate the cost. Indeed it coolly remarked that: 'if all our recommendations are implemented they will add significantly to the cost of providing legal services . . . ' (5–25). And to support this view it asserted: 'the fact remains that legal services call for highly skilled and time-consuming work which *cannot be cheap*' (5–28, my emphasis).

A broader approach to the task might have suggested that at least two crucial assumptions could be challenged in this line of reasoning. First, it is true that *all* legal services call for 'highly skilled and time-consuming work'? It is not the case that already much work in legal offices is of an extremely routine and tedious character which requires little skill? The legal profession may like to give the impression that law and legal procedures are so hard to deal with that intellectual ability little short of Albert Einstein's is a prerequisite for the lawyer; but may not this be part of the mystique of professionalism that we should be dispelling? The Commission, having failed to conduct any adequate study of what services are *actually* provided by lawyers, left us unable to answer this question.

Secondly, whether work is skilled and time-consuming or not, why cannot it be cheap, or at least cheaper than at present? The Commission did obtain some evidence about the cost of running law centres, from which the conclusion was drawn that the average annual cost of running a law centre was in the order of £50–60,000 at 1978–9 prices (II 31–8). Nowhere was this figure used in the body of the main Report as the basis for a discussion of the comparative costs of private practice, as opposed to law centres, in providing particular types of legal services. In short, fundamental questions of cost-effectiveness are wholly ignored.[11] (Cf. Culyer 1973, Ch. 8)

It is true that a number of ideas for reducing the level of costs for potential litigants were briefly considered (see Ch. 16). But contingency fees (16–2, 6), and the Justice proposal for a contingency legal aid fund (16–7, 12) were dismissed. Legal cost insurance was noted to exist, but the Commission rejected the idea of supporting this out of public funds (16–13, 15). It did suggest the establishment of a suitor's fund to reimburse costs incurred by the illness or death of a judge, or to pay the costs in determining a point of law of public importance.

Furthermore, and paradoxically, the claim of the Commission that 'the main aim should be to penetrate areas of greatest need' (44–4) looks somewhat thin when it is realized that its primary strategy for reform is so expensive that no government, particularly in the present economic climate, would be likely to authorize the necessary finance (Glasser 1980).

Had a more consumer-oriented perspective to the work been adopted the Commission might, in addition to considering extensions to legal aid, have also asked whether the legal aid scheme, however expanded, would ever be sufficiently flexible to respond to consumer needs and demands. There is considerable evidence from the operation of the legal aid scheme to date which suggests that simply improving legal aid will result in more of the same kinds of legal services being provided, but that innovation or experiment will not be encouraged. Indeed the whole emphasis of legal aid provision is on uniformity rather than diversity (Pollock 1975).

The desire of the Commission to encourage uniformity of provision can also be seen in its emphasis on equality of treatment of clients. At first glance this might appear a desirable objective. Closer examination reveals that the Commission used the concept as further justification for reducing the role of law centres and supporting the role of private practitioners. Thus there are passages where the Commission sought to imply that clients who go to law centres get an inferior service, as opposed to those who go to private practitioners. However this implication is not justifiable on the facts. For certain classes of case, law centres do work that private practitioners ignore (indeed their waivers from the Rules of Professional Etiquette have been largely negotiated on this basis). Where law centres do engage in the same class of case (e. g. certain types of criminal work, or landlord–tenant work) their service is frequently more effective. As regards overall standards of efficiency, there may have been cases of poor quality of service on the part of law centres. Given the attention they have attracted, and the fact that many of them are run by relatively young and therefore, perhaps, less experienced lawyers, this is not surprising. But until a detailed study of what goes on in the private law office has also been completed, it is not possible to say whether law centre personnel are more or less competent than lawyers in private practice. The implicit suggestion that making private practitioners, operating out of law offices, the principal – if not exclusive – source of legal service, will result in equal treatment for clients, is on closer examination unsustainable.

Again, any general notion that clients have freedom of choice of their lawyers is untenable. The rules against advertising minimise this choice. Furthermore, the client who attempts 'freely' to change the lawyer often finds that freedom is minimal, if not non-existent.

To be sure, the Commission recognized these points and made suggestions for increasing genuine freedom of choice (see Ch. 27 on advertising) and altering the rules relating to the solicitors' lien (1 23–31, 37). However, even if these and other changes were made, it does not follow that encouraging legal service provision through private practitioners is the only method of securing freedom of choice. Indeed it can be strongly argued that the creation of law centres has increased the clients' freedom of choice, not only in relation to the type of work that is conducted, but in the style of operation. There is increasing evidence that many law centre clients *prefer* the informal atmosphere of the centre to what they perceive as the stuffy and formal environment of the private solicitor's office. Thus, in this respect, the creation of a network of law centres and other delivery models would increase, not reduce, fredom of choice.

The failure to consider alternative models for the provision of legal services also results in non-existent or inadequate consideration of two further relevant debates. The first relates to the extent to which law and legal processes may be simplified so that non-lawyers may themselves use the law. The Commission attached a very low priority to this development. 'We believe . . . that the right of every citizen to act on his own behalf in (e. g. small claims, criminal cases or conveyancing), *even though it may be less effective than the employment of a professional adviser*, is a fundamental right which should be preserved' (4–17, my emphasis). The clear implication of this passage is that a service provided by a qualified lawyer will usually, if not inevitably, be better than acting on one's own account. Such sentiments clearly reflect the current state of affairs where complex legal procedures, incomprehensible forms, forbidding buildings constitute major deterrents to those who might wish to act on their own behalf. However, there is now a body of literature which asks whether the place that lawyers have in society is proper, inevitable or desirable.

The dependence of laymen on professionals has been criticized (LAG 1978). None of this body of opinion was even hinted at, let alone discussed, in the Report. While the Report did mention the importance of education in schools, there was no hint as to how this idea would be put into effect, or any discussion of alternative educational programmes.

Part of the reason why it may have been difficult for the Commission to investigate these issues may have been its terms of reference, which precluded it from investigating court procedures (though this did not prevent the Commission making some detailed comments on procedure in Ch. 43). Furthermore, even had it taken the issue seriously, this might not have altered its views in relation to legal services very greatly, for there are huge difficulties in the way of establishing workable systems of self-help in legal proceedings – however structured – which ensure that the 'haves' do not always come out ahead of the 'have-nots' (Galanter 1974, Abel 1980).

Notwithstanding these points, however, the failure to take the issue of self-help seriously is a further indication of the concern the Commission appears to have felt about keeping the existing private legal profession as the main provider of legal services.

A second issue, which the Commission failed to consider, but which is beginning to generate interest in the UK, is the development of 'public interest law.' The boundaries of this concept are far from clear, but in the USA, where the existence of public interest law has been recognized for a number of years, it has been based on the view that, in a pluralist society, it is important that interest groups which would otherwise tend to get ignored, should have as equal access to the rule makers, be they the courts or the legislature or the executive, as do the more powerful, established groups. (Partington 1979) The fact is that in the UK a considerable number of agencies also engage in legal activity as part of their work: the citizens' rights office of the CPAG; shelter; ecology and consumer lawyers. Their object is both to ensure that rules designed to operate in favour of the groups that they may be said to represent (e. g. the poor or the homeless) do work in the way envisaged by Parliament; and they seek to use the legal system to obtain favourable rulings from the courts (Hodge 1979). Again there are substantial problems relating to the impact of such work (Handler 1978). Nonetheless it seems high time that this kind of activity should also be clearly recognized as falling within the proper scope of legal service provision.

The Relationship Between Government and the Provision of Legal Services

In asking about, and attempting to analyse, this issue, one moves into more difficult, and speculative territory. However, in any discussion of legal services, I think it is important to consider also the tasks which government is requesting the law, and thus the legal system, to perform. It may then be asked whether or not those engaged in the provision of legal services should, without question, perform those tasks (Luckham 1980).

Discussion of this issue may perhaps begin by considering the concept of the 'independence of the legal profession.' In a stirring passage, the Commission declared:

a profession has a sense of corporate identity and independence which is of value not only to members but also to the public at large. It is founded on the ability of members to speak with knowledge and authority in a particular field of learning; the right to express professional opinions free from external pressures or fear of reprisals; the power to regulate their affairs so as to enhance the prestige and standing of their calling, not only nationally, but internationally; the sense that its members are directly serving the public to whom they are answerable for their actions; their dependence for their livelihood and advancement on their own talents and abilities . . . We attach importance to the need for independence . . . ; so far as it is compatible with the public interest we recognize it in the recommendations made in this report (3–25).

However, as Zander (1976) has pointed out, 'independence' is a multi-faced concept. It has vices as well as virtues. And, in any event, the actual work of lawyers is by no means as 'independent' as the assertion of independence would have one believe.

For example, the concept of independence – in the sense of lack of interference from the state – has been used to justify the view, re-asserted strongly by the Commission, that it is the legal profession that should determine the kinds of cases it conducts. Yet the evidence of the Commission shows that the vast majority of law firms go to where the money is, and the services they offer are geared to meeting the needs of the propertied classes (4–28, 33, esp. 32). It is frequently stated that the sole reason why work in 'social welfare law' in 'deprived areas' is not done is because of the inadequacies of the legal aid scheme (e. g. 3–26). May it not, however, also be the case that large numbers of lawyers in private practice simply do not wish to do work that they regard as 'trivial' or 'unimportant.' This is not to deny that there are not many individual solicitors who wish to offer this kind of service, but will there ever be enough to provide the level of service that is said to be needed? If this view is correct, may not the public interest demand that there should be a more direct provision of legal services in particular areas by some kind of centralized agency, so that legal services are spread more equitably through the community?

Secondly it may be asked: to what extent do lawyers express professional opinions free from external pressures? Do all solicitors with substantial criminal practices in busy urban centres always act fearlessly in their negotiations with local police forces? Recent research on plea-bargaining is a useful illustration of this problem. One of the reasons why plea-bargaining goes on is so that the criminal courts are snowed under with cases. By engaging in plea-bargaining, therefore, lawyers are assisting the government bureaucracy in its desire to process cases quickly. The near-hysterical reaction of certain senior members of the legal profession to the suggestion that plea-bargaining goes on may be explained, at least in part, by the fact that it seems to be inconsistent with the traditional view of a profession that is independent of government (Baldwin and McConville 1977).

Thirdly, although, as we have seen, the Commission recommended massive increases in provision of public money for legal aid, it failed to consider the likely effect this would have on government control of legal services. Already, we have seen that by withdrawing legal aid for undefended divorce, the Lord Chancellor's office has, in effect, altered the way in which solicitors provide their services on matrimonial breakdown. Pressures to control levels of expenditure on criminal legal aid have resulted in a number of suggestions for changes in criminal procedure. These tendencies would be likely to continue. It should be stressed that the consequences of greater central control over legal services provision need not necessarily be socially undesirable. But what is needed is that the existence of such controls or pressures be admitted and discussed, rather than be assumed not to exist because of some vague suggestion of 'independence.'

Fourthly, it cannot be said that the Commission was itself consistent on the question of independence. Those lawyers who have taken seriously the concept of independence, in the sense of being able to express opinions free of the fear of reprisals, and set up law centres designed to fight for their client groups in the most effective ways possible, have found themselves subject to considerable criticism. Thus the Commission noted:

these centres like to work for the community at large or a section of it, rather than for individuals. They often seek to attack the roots of problems by organizing groups to bring pressure to bear on landlords, local authorities and central government, either to improve working, housing or living conditions or to urge changes in priorities of public expenditure so as to meet urgent needs or to promote changes of a similar character . . .

However, it then proceeded to state, unequivocally:

whatever opinion is held as to the value of work of this kind, we firmly believe that if it is to be carried on, it should be . . . carried on by local or national groups, by political parties or by members of the local authority. *We consider that this type of work is not appropriate for a legal service.* [My emphasis] [However] there can be no objection to a law centre providing advice and assistance on legal matters to individuals on how best to proceed . . . (8–19, 21).

In so doing, the Commission ignored other evidence submitted to it. For example, the Law Society has a number of standing committees, revenue law, criminal law, town and country planning, land law and conveyancing, and company law, all of which include, in their terms of reference, the possibility of campaigning for changes in the law. (*Law Society Memorandum No. 3, pp. 8–10*). Similarly the City of London Solicitors' Company in its *Memorandum of Evidence* emphasized the importance of law reform in its work. However, since substansive law reform is, inevitably, going to involve changes in policy and, thus matters of political judgement, is this too beyond the scope of what is 'appropriate for a legal service'? Surely, if the concept of independence is to be taken seriously, the freedom of law centres to act for their client groups must be supported as much as the freedom of Law Society's standing committees or the City of London Solicitors' Company to act for their client groups.

Furthermore, insofar as the Commission seeks to imply that only private practitioners can be independent, it should be noted that although a number of law centres have been closed down by local authorities withdrawing their funding, apparently on the grounds that those authorities were fed up with attacks being made upon them, nonetheless the vast majority of law centres have continued to stay open, and to fight for their client groups against often well-established interest groups (e. g. local authorities, the police, landlords, local traders and employers) in a truly independent way – so much so that one is at least forced to ask why 'independent' private practitioners were not already doing this work?

If the points made above are accepted, it can be seen that all too frequently the notion of independence has been used to justify arguments which ensure that the maximum amount of finance is available for the legal profession; it has not, however, been used to justify a more comprehensively critical view of the functions of government. There are too many examples of lawyers either failing to make fearless stands, or if they do, being criticized for their pains.

I believe that this question of the nature of the lawyers' independence is likely to become even more important in the 1980s. If we ask what the relationship between government and law is, the Commission adopted an extremely narrow viewpoint. Its summary of the shift from a laisser-faire society to a welfare society (p. 129 above) is both crude and misleading, particularly in its assumption that all current legislation is designed to improve the life and welfare of the population.

The fact is that the dominant, if not exclusive, activity of government today is the management (or the attempt at management) of the economy. Governments of all political complexions are operating within a self-imposed framework of economic policy that demands expenditure cuts, or at least severe restraints in the growth of the public sector. Although the theory may claim that this will lead to greater long-term prosperity, there seems little doubt that at least in the short term, and maybe permanently, the standards of welfare provision that we have come to expect will fall.

This might not matter to lawyers, were it not for the fact that governments are using the law as one of the principle means of effecting these cut-backs. Take, for example, the supplementary benefits (SB) scheme. The Social Security Act 1980 changed the nature of SB from a scheme based on discretion to one based on legal rules. At first glance, it might seem that this shift to 'legal rights' represents a substantial victory for those who have campaigned for welfare rights. But it can be argued that apparently desirable changes in the legal form are in fact being used to mask regressive social policies. In the case of SB, the result of the shift to rules is likely to be that SB officials and appeal tribunals will be able more easily to say 'no' to claimants.

Unless they are careful, therefore, lawyers will, far from being able to assist the deprived – the group who are said to be the primary concern of the Commission – have to perform the task of informing the poor that they cannot get various additional benefits. Lawyers will find themselves co-opted to work for the government (or state, if you will) in order to explain why claimants have no legal entitlement, rather than be able to work *for* claimants, who are striving to obtain a greater share (albeit limited) of material resources. In this context, the traditional ideological position of the legal profession, that they simply administer the law as it is now, and do not question its content (which the Commission appeared to endorse), may be seen as inadeqate. However, the development of a more consistently and genuinely 'independent' legal profession would support the position of those lawyers who seek not only to administer the law as it now is, but also to press for changes in the law for the benefit of their clients (see also Elliott 1980).

Conclusions

It was noted in passing, that the Royal Commission on Legal Services is effectively dead. It may be wondered, therefore, why this paper has concentrated on the Commission's views, and criticism thereof. The reason why this approach was adopted is that I have assumed that the views of the Commission reflect those of many legal practitioners. Insofar as developments in legal services will be dependent on the goodwill and imagination of those practitioners, it is necessary for those who seek more fundamental changes than those envisaged by the Commissioners, to point out the limitations of their views, and to indicate ways in which they may develop.

This paper has not purported to offer blueprints for the future development of legal services. However, a few remarks on this are proper.

(i) It is inconceivable that, for the immediate future, private practice will not, in fact, continue to be the main source of legal service provision. A sudden shift to any other model is unlikely as a matter of present political reality; in any event, it would be undesirable.

(ii) Change, when it comes, is likely to be incremental rather than sudden and dramatic. Thus it remains important for experiments in legal service provision to continue to be run and monitored. We also need much more information about the current scope of legal services. It will be easier to build on existing models than create fundamentally new structures.

(iii) I think that the case for the development of a network of publicly funded law centres is still compelling. (The model of 'Citizens' Law Centres' envisaged by the Commission is inadequate.) The government already supports a number of specialist agencies to assist in the enforcement of particular sets of legal rights – rent officers, trading standards officers, public health inspectors, the Health and Safety Executive (4–20). The Commission itself has called for the creation of a national structure of generalist advice agencies (Ch. 7).[12] Why not a national structure of legal services?

Although there may be the theoretical possibility of conflicts between publicly-funded agencies who seek to enfore the law against other public bodies, one must ask whether or not and to what extent it will happen in practice; and at the same time, one must be critical of any assumption that an 'independent' legal profession always operates in the public interest and it is always immune from pressures which limit their independence. What is needed is a strong public sector to provide in an efficient way legal services that private practice cannot, or is unlikely to offer. If such a public sector was sufficiently strong, it should be able to resist, through existing political channels, any encroachments upon its essential independence, either on its own behalf or with the support of the representatives of the private profession.

(iv) Insofar as legal services should develop to take on a more critical stance representing the rights and claims of those groups who tend to be ignored, it is likely that governments may resist funding such activity. However, issues are not as obvious as one might think. If we assume that the fundamental issues of the 1980s relate to major changes in society stemming from decline in world trade, 'structural' unemployment, high rates of inflation, the impact of new technology, cutbacks in welfare provision and so on, it may be suggested that many people's standards of living will be under threat. Disputes relating to the distribution of material resources in society will become more overt and more potentially conflict-ridden. On such a view, the case of the disadvantaged must be made as strongly as possible.

It is not plausible to suggest that private practice will be able to take on this role. At the same time it is important for lawyers even in the public sector of legal services, to resist attempts by the government to use them as a tool for the enforcement of socially-regressive policies. True 'independence' should engender a willingness to see that criticism of laws, particularly in the context of policies affecting the socially deprived, is a proper task for lawyers (as well, of course, as for all the other pressure and political groups with interests in such matters).

(v) Notwithstanding the last point, the limits of legal service provision must also be recognized. The basic questions that affect economic and social policy will remain political – not legal – questions.

The provision of legal services may make a useful contribution in the achievement and development of social policy goals; but they are always likely to be of secondary importance. However much the legal profession is reformed, and the scope of legal services provision is refined, there will be major limitations on what the law and legal procedures on their own can achieve (Abel 1979).

Notes

1. HMSO (1979), Cmnd. 7648.
2. Their list included 'trusted acquaintances', government officials, other professionals, organizations (e.g. tenants' groups), advice agencies and citizens advice bureaux (2–4, 12).
3. Details of caseloads in the courts are in Annex 2.1.
4. See further, Table 8.14, Users' Survey, Vol. 2, p. 198.
5. 'Social welfare law' was perceived by the Commission to be concerned largely with social problems such as housing (including evictions, public health and the rights of tenants and landlords), claims for social security benefits, problems involving family relationships, loss of employment, environmental problems, and, in some areas, juvenile crime and some forms of adult crime. It is a feature of cases of this type [and no others?] that legal problems do not arise in isolation and that in many instances, although a legal element exists, personal and social problems predominate . . . (2–10).
6. The means-tests were too stringent; and the scheme did not extend to certain issues, e. g. tribunal hearings.
7. Lack of knowledge that law might be able to help solve particular problems; lack of lawyers in certain areas of the country; lack of information about how to get a lawyer; fear of lawyers, particularly of their costs; and the public image of lawyers, which it was suggested might inhibit use of lawyers.
8. See Stephens, M. pp. 107–126, Law Centres and Citizenship: The Way Forward.
9. Certainly the response of the professional legal press was broadly supportive of the Commission's approach. There is a certain irony in this, since a majority of those on the Commission were not lawyers.
10. HMSO (1980), Cmnd. 7846. For a valuable summary of this much neglected document, see LAG Bulletin (1980), pp. 126–7.
11. So too was the body of American research literature which points to the same conclusion.

12. At first sight it seems a contradiction that the Commission recommended a national advice agency, but rejected a national legal service. However this can be easily explained in that, in the Commission's terms, the primary function of the advice service would be to encourage clients to go to lawyers.

References

Abel, R. (1979), Socializing the legal profession 1 *Law and Policy Quarterly*, pp. 5–51.

Abel, R. (1980), Delegalization in *Alternative Rechtsforem und Alternativen zum Recht* pp. 27–48.

Baldwin, J. & McConville, M. (1977), *Negotiated Justice* Oxford, Martin Robertson.

Cappelletti, N. (ed.) (1978–79), *Access to Justice* Holland, Sijthoff/Giuffre.

Cottrell, J. (1980), From Ruschiffe to Benson – and Back 43 *Modern Law Revue* 549–58.

Culyer, A. J. (1973), *The Economics of Social Policy*, Oxford, Martin Robertson.

Elliott, M. (1980), The Royal Commission on Legal Services: the theoretical background, *J. Social Welfare Law*, 1–12.

Galanter, M. (1974), Why the 'haves' come out ahead: speculations on the limits of legal change, 9 *Law & Society Rev*, p. 95.

Glasser, C. (1980), After the Report – remuneration, *LAG Bulletin* 29–32.

Handler, J. (1978), *Social Movements and the Legal System*, New York, Academic Press.

Hodge, H. (1979), A test-case strategy, in Partington and Jowell (eds.) *Welfare Law & Policy*.

LAG (1978), *Life Without Lawyers*, Legal Action Group.

LAG (1980), *Legal Services _ A New Start*, Legal Action Group.

Luckham, R. (1980), The final report of the Royal Commission on Legal Services: a sociologists view, 43, *Modern law revue*, pp. 543–8.

Partington, M. (1979), Public Interest Law, *LAG Bulletin*, pp. 225–7.

Pollock, S. (1975), *Legal Aid: The First 25 Years* London, Oyez.

Zander, M. (1976), Independence of the legal profession – what does it mean?, 73 *Law Society's Gazette* 758–9.

Zander, M. (1980), The Royal Commission on Legal Services, *Current Legal Problems*, London, Sweet & Maxwell.

CHAPTER 6

Advertising: Professional Ethics And The Public Interest

Phil Fennell

'There is a sensitive area in the subject of advertising. The chapter on advertising has been drawn with moderation. . . . The professions have too long laboured under a cloak of anonymity and mystery' (Sir Henry Benson[1].)

Introduction

There can be no doubt that the question of advertising by professional bodies is, as the Chairman of the Commission described it, an extremely sensitive area. It is one of the proudest claims of the solicitors' profession that its members are forbidden to engage in such practices. I shall seek to outline the origins and the historical role played by this prohibition of advertising as it has affected the solicitors' profession in England and Wales, and to attempt to explain the importance of the Commission's recommendations on advertising in terms of their overall strategy for the regulation of the legal services market.

The main body of the paper begins with an analysis of what Larson (1977, pp. 53–65) calls 'market' and 'anti-market' elements in professional ideology, elements which might be more appropriately dubbed 'entrepreneurial' and 'anti-entrepreneurial'. In this section I stress the point made by Larson (1977, pp. 53–65), Reader (1969, pp. 158–9) and others (Rueschmeyer 1973, Johnson 1972, Hadfield 1975, Zander 1968) that professional ideology is not exclusively anti-entrepreneurial, but that it incorporates elements of the value systems of both the 'pre-industrial gentleman' and the tradesman. I also note in this section the point which is re-iterated later, that anti-entrepreneurial ideologies played an important function in the organization of solicitors' markets. In the sections which follow, I deal in turn with the different forms of advertising upon which the Commission made recommendations – individual advertising, referral lists and corporate advertising – referring where appropriate to the theme of market regulation and its relation to professional ideology. In conclusion, I offer a tentative evaluation of the Commission's recommendations in terms of the goals as spelt out by Sir Henry Benson in his address to the Law Society in Jersey in October 1979.

Before embarking upon the course outlined above, it is important briefly to outline these goals. First, Sir Henry was at pains to make it clear (Benson 1979, p. 1030) to the Law Society that the recommendations of the Commission on advertising were to be regarded as 'the necessary concomitant of our stated conclusions on conveyancing.' Conveyancing remuneration levels and the conveyancing 'monopoly' were among the areas of report where most criticism had been directed at the Law Society. On the subject of 'monopoly', Sir Henry had this to say (Benson 1979, p. 1030): 'there are 6,500 firms of solicitors in practice, and partners in most of them ready to do conveyancing, so that it is misleading to speak of a monopoly particularly if, as we propose, there is greater freedom of advertising and the public are able to shop around.' Clearly, the Chairman saw individual advertising as a means of fostering efficiency and competitiveness, and as a way of avoiding the more dramatic expedient of ending the 'monopoly.'

The second aim of the advertising recommendations is to publicize the services of lawyers to 'the less well-to-do.' The Report (4–24–26 and 27–1) identifies lack of knowledge that a particular problem requires legal advice, and lack of information about the availability, location and expertise of solicitors, as key factors in producing 'unmet legal need.' The key element in the Commission's strategy here is 'generalist advice services' which would (Benson 1979, p. 1029) 'funnel enquiries to lawyers who are competent to provide the legal services which are required.' As a result of these arrangements, in which legal aid referral lists will play a major part, the Chairman of the Commission promised that (Benson 1979, p. 1029): 'the profession has a great opportunity here to receive a regular flow of work into its offices, much of which will be legally aided.'

In order to place the whole question in its proper context, it is important that we examine the attitude of the profession to advertising. It is to that aspect of professional ideology that I now turn.

Market and Anti-Market Principles

As the Commission points out, (27–25) 'the prohibition of advertising by individual practitioners has long been regarded as a characteristic of a profession.' Certainly the Law Society regards it as an essential point of differentation between a profession and other forms of corporate and occupational organizations. The majority opinion of the United States Supreme Court in *Bates v. State Bar of Arizona*[2] saw the ban as originating as a rule of etiquette and not a rule of ethics: 'early lawyers in Great Britain viewed the law as a form of public service rather than as a way of earning a living and they looked down on 'trade' as unseemly.' As we shall see, a persistent and important theme in the ideology of the solicitors' profession is the intrinsic value placed upon work and upon service to the public, rather than the more entrepreneurial values of making money.

The well known views of Emile Durkheim (1957, pp. 1–28) – who saw in the professional organizations the potential for the establishment of a morally regulated zone, in contrast to the 'anarchy' of the capitalist commodity markets – find contemporary expression in many areas. Among these is the evidence of the Law Society to the Monopolies and Mergers Commission which examined the question of solicitors' advertising in 1976 (Monopolies and Mergers Commission, 1976a, para. 74).

'A professional man was expected to observe certain obligations out of the trust reposed in him. Certain common commercial practices were incompatible with the rendering of professional services, and from these practices, the professional man was required to abstain. In particular, while professional men competed in reputation for ability, they did not compete by way of advertising, price cutting, or other methods familiar or unobjectionable in the business world.'

It is this anti-entrepreneurial – or what Larson (1977 pp. 53–65) calls 'anti-market' – principle, often repeated in professional ideologies, which is of central concern to the study of professional ethics in general and advertising in particular.

Yet, despite this ideological espousal of anti-market principles, we shall see how modern professions share many of the attributes of large corporations in the way in which they attempt to regulate the markets for their services. Furthermore, Larson (1977, pp. 61–2) finds it helpful to distinguish two dimensions of Weber's 'bourgeois economic ethic' in analyzing this particular aspect of professional ideology. These two dimensions are the entrepreneurial aspect and the notion of calling or vocation, which, as she notes (1977 p. 62) 'are analytically distinct, but . . . appear fused in the early modern professions. . . . The function of vocational and entrepreneurial orientations generates tensions both for the individual professional and for the profession as a whole.' It appears that it would be more accurate to describe professional ethics as a system of morality which overlaps significantly with the entrepreneurial morality of commerce, rather than as a completely anti-entrepreneurial morality. As Reader (1966, pp. 158–9) describes it, 'the new professional men brought one scale of values (the gentleman's) to bear upon the other (the tradesman's), and produced a specialized variety of business morality which came to be known as 'professional ethics' or 'etiquette.' Furthermore, this particular hybrid ethical structure was of considerable use in organizing the most lucrative market of the solicitors' profession, that of conveyancing. It is therefore important to recognise that the stark contrast drawn by many ideologues between professional and commercial morality is severely stylized, and further to note that the particular ideological components of professional ethics were useful to the profession, not only in the establishment of social credit as a *sine qua non* of market organization and control, but also as a means of regulating such markets once they had been carved out and organized.

It is perhaps best to leave the final word here to Larson, who (1977) views professionalization as a project which involves the leaders of the occupation in the conscious pursuit of a series of goals, including market control, autonomy, high status and economic security. She concludes that (1977, p. 63): 'anti-market and anti-capitalist principles were incorporated in the professional task of organizing for a market because they were elements which supported social credit, and the public's belief in professional ethicality.' Thus at the core of the professional project we find the fusion of anti-thetical ideological structures and a potential for permanent tension between civilizing functions and market orientation, between the protection of society and the securing of a market.

**The Commission's Recommendations
and their Background**

Having examined the ideological basis of the prohibition against
advertising, I turn to the Commission's findings and recommendations. Chapter 27 actually deals with a much wider area than that of
advertising by individual solicitors. This chapter entitled *Information for the Public*, concentrates on the solicitors' profession, the
Commission seeing no need for any change in the restrictions currently operative with regard to barristers' services (27–44, 9). The
only exception to this general position was that the Commissioners
felt that barristers who establish a new set of chambers, or whose
chambers change address, should be allowed to issue an advertis-
ment in legal journals stating the fact. In adopting this position, the
Commission was expressly following the Report of the Monopolies
and Mergers Commission on Barristers' Services (Monopolies and
Mergers Commission 1976b, paras. 64–78).

The Commission also had the benefit of a recent Monopolies and
Mergers Commission Report on advertising by solicitors (Monopolies and Mergers Commission 1976a), and indeed its recommendations are substantially in line with those of the Monopolies Commission, with some significant modifications. For the remainder of this
paper, I follow the Commission's categorization of the issues involved in the provision of information for the public. The question
is tackled in three sections: corporate advertising, referral lists, and
individual advertising. I deal with them in the reverse order since
that appears to be historically logical. In the sections on individual
and corporate advertising, I outline the historical background
against which the Commission's Report must be set, as well as
re-introduce some of the themes dealt with in the preceding section
on anti-market ideology and its connection with market control.

Individual Advertising

The first specific rules against advertising, touting and price cutting
are contained in the Solicitors' Practising Rules of 1936, although
'touting' had previously been prohibited under the general heading
of 'professional misconduct.' Under the Solicitors Act 1888, complaints of 'professional misconduct' were heard by a Disciplinary
Committee elected from members of the Council of the Law Soci-

ety. Miscreants could be sent to the High Court 'to be suitably dealt with' (section 13). The courts were quite content to leave the question of what constituted 'professional misconduct' to the discretion of the Disciplinary Committee.[3] The Solicitors Act 1919 extended the power of the Disciplinary Committee to allow it to mete out punishment subject only to appeal to the High Court. In the first ten years of operation of the Act, there were only 12 appeals, in 11 of which the orders of the Committee were confirmed.[4] So, by the 1920s the Council of the Law Society had acquired considerable autonomy from outside scrutiny of its disciplinary proceedings. Events in the 1920s and 1930s were to strengthen this autonomy and to see the introduction of a power upon the part of the Council of the Law Society to legislate for the profession. These events (Abel-Smith and Stevens 1967, pp. 188–92) took place in response to a rising tide of public unrest over solicitors' defalcations. They were to result in the promulgation of a code of ethics, The Solicitors Practising Rules, which were ultimately be used as market regulators by the Council of the Law Society.

By 1930 there were two major problems for the Council of the Law Society. The first was the shadow cast over the profession by the defalcations scandal, and the second was that solicitors were being used by building societies as a way of competing with each other for business. The latter problem, that of 'undercutting', was a practice by which building societies published scales of charges at which solicitors engaged by them were prepared to carry out conveyances. Undercutting, as Abel-Smith and Stevens point out (1967 pp. 204–5) was seen by the leaders of the profession as an unhealthy incursion of market forces into the primary source of income of the profession.

Eventually, after a number of abortive attempts at legislation on solicitors' frauds, an Act was passed in 1933 which gave the Council of the Law Society the power, not only to make and enforce rules governing the keeping of accounts (to deal with frauds), but also to make and enforce rules regulating any matter affecting the professional conduct, discipline and practice of solicitors. It had already been established in 1930 by the Disciplinary Committee in a case involving a Lancashire solicitor that 'soliciting professional business is inconsistent with the dignity of an honourable profession and tends to bring it into disrepute', the solicitor in question being suspended for 6 months for 'undertaking professional work for remuneration lower than the scale fee, and so low, and in such circumstances as to bring the profession into disrepute.[5] Furthermore, the Council had announced in 1934 that 'touting' was considered to be an offence under Section 5 of the Solicitors' Act 1932.

In 1936 the Council proposed more detailed regulations, to be made under the Solicitors Act 1933. These prohibited solicitors from obtaining, or attempting to obtain, professional business by (a) directly or indirectly inviting instructions for business, (b) doing or permitting to be done anything which by its manner, frequency or otherwise, advertises his practise as a solicitor, or (c) doing or permitting to be done, anything which may be reasonably regarded as touting. Wider power was then given under rule 1 (c) as its impact was to render the statutory appeal of little or no effect. The rules also made it an offence for a solicitor to hold himself out as prepared to do work at less than the scale fee, and for a solicitor to share profits with non-solicitors. These rules were aimed against undercutting and working for legal aid societies.

Legal aid societies, sometimes disparagingly referred to as 'ambulance chasers', mainly operated in the sphere of personal accident cases. Solicitors, or their representatives, would often offer to take on cases on a contingency fee basis. Sometimes the plaintiff was already a member of a legal aid society. On other occasions, the business seems to have been sought out in hospital casualty departments. The practice of charging on a contingency fee basis was illegal, constituting the offence of champerty, but, as Abel-Smith and Stevens have noted (1967 p. 139) 'this was not the main aspect which worried the Law Society. The Societies were being used as a cloak for advertising or touting for cases by speculative firms of solicitors. . . . Ordinary solicitors were said to be losing the work arising out of personal injury cases, owing to the fear of extortionate charging.'

Announcing the new rules on 10 July 1936, the President of the Law Society justified the rules as not only being in the professional interest, but the public interest as well, since 'we shall not be able to maintain the high standard of our profession, the maintenance of which is necessary in the public interest, unless those proposing to enter the profession can be assured that they have a reasonable prospect of making a living.'[6] Thus through the creation of a series of ethical offences, the Law Society was able to deal with threats to the two areas of business in which the profession enjoyed statutory monopolies. Since no-one who was not a solicitor could institute legal proceedings or convey property for gain, these areas of activity were secured for the profession. However, there was no existing guarantee that these areas would remain remunerative. Legal aid societies, building societies, and 'speculative builders' threatened to bring about a general lowering of remuneration for these areas of business. Through the introduction of the rules against advertising and undercutting, the Law Society was able to combat those threats. As Abel-Smith and Stevens (1967 p.205) summarise it:

the system of state regulation of solicitors' charges had been introduced to protect the public from excessive charges. Such protection was needed because in many matters clients could not know in advance the costs they were about to incur when they engaged a solicitor and because solicitors were potentially able to increase the work they did in order to magnify their own profit. In the 1930s the Law Society began to take steps to turn what had originally been a system of maximum price regulation into a system of minimum price regulation.

The scale fee system to which they refer had been in operation since the passage of the Solicitors' Remuneration Order 1883. In 1950, a rule was introduced which made charging less than the scale prevailing in a particular area, *prima facie* evidence of a professional offence. The burden of proof rested on the solicitor to show that the charge was unlikely to attract business unfairly. In this way, the Law Society was able to ensure the economic prosperity of the profession through a combination of the Solicitors' Practising Rules and the Solicitors' Remuneration Order.

Throughout this period, the Law Society had laid great stress upon combatting 'a particular class of profiteering solicitors' and 'speculative firms' who were set in stark contrast to the 'ordinary solicitor.' Yet there were ways in which solicitors could seek business without falling foul of the professional rules. As Lewis and Maude wrote (1952, p. 107) 'a professional man with a keen business instinct is not prevented by the advertising ban from going out and getting custom. There are contented and prosperous partnerships in accountancy, architecture and several other professions, in which the labour is shrewdly divided between the partner who plays golf, bridge and billiards, attends cocktail parties and dances, and the partner who just does the work.' This point is underlined by Abel-Smith and Stevens (1967, pp. 142–3) who state that it is 'impossible to prevent indirect forms of touting. Solicitors have an incentive to participate in any type of social activity which is likely to bring them the right kind of contracts. Thus solicitors tend to be active members of rotary clubs, golf clubs, rugby football clubs, and to become freemasons and leading churchmen.'

Abel-Smith and Stevens were prominent members of a group of academics whose concern it was to evaluate the extent to which the legal profession operated in the public interest. From the middle of the 1960s onwards, this group published works in which price fixing, the rules against advertising, and other restrictive practices were subjected to detailed critical scrutiny. In the van was Michael Zander, whose book *Lawyers and the Public Interest* (1968 pp. 185–233) contains a sustained attack upon the way in which the Law Society used advertising rules to impose a minimum conveyancing rate. Zander's argument was that the relaxation of the rules against advertising could only introduce a healthy and realistic element of economic competition into the affairs of the solicitors' profession. An equally important argument by this group (Abel-Smith, Zander and Brooke, 1973) was that the rules against advertising prevented the poor from using lawyers, since they would be unlikely in their social milieux to encounter lawyers or other professional people. Thus the advertising restrictions were perceived as a major factor in generating 'unmet legal need'. Without overestimating the impact of academic research on official policy these events did provide the basis on which the supply of solicitors' services was referred to the Monopolies and Mergers Commission in July 1974.

That Commission reported on the question of solicitors' advertising in July 1976. It found (Monopolies and Mergers Commission 1976a, paras. 114–30) that the prohibition of advertising was a restrictive practice in that it prevented the public from being given information about the services of solicitors; that it was likely to have a disadvantageous effect on the competitiveness and efficiency of the profession generally; that it was likely to impede the introduction of innovatory methods; that it was likely to some degree to enhance the importance of other less open and challengable methods of attracting business; and finally that the operation of the rule by the Law Society had on occasion impeded the operation of law centres. The Commission went on to recommend that the restriction be replaced with a rule which permitted any solicitor to use such publishing as he might think fit, as long as he did not claim superiority for his practice over any other, the publicity contained no inaccuracies or misleading statements, and the publicity was not of a character which could be reasonably regarded as likely to bring the profession into disrepute. Despite the fact that these proposals left effective control with the Law Society, the Council reacted unfavourably to the report on three major grounds. First, that advertising would have an adverse effect upon the relationship between the solicitor and client and upon the solicitor's duty to the court. Second, that competition could not raise standards but would increase overheads to the detriment of smaller practices and clients. Finally, the Council felt that if advertising led to excessive competition and undercutting, the standards of the profession would decline. Zander (1968, p. 47) gives such arguments short shrift: 'If solicitors felt themselves under the pressure of informed shopping around, it is likely that they would respond with improved standards and lower charges, as in any other field of human activity.' This writer finds it hard to share Professor Zander's enthusiastic view of the bracing effects of competition by advertising.

On individual advertising the Royal Commission followed the Monopolies Commission in finding the current restrictions on advertising 'too restrictive' on a number of grounds. First, they felt that the attitudes of the Law Society were over-cautious because the mere fact that some advertising is bad, does not mean that it is all bad and more important, (27–31) 'because advertising is inherent in any free or mixed economy and helps the consumer exercise the choice between competing products or services.' Not only was advertising felt to inhere in any mixed economy, it was also felt by the Commission to be necessary in order to enable the client to exercise a properly informed choice. However, despite this general enthusiasm for advertising, the Commissioners (27–34) were concerned that a 'proper balance' should be achieved between the needs of the public to be informed and the need for the standards of the profession to be maintained. The restrictions are designed to conform with the principles set out in the Monopolies Commission Report and (27–35) limit the information to: name, address and telephone number of the firm; names and qualifications of the partners; opening hours; types of work undertaken; details of fixed charges; knowledge of foreign languages or languages of ethnic minorities. Thus, whilst the Commission was anxious to assist the consumer in the decision between competing services, they were also concerned not to allow too much licence. The evils which they were concerned to avoid were (27–36) 'claims of superiority', and whilst competition seems to be encouraged, 'excessive competition' is to be deprecated.

In order to achieve this balance, the Commission recommends (27–38) that control of individual advertising should rest with the Law Society which would regulate such matters as style, timing, frequency, and annual budget. The Report also recommends that solicitors should not be allowed to advertise publicly the quality of their service, number of staff other than partners, income, case-load, fee charges (other than fixed fees), nor to make any reference to clients of the firm. The type of advertising which is to be permitted is not the type which promotes the services of one firm at the expense of others, but whose purpose is to 'inform the public.'

One of the main areas of difficulty with which the profession had to contend was the intangible nature of professional services by comparison with products or commodities, a fact which, as the Report mentions, leads to a greater potential for deception and makes this type of advertising more difficult to control effectively. For this reason, the Commission has insisted upon a high degree of restriction upon the style and content of advertisments. This left the dilemma of how to permit the provision of some information on the basis of which some discrimination could be made between practitioners. The proposed rules make price discrimination an impossibility since they prohibit mention of price, except where fees are fixed. The basis of discrimination selected by the Commission was the use of a register of specialists. The proposals is that any solicitor of at least five years standing should, on application to the Law Society, be eligible to be designated a specialist in a particular subject, provided that he has spent not less than a quarter of his time in each of the last five years on that area, and that he shall not be designated a specialist in more than two areas. As Zander points out (1978, pp. 154–7), the advantages of such a scheme are likely to be outweighed by the disadvantages. First, the scheme is likely to be based on little more than self-credentialling. Secondly, there may be practices which will be as expert as the registered specialists, who wish to participate neither in the scheme nor in the affairs of the Law Society. However, Sir Henry Benson has said (1979, p. 1029) one of the objects of the Commission was to encourage participation in the affairs of the Law Society. Thirdly, such a scheme will be costly to administer and will discriminate against new entrants to the profession.

As I stated earlier, there has always been an integral connection between advertising and conveyancing, a connection which is maintained by the Commission's Report. On conveyancing, the Commission recommends that the monopoly should be maintained, but that standard charges should be re-introduced (scale fees having been abolished in 1972) which would be fixed by a new Fees Advisory Committee. These fees will be fixed maximum fees, presumably to be mentioned in advertising. However, from the guidelines on advertising it appears that any mention of a lower fee would attract punishment as an ethical offence. It is therefore difficult to imagine how the advertising proposals will lead to any changes in the position on conveyancing. As Glasser (1980, p. 30) has noted, it is unlikely that the failure to spell out the connections between these two areas will have the effect of engendering continuing disagreement. Hence the advertising recommendations appear to be a part of the general Commission strategy of preserving the autonomy of the profession and their traditional business areas, whilst encouraging the promotion of increased efficiency and cost effectiveness through the promotion of professional associations and through the introduction of very limited competition. Whether the strategy will be successful remains to be seen.

Referral Lists

As I outlined earlier, one of the major elements in the academic critique of the advertising regulations was the effect which they had upon the availability of legal services to the poor. The arguments are so well rehearsed that they scarcely require re-iteration. Their essential elements include the propositions that lack of knowledge that a problem has a legal solution, and that lack of information about the availability, location and expertise of solicitors are key causes of 'unmet legal need' among, what the Chairman was pleased to call (1979, p. 1029), 'the have-nots'.

This lack of information afflicted not only the 'have-nots' but also referral and other advice-giving agencies which lacked information about which lawyers were willing to undertake legal aid work of various categories. It has been one of the achievements of the reform lobby and of the Law Society in recent years that in 1976 the

Law Society took steps to rectify this gap in the provision of information by publishing legal aid referral lists. These are published on a regional basis, one for each of the 28 areas and they indicate which firms in each area are prepared to do any of the 14 categories of legally aided work. These lists are distributed to various agencies likely to be approached by the public for information about solicitors, including citizens' advice bureaux, consumer advice agencies, the probation service, social services departments, police stations and public libraries. The second and third editions contain details of those firms prepared to conduct the fixed fee interview of 30 minutes for £5. The Commission was very impressed by the Law Society's achievement in publishing these lists, and certainly they seem to have gone a long way towards reducing the sort of obstacle course which had become all too prevalent where the bewildered citizen was shunted from one advice agency to another, and turned away from several solicitors' offices in the course of efforts to have the problem dealt with.

Referral lists are a key element in the Commission's strategy on 'unmet need' which consists of a reliance on 'generalist advice agencies' like CABx as agencies through which appropriate legal aid clients can be channelled towards private solicitors. This strategy appears to be a supplement to the establishment of law centres which have a deservedly high reputation in providing innovatory methods of delivering legal services to poor communities.

Collective Advertising

Before embarking upon an analysis of this area of advertising, it seems appropriate to remark upon what seems to be an anomoly in the attitude of the Council of the Law Society to the question of advertising. The anomaly lies in the fact that, despite its implacable opposition to individual advertising the Council has, since 1964, been vigorously pursuing collective advertising or public relations campaigns, culminating in 1977 with the 'Whatsisname' campaign, and in 1979 with the hiring of the famous public relations consultants Saatchi and Saatchi. Bennion (1969, p. 90) finds this somewhat puzzling, noting that what appears to be undignified for an individual somehow acquires dignity by being carried on by a professional body. On the subject of collective advertising the Report

(27–5) praises the work of the Law Society, considering that 'as a general principle it is a proper function of a governing body of a profession to improve public knowledge of the services provided by its members.'

It is possible to explain the anomaly alluded to above if one examines the different roles of individual and collective advertising market regulators. Whilst clearly there was a realization on the part of the Council that restrictions on individual advertising performed a valuable function in regulating markets already monopolised by the profession, since 1960 there has been an equally clear recognition of the value of collective advertising as a vehicle through which these markets might be protected and expanded. As I have noted elsewhere (Fennell 1980, pp. 9–26), one of the salient features of the Council's activities in the last two decades has been the rapid development of a sophisticated corporate machinery through which the economy of the solicitors' profession may be planned and its image simultaneously enhanced.

The development of a fully fledged public relations machinery for the profession began relatively humbly in 1956 with the establishment of a public relations department which grew slowly over the next eight years to boast a staff of (Lund 1964, p. 464) 'one solicitor, two girls and an unadmitted man.' By the end of 1963 the profession had come under heavy attack in the press over the issue of conveyancing remuneration. In June 1964 an editorial in the *Law Society's Gazette* referred to the fact that the Council had sought the advice of a leading firm of public relations consultants on the question, and they had stated that the Society was doing a great deal of good work. This was a new departure in that it was the first time that the profession had hired public relations experts in order to defend its markets and enhance its public image.

In 1976, after the report of the Monopolies Commission on advertising, the Law Society launched another public relations campaign. Entitled 'the national information campaign', its aims included (according to the managing director of the firm selected to act as agents) increasing the public's awareness of the whole range of solicitors' services, increasing public understanding of solicitors' contribution to the community and obtaining the active support of solicitors. He described the longer term aims as (Neill 1977, p. 883) 'the safeguarding of solicitors' existing markets and building a platform for increasing their share of these markets and any new markets created by legislation.' The medium for the campaign was the cartoon feature entitled 'Whatsisname' which consisted of a series of nightmarish vignettes illustrating the pitfalls of buying a house, establishing a business, or investing money, without first seeing a solicitor.

This campaign was adjudged a sufficient success to merit continuation of the public relations work and in 1978 the Master of the Rolls gave permission for the levy on the profession to be increased to £20 per head to finance a new campaign to be directed by the firm of Saatchi and Saatchi. Two observations may be made on the subject of collective advertising. First, it is clearly intended by the Law Society that it should be a vehicle through which the image of the profession may be enhanced and the markets of the profession protected and expanded. It has been an integral part of the plan to increase the professional market to keep pace with the rapidly increasing recruitment to the profession which has taken place since the mid-1960s. Second, the advertisments have been aimed primarily at areas of business normally associated with solicitors, such as divorce, conveyancing and the establishment of businesses. This being the case, they are unlikely to go far in expanding the public conception of the range of services provided by solicitors.

Conclusion

The recommendations of the Commission on advertising are best viewed in the context of the overall strategy adopted in the Report to reform of professional services. This strategy, which proceeds logically from the definition accepted by the Commission of what a profession is (3–18, 19), is based on the belief that reform can best be achieved by preserving professional autonomy from outside supervisory agencies, whilst strengthening the powers of the professional bodies to implement the blueprint of reform. This strategy rests upon two assumptions. The first of these is that, in this case, the Law Society possesses the political will, and the political muscle to implement the recommendations on advertising. The second is that the implementation of their recommendations will have an impact upon the competitiveness of conveyancing rates. The latter is doubtful, given the inability of the Commission to decide upon the degree of competition which they would be prepared to tolerate. Whether the former assumption is justified only the events of the next few years will tell.

Notes

1. Benson, Sir H. (1979), Speech to the Law Society's Annual Conference, *Law Society's Gazette* 24 October, pp. 1029–30.
2. *Bates v. State Bar of Arizona* 53 L. Ed. 2d. 810–50.
3. See *In re a solicitor, The Times Law Reports* 17 November 1911 pp. 50–1 in which Mr. Justice Darling applied to the Solicitors' Disciplinary Committee the following dictum of Lord Justice Lopes in *Allinson v. General Council of Medical Education and Registration* (1894) Q. B. p. 750. 'As long as conduct could reasonably be regarded as disgraceful or dishonourable by his professional brethren of good repute and competency, then it is open to the Council to say he has been guilty of professional misconduct.'
4. *The Times*, 2 October 1929.
5. *Law Society's Gazette* (1930), p. 62.
6. *The Law Society's Gazette* (1936), p. 167.

References

Abel-Smith, B. & Stevens, T. (1967), *Lawyers and the Courts* London, Heinemann Educational Books.
Abel-Smith, B. Zander, M. & Brooke, R. (1973), *Legal Problems and the Citizen: A Study in Three London Boroughs* London, Heinemann Educational Books.
Bennion, F. (1969), The plight of the profession *Law Society's Gazette*, pp. 87–91.
Benson, Sir H. (1979), Speech to the Law Society Annual Conference, *Law Society's Gazette*, 24 October, pp. 1029–30.
Durkheim, E. (1957), *Professional Ethics and Civil Morals* C. Brookfield (trans.) London, Routledge & Kegan Paul.
Fennell, P. (1980) Solicitors, their markets and their ignorant public in Z. Bankowski & G. Mungham (eds.) *Essays in Law and Society* London, Routledge & Kegan Paul.
Glasser, C. (1980), After the report-remuneration *LAG Bull.* p. 30.
Hadfield, B. (1975), Two models of the legal profession, *Northern Ireland Legal Quarterly*, pp. 94–105.
Johnson, T. J. (1972), *Professions & Power*, London, Macmillan.
Larson, M. S. (1977), *The Rise of Professionalism: A Sociological Analysis* University of California Press.
Lewis, R. & Maude, A. E. U. (1952), *Professional People* London, Phoenix House.
Lund, Sir T. (1969), Public relations and the profession *Law Society's Gazette*, p. 464.
Monopolies and Mergers Commission (1976a) *A Report on the Supply of Services of Solicitors in England and Wales in Relation to Restrictions on Advertising*, London, HMSO, HOC 557.
Monopolies and Mergers Commission (1976b) *A Report on the Supply of Barristers' Services in Relation to Restrictions on Advertising*, HMSO, HOC 559.
Neill, R. (1977), The national information campaign, *Law Society's Gazette*, p. 883.

Reader, W. J. (1966), *Professional Men: The Rise of the Professional Classes in 19th Century England*, London, Weidenfeld & Nicholson.

Rueschemeyer, D. (1973), *Lawyers and Their Society: A Comparative Study of The Legal Profession in Germany and the United States*, Harvard University Press.

Zander, M. (1968), *Lawyers and the Public Interest – A Study in Restrictive Practices*, London, Weidenfeld & Nicholson.

Zander, M. (1978), *Legal Services for the Community*, London, Maurice Temple Smith,

CHAPTER 7

Public Accountability of the Legal Profession

*H. W. Arthurs**

The legal profession is a relatively powerful group in any Western society. Its power may derive from a variety of sources:

(1) knowledge monopoly – lawyers possess a congeries of skills and a body of knowledge which enable only them to do jobs;

(2) legal monopoly – judge-made and statutory laws prevent other people from undertaking many tasks which lawyers perform without regard to whether such people are actually able to perform them;

(3) client dependency – clients who, by default or willingly, consult lawyers often come to depend upon them not merely for the performance of legal services, but for personal, financial, or policy advice as well;

(4) moral stature – the perceived willingness of individual lawyers to provide help to those who need it, regardless of their own profit or preference, and without abuse of trust, provides the basis of a claim by the profession as a whole to moral rectitude and civic mindedness; a special instance of this is the lawyer who acts as spokesperson for the individual in conflict with the state;

(5) economic and political leverage – lawyers occupy many critical positions in, or act as spokespersons for, business and government, thus permitting them to participate in important public policy decisions;

(6) social prestige – as a relatively affluent, educated and visible group, lawyers assume a variety of community leadership roles.

* I wish to make clear that I do not speak on behalf of, nor – except as indicated – even primarily about, the governing body of which I happen to be a member, the Benchers of the Law Society of Upper Canada.

However, to say that the legal profession possesses power, and to identify the sources, is not to locate accurately the institutions or individuals who wield that power, or the means by which they do so. Some lawyers, as individuals or as members of informal networks, are obviously more influential than others in the affairs of their clients and the community. Some voluntary groupings of lawyers, such as law firms, Inns, and local lawyers' associations, make their particular primary impact upon the internal organization and relationships of the profession, although with obvious ultimate public consequences.

Moreover, special attention should be paid to the formal organizations which exercise powers of self-government over the legal profession. They are thought to possess considerable, if not complete, powers to control the other professional actors. And given the existence of such powers, one would expect, in principle, that Williams' Law of Power Abuse must be right:

the degree by which power will inevitably be abused by the professional self-governing body operating under statutory authority varies inversely with the degree of public accountability provided in that statute (Williams 1979, p. 345).

But the evidence suggests that Williams may both overstate and understate his case. That considerable power exists is indisputable, but it does seem to be exercised so erratically: as often benignly as selfishly, as often insufficiently as egregiously, as often by indirection as by overt, formal act. Legal professions, on the one hand, often demonstrate appropriate regard for the public interest, although their constituent statutes provide no mechanisms for public accountability. Yet, on the other hand, institutional arrangements which seem to be well-designed may fail to accomplish their purpose of securing such accountability.

The connection between institutional forms and social results is, no doubt, always difficult to assess. The task is particularly difficult when the institutional form, such as a professional governing body, is obscured by a spider's web of history and folklore, social customs and political ideologies, economic commitments and legal rights and obligations, expressed and implied.

Three choices are thus presented. One can seek to trace the strands of the web, and brush aside those which obscure or interfere with the desired functioning of the institution. This is a difficult and problematic exercise. Or one can address the question of institutional form directly, and as a matter of principle. What sort of governing body should one design in a mixed economy, in a society which is devoted to democratic values, in a legal–administrative system which adheres to the rule of law? Such a question would be politically naive, and quite un-British. Or, finally, one can essentially ignore the institution and the spider's web, and focus on the social results. A lawyer has been defined as someone who can think of a thing which is connected to something else, without thinking of the thing to which it is connected. In this sense, although neither its chairman nor the majority of its members were lawyers, the Report of the Commission is a very lawyerly document.

The Report neither poses, nor answers, the question of whether greater accountability would enhance the quality of services the public receives from its lawyers. It does not address in any systematic way, as a matter of principle, the question of whether the legal profession ought to be made formally accountable for the manner in which it exercises its privilege of self-government. What the Report does do is to deal with a series of discrete issues to which discrete solutions are proposed.

The Benson Commission Report

Although the Commission was mandated 'to consider whether any, and if so what, changes are desirable in the public interest in the structure, organisation [and] regulations of . . . the legal profession . . .' (Benson 1979, p. iii), accountability is a *leitmotif*, rather than a dominant theme, of the Report. At numerous points, the Commission reminds us of the need to protect public interests in all of the processes of professional government. But when the public interest collides with professional interests, the Commission is not always unequivocal in subordinating the latter to the former. And, above all, the Commission is diffident about any institutional solutions which might materially dilute professional control or subject it to searching external scrutiny.

Let me first consider the Commission's perception of how a balance might be struck between public and professional interests. The Commission states that it wishes to protect the profession's 'corporate identity and independence which is of value not only to its members but to the public at large' (Benson 1979, p. 32). While the Commission does, in the same breath, acknowledge the risks of self-regulation, this easy assimilation of public and professional interests tends to blur the areas of divergence.

Some examples may be pertinent. The Commission refers to a public perception of professional self-interest flowing from the overt antipathy of professional bodies to the emergence of law centres (29–20). Yet it stresses the maintenance of such professional values as the cab rank principle and abstention from unseemly efforts at community organization in its prescriptions for the conduct of lawyers associated with such centres (8–20–34). To be sure, the Commission contemplates that other rules of professional conduct might be relaxed to facilitate the work of law centres, but only at the discretion of the relevant professional governing body (Benson 1979, p. 88). To overstate the case somewhat, in the event of a conflict between professional values and effective representation, the Commission has preferred to maintain professional values.

Even where the Commission has apparently accepted the pre-eminence of public interests, as for example in recommending more extensive advertising in order to improve the accessibility of legal services (27–34), in a sense it may be seen to be relieving the profession of the consequences of its own traditional folly, with ensuing financial benefits. Here again, the Commission's language is instructive: 'the need to inform the public about available legal services must not be allowed to conflict with the need to maintain high standards of integrity and performance by members of the legal profession . . .' (27–2). To ensure that its recommendation concerning more extensive advertising will be implemented in a manner consistent with this principle, control over advertising is vested in the Law Society itself (27–38), rather than in a body which would include lay representatives.

It is not surprising, therefore, that when the Commission turns from a discussion of specific policies to consideration of the institutional forms through which these policies are to be promoted, it gives at best limited and tentative endorsement to mechanisms of public accountability.

The Commission's solicitude for the profession is captured in its plea that, during the period of implementation of the Report's recommendations, '. . . the profession should have a period of orderly development free, so far as possible, from external interventions' (Benson 1979, p. 36).

To be sure there is to be established a new Council for Legal Services which will comprise lay and legal representatives, and which will be well-supported by the staff and budget necessary to enable it both to conduct research and to launch pilot and experimental schemes (6–15). But the Council's mandate to develop 'long-term policy based on adequate data and coherent planning' is somewhat circumscribed by the fact that the Council will have no executive functions, and will simply render advice to the Lord Chancellor.

In a similar vein, the Commission proposes the establishment of a Fees Advisory Committee, including lay representatives, which would review all tariffs of fees 'to ensure that where the level of fees is directly controlled by scale or taxation, the lawyer receives fair remuneration for the work done' (37–95). This somewhat ironic twist on the usually-perceived function of lay representation is underlined by the admonition that the Fees Advisory Committee 'should not operate or be seen to operate as a means by which government policy, on incomes or on the provision of services, may be imposed (37–93). The function of lay representation, in other words, is to legitimate, rather than scrutinize from a public perspective, the level of remuneration sought by lawyers.

Yet again, the Commission proposes that Solicitors' Practice Rules – which deal with such important matters as conflicts of interest, contingency fees, etc. – ought to receive public scrutiny. However, proposed rules are to be reviewed not by any special, formal body – an alternative explicitly rejected – but by circulation amongst interested groups such as the National Consumers' Council. Their representations are to be made not directly to the profession, but to the Master of the Rolls, who will take them into account in ultimately determining whether to approve or disapprove proposed new Practice Rules.[2] And the proposed new professional standards for barristers and solicitors, while available for public comment, are not to be subject to external approval of any sort (22–58).

The Report expressly endorses the view that the profession must have freedom to frame the rules which govern it 'because the profession itself bears the responsibility for maintaining the standards which the public interest requires' (25–21).

No doubt *noblesse oblige* will usually lead the profession to 'do the right thing'; but obviously no process of serious, structured debate is envisaged, and no mechanism exists even for ensuring that public comment is solicited and considered.

The Commission is indeed firm on the issue of lay participation in one area, complaints against lawyers, and subsequent disciplinary proceedings (Benson 1979, p. 347 ff.). Direct lay representation on various professional committees and tribunals is no doubt an important form of symbolic reassurance to complainants that their concerns will receive objective consideration by at least one disinterested member. However, the Report also envisages the withering-away of the Lay Observer who now functions as a 'mere adjunct to the complaint procedures' (25–45). Why greater internal lay participation should necessarily diminish external scrutiny is not made clear. Nor does the Commission address the possibility that the single lay member who will serve in each disciplinary matter may be unduly deferential to his legal colleagues – and outvoted if he is not. And finally, it is at least slightly ironic that the Commission should have mandated lay participation in the area of professional government which is most distinctively 'legal' – adjudication of complaints – while failing to do so in other areas involving the formulation and adoption of policy, where lawyers' claims to expertise and objectivity are rather less compelling.

The ultimate test of the Commission's views on accountability is its prescription for the constitution of the governing body of the Law Society, and that of the Bar: 'it must be responsive to lay opinion' (29–16). But not too responsive: the Commission rejected a proposal for lay membership of the Council of the Law Society (and the Bar Senate) '. . . because it is contrary to the principle that the governing body should be elected by the members of the profession' (29–40, 32–77). In effect, the Commission concludes that the governing bodies are to be ultimately accountable only to their own professional constituencies. By inference, it also concludes that neither the public nor the state should have a responsible role in the adoption and execution of the great residue of policies which, notwithstanding other recommendations, remain firmly within the profession's control.

In the light of these conclusions the objective, if uninformed, observer might view those other recommendations somewhat cynically. How effective are wide consultation and lay committee membership likely to be in influencing the course of events when undiluted professional governing bodies retain final powers of decision? How important is the retention of veto powers by the Master of the Rolls and the Lord Chancellor likely to be when the range of possible departures from the *status quo* will be determined by the initiative of the profession itself?

It is at this point in the analysis that one wishes the Commission had acknowledged the presence of the spider's web. Will the Law Society Council, for example, adopt a tacit, self-denying ordinance by which it will avoid policies which offend the National Consumers' Council? Will a wink and a nod from the Lord Chancellor's office send the Senate of the Bar down the road to virtue? Stranger developments than these have provided the invisible glue of British institutions in the past.

It would be unfair to the Commission, moreover, not to stress that it does speak to the issue of internal accountability: 'the governing body . . . should be compact and readily identifiable. . . . The different sizes and types of practice and the various specialisms in which members are employed should be represented on it. . . . '[3] Moreover, particularly in the case of the Law Society, the Report stresses the need for internal communication and debate and decentralization of activity (29–21, 29–43), which should stimulate a higher level of rank-and-file participation. In the case of the Bar, the Report urges a shift in responsibility for professional government to a renewed, and predominantly elected, Senate which would also contain representatives of the Inns and the bench (32–70).

These proposals are praiseworthy, but it must not be thought that by enhancing the internal democratic procedures of the governing body, it is thereby likely to be made more responsive to the public interest. On the contrary: it is entirely possible that grassroots opinion will be more self-interested, less civic-minded, on some issues than the profession's elite. For example, the question of unauthorized encroachments on the profession's conveyancing monopoly is more likely to agitate country solicitors than city firms; higher fee tariffs are of more concern to the mass of junior *lumpen*-practitioners than to the *haute bourgeoisie* of established seniors. Greater internal accountability, therefore, may have the unintended result of generating greater pressures for external accountability.

In one matter, the Commission does evince commendable concern to bring professional practice into line with public policy. A series of recommendations are designed to secure the elimination of racial and sexual discrimination, and to include the reservation 'if necessary' of places on the governing bodies for representatives of women and ethnic minorities (35–43). But again, while members of the minorities within the profession may be generally more sensitive to the needs of their external 'constituencies', there is no particular reason to expect that they will display greater concern for the public interest, in other respects, than the traditional governors of the profession.

In summary, it can be said that the Report stops well short of recommendations, or even analysis, which would portend a fundamental change in the profession's accountability to the public.

Institutional Arrangements to Secure Accountability: A Comparative Perspective

The Commission makes occasional reference to foreign experience, yet it obviously regards the structure of the governing bodies themselves as impossible of external comparison. Perhaps this is wise; institutional transplants are no less problematic than organic transplants. But as the legal professions of Canada and Australia have already begun to turn away from their former imitation of English arrangements, consideration of developments abroad might have at least raised questions of principle and stimulated further analysis.

The legal professions in Canada especially have accepted the practice, if not the principle, of accountability. But the principle itself has become a central tenet of public policy relating to the professions.

Three public documents in the late 1960s – none of them primarily directed towards the legal profession *per se* – accomplished this change in public policy. The McRuer Report stressed that 'the granting of [professional] self-government is a delegation of legislative and judicial functions and can only be justified as a safeguard to the public interest' (McRuer 1968, p. 1162). The Economic Council of Canada's Interim Report on Competition Policy (1969, pp. 148–9) demonstrated the anti-competitive, and potentially injurious, nature of various professional conduct rules and practices. And the

Castonguay-Nepveu Report[4] proposed a new structure of professional government in order to effect an accommodation between traditions of professional self-government and the need for protection of the public. Since the latter Report has resulted in the most far-reaching changes in Canadian law, these might conveniently be contrasted with the present and proposed structures of professional self-government in England.

The Quebec Professional Code[5] was adopted in 1973 following prolonged controversy, and ultimately a negotiated compromise, with that province's lawyers. At the apex of a complicated regulatory structure it establishes an Inter-professional Council comprising representatives of each of the recognized professions. The Council has the obligation of recommending that professional status be conferred on new groups, and of reporting annually to the legislature upon the state of the professions. It also nominates a majority of the members of a Professions Board, all of whom are members of some profession, and all of whom are ultimately appointed by the Cabinet.

The Professions Board is a powerful and active body. It is enpowered with ensuring the discharge by each professional group of its statutory obligations, protecting the public, approving regulations proposed by each profession (or enacting regulations for that profession, if necessary), setting fee schedules, and publishing decisions in disciplinary cases.

Within this overarching framework, each profession is organized into a corporation, the constitution of which conforms to a statutorily required pattern. Administration of the professional corporation is entrusted to a general council whose directors are elected by the members, save for a small group (four out of 34, in the case of the Bar). The non-elected directors are appointed by the Professions Board, following consultation with the Council and various socio-economic groups; at least two of those appointed must be laymen.

Each corporation is required to establish, subject to ultimate cabinet approval, a fund to indemnify clients injured by malpractice, a procedure for the arbitration of disputes over accounts, and a code of ethics. Disciplinary proceedings are conducted, in the first instance, before the corporation's Discipline Committee comprising three members, one of whom must be an experienced barrister appointed by the provincial cabinet. An internal appeal is provided, with ultimate recourse in the case of all professions to a Professions Tribunal comprising three judges.

By way of contrast with the present British arrangements or the Commission's proposals, the Quebec scheme appears to be far-reaching indeed. However, in practice, professional autonomy seems to co-exist quite happily with public accountability (Issalys 1978). Although a number of concessions were made especially to the Bar, during the controversy over adoption of the Professional Code, there can be no doubt that if the public interest does not receive attention in the processes of professional government in Quebec, it will be because of shortcomings in the performance of the participants, rather than in the machinery itself.

The experience in Ontario with a similar strategy[6] may be briefly described. In 1970, at the request of the Law Society, and in the context of a general revision of its constituent statute, there was established a Council whose mandate was 'to consider the manner in which the members of the Society are discharging their obligations to the public and generally matters affecting the legal profession as a whole'.[7] Membership of the Council comprised laymen (about 10 per cent of the total) and the various estates of the profession (the law schools, local lawyer's associations and, predominantly, members of the governing body). The Council was unwieldy, lacked staff or finances, had no powers save that of making a report twice annually to the provincial cabinet and the Society, and soon grew comatose and died. A vestigial remnant of the Law Society Council is now found in a statutory requirement for an annual meeting of the various legal groups involved.[8]

But the death of the Law Society Council did not end the profession's obligation of public accountability. Rather, it led to the introduction of direct public representation in the government of the Law Society. As from 1974, four lay benchers (out of a total of 44) were appointed by the provincial cabinet to Convocation, the Society's governing body; they enjoy all the rights and privileges of elected benchers.[9]

This strategy of direct public representation has been adopted in several Canadian provinces, a development facilitated by the relatively supportive attitude of the organized bar. The Federation of Canadian Law Societies in 1972 announced:

[t]he Federation confirm(s) the principle that in order to ensure a source of independent legal advice and representation for the public the lawyer in the

practice of his profession must remain free of direct day-to-day interference by the state or its agencies but subject to the discipline of law societies controlled by members of the legal profession.

However, another principle was simultaneously confirmed: '[t]he governing bodies of the law societies are under the obligation to satisfy the public that the powers vested in them by law are being exercised in the public interest' (Federation 1973). Specific endorsement was given to the appointment of small numbers of responsible lay members to professional governing bodies, subject to the preservation of confidentiality in discipline proceedings.

Direct public representation has also begun to appear in various professional bodies with specialized concerns. In Ontario, for example, public representatives are to be found on the committees which monitor the profession's operation of the legal aid system and on the board of trustees of the Law Foundation, which collects and disburses, for public purposes, interest generated by solicitors' trust accounts.

It would be pleasant, but inaccurate, to report that the debate on public accountability has come to rest in Canada. Surprisingly, it has been renewed not in Quebec, where battle lines were initially drawn most dramatically, but in Ontario, which seemed at first so amenable to change.

A preliminary skirmish over control of legal aid appears to have been won rather handily by the Law Society which, however, moved to defuse criticism of its administration by several important innovations (Zemans 1978). But the issue of autonomy versus accountability is now joined at the level of principle.

A staff study issued by a government inquiry, the Professional Organizations Committee, made its stand clear:

it is a fundamental principle of our political system that those who make public policy decisions ought to be held accountable to those who are affected by their decisions. . . . Where governmental powers are delegated to professional or other regulatory bodies, the same principle . . . obtains. And no governmental powers ought to be exercised simply on the basis of a *pro forma* accountability. Public accountability will be effective only to the extent that all affected interests are informed about the actions of political decision-makers and can give or withhold support of those decision-makers accordingly (Trebilcock 1979, p. 42).

The Law Society's response was equally clear. Asserting on legal–historical grounds an independence inherited from the English Bar, the Society rejoined that 'to speak of the Law Society making "public policy" [was] a misconception of its role and function.' The implications of this position are far-reaching:

the protection of rights has been an historic function of the law and it is the responsibility of lawyers to carry out that function. In order that they may continue to do so there can be no compromise in the principle of freedom of the profession from interference, let alone control, by government (Law Society 1979, pp. 3–5).

Predictably, therefore, the Law Society expressed no enthusiasm for various proposals of the staff study. In relation to the composition of the governing body, these included an increase in lay membership and a decrease in professional membership; nomination of lay representatives by client, paralegal, and other interested groups; and creation of specific professional constituencies to ensure greater diversity of interests within Convocation (Trebilcock 1979, pp. 194–204). Of greater significance was the establishment of more specific channels of accountability to aid external scrutiny: access by dissatisfied clients to the Ombudsman; annual reporting to, and review by, a standing committee of the legislature; and abandonment by the Attorney-General of his present status as an *ex officio* bencher representing the public interest, in favour of his assumption of more clearly defined responsibility, in his ministerial capacity, for the ongoing scrutiny of professional organizations (Trebilcock 1979, pp. 239–43). These latter arrangements, the staff study proposed, would help to create 'opportunities for informed public debate and discussion of professional policy by affected interests, and for bringing this debate to the attention of public authorities' (Trebilcock 1979, p. 242).

Compared to the arrangements in Quebec – indeed compared in some respects to the present or proposed English arrangements – these seemed to be mild medicine indeed. The present structure of professional government would remain, in essence, undisturbed. One can only assume that it was the package rather than the contents which provoked the Law Society's negative reaction.

The Committee's formal Report, obviously intended to mollify the Law Society, acknowledged '. . . an inevitable, and in many ways healthy tension between two equally fundamental constitutional values: the independence of the judiciary and the bar, and the supremacy of the legislature'. (POC Report 1980, p. 26). Indeed, the Committee virtually accepted the *status quo* in all matters pertaining to the Society's internal government and policies.[10] However, two new devices to facilitate external scrutiny were proposed. A Lay Observer would be established to investigate complaints against various self-governing professions,[11] and each of those professions would submit an annual report through a designated Minister to the Legislature, relating to a number of specific matters.[12]

The accountability controversy has also surfaced in Australia. In its recent Discussion Paper on General Regulation of the Legal Profession, the New South Wales Law Reform Commission steps off to the resounding drumbeat of the McRuer Commission, quoted earlier, but marches farther and faster, albeit inexorably, down the road already traversed in Ontario and Quebec.

The Commission's 'tentative views' are set forth in a series of propositions (NSW 1979, pp. 5–8). Professional regulation is necessary, but must be undertaken with due regard for various, and sometimes conflicting, public interests. Resolution of such conflicts should not be left to one interested group, the profession or its clients. The safeguarding of professional independence is one of a number of important goals of any regulatory machinery: 'it is not a justification for excluding non-lawyers from the regulatory machinery, or for turning the regulatory function over to a professional association' (NSW 1979, p. 6). Neither the government nor the courts are appropriate bodies to undertake professional regulation.

What affirmative principles should shape professional regulation? The profession's participation is essential both to ensure informed decision making and to secure its co-operation and sense of responsibility; such participation should be shared amongst various sectors of professional interest. It must also embrace 'significant participation' from outside the profession. However, 'it would not be satisfactory merely to add lay people to the governing bodies of professional associations' (NSW 1979, p. 7); an independent, regulatory body established by statute is the 'best instrument' for professional regulation. And, finally, public participation in such a body would be aided by an adjunct, non-regulatory, predominantly lay body which could select, support and stimulate an authentic constituency for the lay members of the regulatory body.

Accordingly, the Commission proposes the establishment of two bodies, a Legal Professional Council and a Community Committee on Legal Services. The Legal Professional Council (NSW 1979, pp.

158–87) would include only a bare majority of professional practitioners, the balance being elected or nominated by other interests including the Community Committee on Legal Services, the Attorney-General, the Commissioner for Consumer Affairs, and the legal academic community. It would succeed to the Law Society's regulatory functions, including the establishment and enforcement of professional standards.

The Community Committee (NSW 1979, pp. 187–93) would comprise lay members almost exclusively, to be nominated by various community groups, interested governmental agencies and advisory bodies, and 'client' constituencies. It would maintain a continuing interest in the law, the administration of justice, law reform, and the legal profession, and would supply informed lay members to the Council. Of course, lawyers would continue to belong to their own independent associations 'to promote their own professional interests, and to advance their view of the public interest' (NSW 1979, p. 12).

This brief summary does not do justice to the New South Wales Commission's well-researched and far-reaching examination of the prospects and problems of professional accountability. It may suffice, however, to demonstrate that the Benson Commission's analysis did not plumb the depths of this issue, and that there is movement in countries closely identified with the British professional tradition towards a radical revision of the very notion of professional self-government. Needless to say, one should not confuse 'tentative proposals' with final recommendations, draft bills, or enacted law. To do so would be to underestimate the force of inertia, the appeal of tradition, and the political power of an aroused legal profession. Yet one cannot imagine that developments in Canada and Australia will fail to make some impression upon British consciousness at some future time.

Institutional Options: Abstention, Accountability and Regulation

There should not be considerable controversy over the general principle that significant centres of private power in a democratic society ought to be made answerable for its exercise to someone other than their proprietors. The range of rational options in the application of that principle, however, might produce very different arrangements relating to the legal profession. These run along a spectrum from deliberate abstention, through accountability at the mid-point, to direct regulation.

Lawyers often argue that the state should largely abstain from interference with the profession. Such an argument might proceed on the basis that the power exercised by the profession is too insignificant to warrant special legislative treatment, or that it has been so satisfactorily exercised that no special arrangements are required, or that the social costs of intervention, in terms of interference with the profession's function, are excessive, relative to the potential gains.

But these are difficult arguments to sustain. Insofar as the profession's power rests on a legal monopoly, at least, the Rubicon of abstention has already been crossed. Almost all legal monopolies are granted conditionally, and on terms, to prevent abuse. Moreover, insofar as its power rests on economic and political leverage or social prestige, the legal profession can expect to attract political demands for some form of public control, at least in the present mood of our society. And, it must be said, the profession's response to problems raised by client dependency, and to challenges to its own moral reputation, has not been so fulsome as to stifle such demands. On the contrary, the profession has sometimes been slow to grasp the notion that it will only be left alone if it is seen to be discharging its responsibilities at an acceptable level.

This leaves the question of whether the costs of intervention exceed the gains. The argument is almost always couched in the form of resistance to encroachments upon the independence of the profession, from which, it is said, will inevitably flow encroachments upon the independence of the judiciary, and then the demise of the rule of law.

The argument tends to claim too much. It is obviously true that lawyers who are involved in representing citizens against the state are particularly vulnerable to pressures, subtle or direct, which might inhibit their representational functions. But, in fact, relatively few lawyers are involved in serious contention with the state (as opposed, for example, to tax planning). Moreover, some who do oppose the state have powerful clients who can resist pressures brought against their legal representatives. And many of those who represent poor and weak clients, typically at the state's expense,

will hesitate to complain of the enervating effects of state intervention, since before the advent of legal aid such clients generally
lacked representation altogether. This is not to say there is nothing
in the independence argument; it obviously has great weight in
relation to possible specific manifestations of state control of the
profession. But it cannot be accepted as a magic spell whose mere
incantation will ward off all forms of interference with undiluted
professional self-government.

Abstention, then, is not likely to carry the day. Accountability,
by contrast, has much appeal. As has been shown, the various forms
of accountability adopted or proposed in Canada and Australia
contemplate the survival, in varying degrees, of professional autonomy. In Ontario, that autonomy is diluted, at present, only by the
symbolic presence of lay benchers, but daily administration and
most policy initiatives, are left in the hands of the profession's own
governing body. In Quebec, essentially the same situation prevails,
but with the theoretical possibility – as yet unrealized in practice – of
egregious intervention by the Professions Board.

It is the New South Wales proposals which appear to envisage the
most stringent requirements for accountability, by an almost evenly
balanced body of lay and professional members. The proposed
Legal Professional Council is not a revised or diluted version of the
profession's governing body – it is a thing apart, and it is to exercise
primary control over the profession. In formal terms, such an
arrangement might be said to signal the end of accountability and
the beginning of external regulation. But would such a clean break
actually occur, and would the profession in fact be deprived of the
privilege of self-government? Probably not.

The Law Society is not to be disbanded. It is to become an
advocate for lawyers' interests before the Council and elsewhere; it
would operate in effect, as a trade union. The analogy is instructive.
Trade unions have been described as private governments, with
considerable power over their members and, because of their status
as spokespersons, with considerable – even definitive – influence
over matters which nominally reside within the joint control of
labour and management. There remain prospects of similar *de facto*
power for the Law Society, especially since professional representatives are to constitute a bare majority of Council members. Because
they are likely to be united, well-briefed and long-serving, they may
well come to dominate the Council. And the apparently far-

reaching institutional change proposed in New South Wales is likely to produce the more modest result of a regime in which the profession persuades and pressures the Council into accepting its views, subject to the reciprocal concessions and moderating influences which might well emerge in a system like Ontario or Quebec.

Regulation, in the pure sense, would require the appointment of a statutory body whose members owed no loyalty to the profession, and whose mandate for fundamental change was expressed in clear terms. Any less drastic departure from the present system is unlikely significantly to alter the behaviour, or impinge upon the power, of the profession. Yet even the most zealous and fiercely independent regulatory agencies, as expereince shows, are sometimes surprisingly vulnerable to 'capture' by those they are meant to regulate. And, finally, the very existence of the power of the legal profession, which is used to make the case for strict regulation, doubtless makes it politically improbable. A government which tried to impose it would certainly alienate an influential group and its allies, and could be made to appear highly repressive indeed.

What possibilities remain, if effective control of private power is the goal?

External Challenge: Internal Response

Whichever institutional approach is adopted towards its governance, the legal profession will also remain, for the most part, subject to laws of general application. However, reliance upon laws of general application does present difficulties: litigation is costly and time-consuming; outcomes are problematic and usually directed towards narrowly-stated ratios and specific remedies, rather than broad, structural reforms; and no overall integration or rationalization of law and public policy affecting legal services is accomplished. Even periodic legislative intervention to resolve particular problems within the profession suffers from this latter defect. Can we say, then, that such 'external' pressures are more likely to ensure accountability than internal, institutional reforms?

As the Commission points out, the English and Welsh legal profession has in fact recently been the subject of several 'external' inquiries (Benson 1979, p. 29). Some of the enquiries terminated long-standing practices, while other professional policies were altered to mollify critics and forestall formal, state intervention. But it would not be accurate to say that direct state intervention has been a serious problem for the legal profession.

Although the Lord Chancellor and the Master of the Rolls are mandated to exercise formal control over certain professional affairs, they seldom appear to arrive at a position of confrontation or conflict with the Bar or the Law Society. On the contrary, the legal profession has usually had its way, although willing on occasion to make concessions either on their merits or in anticipation of the inevitable. Nor has litigation by or against the profession had a profound impact on its organization, powers or responsibilities. Sometimes professional privileges have been upheld;[13] on other occasions they may have been slightly imparied.[14] It seems clear, even in the Commission's relatively benign view, that the profession has, up to now, been allowed to ignore such critically important issues as competence.

Nonetheless, externally generated change does seem to enter the English legal profession, perhaps by capillary action. On the surface, nothing appears to happen, but under microscopic examination it will become obvious that an idea has actually passed through the thick, protective membrane of professional autonomy and now resides within the minds of the governing body. In such a process, even agents of change, who are viewed in certain quarters as possessing demonic qualities, upon analysis prove to comprise only sweet reason diluted by gentle persistence.[15]

The Canadian picture is rather different. As in England, several recent investigations have been made into the professions.[16] But in Canada these have resulted in legislation significantly altering at least the forms of regulation. Whether these changes have in turn produced changes in substantive policies is problematic. For example, Canadian law societies had already been drawn into legal aid before the 1970s' reforms in professional government, although no doubt continuing external pressure has helped to persuade them to involve laymen more deeply in policy-making, and to expand the role of community law clinics in the delivery of services. Again, in recent years, a concern for professional competence has become increasingly evident (Hurlburt 1979), but not necessarily as a result of overt external pressure. It is true that recently Canadian courts have been imposing civil liability for negligence upon lawyers somewhat more frequently,[17] but even before this trend had become apparent, the Canadian Bar Association's Code of Professional Conduct had been amended to create a duty to perform competently.[18] And recently various initiatives to promote competence, and prevent incompetence, have been launched in several provinces.[19] On the other hand, to the extent that those initiatives are the most credible evidence of professional concern, they have been primarily stimulated by increasing client claims and the spiralling cost of malpractice insurance; external forces obviously are at work as well.

The problematic connection between external pressures and internal responses, in the new climate of accountability, is illustrated by the contingent fee issue. Until the 1960s, it was generally accepted that contingent fees were illegal at common law. However, it was belatedly discovered that the complete codification of Canadian criminal law in 1955 had abolished champerty and maintenance, along with all other common law offences. The provincial law societies could have then stepped into the breach and prohibited contingent fee arrangements as unprofessional, but they generally did not do so. On the contrary, today contingent fees are permitted in most Canadian provinces (Arlidge 1974).

One obvious, but as yet relatively unexploited, breach in the profession's control over its members was accomplished by the amendment of federal competition legislation to bring professional services within its prohibitions,[20] thus outlawing such anti-competitive practices as price-fixing and restraints upon advertising. Litigation over its interpretation and constitutionality is under way in several lower courts, and law societies are now having to contend with private law clinics advertising standard legal services at posted rates.[21] But litigation has been relatively conspicuous by its absence, and most provincial Bars now at least concede that lawyers are free to advertise their location, areas of practice, and other pertinent factual information.

In each of these developments, external pressures are matched by relatively reasonable internal responses. But it is difficult to determine whether the new institutional arrangements for accountability have played any significant role in the shaping of these responses. Evidence to support such a claim is lacking. The new Quebec regime apparently functions without much direct intervention in the profession's affairs. In Ontario, neither the lay benchers nor the Attorney General, in his role as a bencher *ex officio*, appear to have taken any policy initiatives. At best, one might speculate that a profession which is told that it is accountable comes to believe that it is, and acts accordingly. At worst, one might suspect that professional governing bodies in Canada, which lack the traditions, prestige and power of their English counterparts, more than compensate by heightened political sensitivity and responsiveness.

When we seek the clearest examples of dramatic external pressures on the legal profession, we must look to the USA. Here we see a virtual transformation in professional conduct accomplished by the application of constitutional standards, of federal anti-trust law, and of tort doctrine. For example *NAACP v. Button*[22] licensed civil rights lawyers, on constitutional grounds, to stimulate test cases and to recruit prospective plaintiffs, notwithstanding local legal and professional constraints upon stirring-up litigation and soliciting business. In *Bates v. Arizona*,[23] again on constitutional grounds, restrictions upon advertising the availability and cost of legal services were struck down. In *Goldfarb v. Virgina*,[24] minimum fee schedules published by a state Bar were held violative of the federal anti-trust laws. And new standards of competence are being hammered out in malpractice suits of vast dimensions.

Nor do these well-known cases exhaust the areas of impact. Access to professional education must meet constitutional norms of equality and may, perhaps, be subject to the requirements of affirmative action to redress past discrimination. Duties of disclosure to the court, the resolution of conflicts of interest, and the diligence required of court-appointed counsel are all grist for the judicial mill.

Is the relatively great impact of external pressure upon the American legal profession only a special instance of a general tendency in that country to resolve issues by litigation which are elsewhere resolved by other, less contentious, means? Or does it reflect deep-seated populist hostility to professional perquisites and privileges, or the high degree of stratification and dissensus, the low level of deference and collegiality, within the American legal profession?

Or is there, perhaps, a simpler explanation? Do external pressures appear to play such an important role because institutions and structures within the profession are relatively weak? While somewhat over half of the American states have 'integrated Bars', of which membership is required as a condition of practice, their origin, organization, functions and powers often differ from the legal governing bodies of England and English-influenced Commonwealth Countries (Johnstone and Hopson 1967). To generalize – perhaps illicitly – from a variety of American state experiences, legislative, and especially judicial, control over lawyers' admission to practice, ethical standards and discipline, is more common than self-regulation.

The external forces which have the greatest potential for impact upon the profession, however, are not those which have been experienced in the USA. Rather, they are forces which might alter the technology or the deep structures of law itself, or the social context of the profession and its work.

One can imagine that significant changes in law might dramatically affect the power of the legal profession. For example, the abolition of personal injury litigation or radical revision of the law of real property might deprive the profession of two of its principal sources of income. The resulting dislocation of the profession might see a redeployment of its energies in the direction of a new, and perhaps less affluent, clientele. Certainly, removal of these two important sources of professional income would diminish an important source of the profession's power. At the same time, it is not inconceivable that a new power base might be found.

Again, one might contemplate the impact upon the profession of a dramatic change in its socio-economic composition. Such a change, as the American experience suggests, is unlikely to be accomplished by legal commandment alone, or even as a result of internally-generated initiatives. It can only flow from a fundamental – hence improbable – change in the structure of the entire educational system. But if such a change were to take place independently of changes aimed at the profession, it would obviously have an impact of enormous dimensions upon the behaviour of lawyers individually and collectively.

Take a third example, one which provoked significant dissent[25] within the Benson Commission: deprofessionalization and demystification of the work of lawyers which might radically alter the profession's power base and social role. Deprofessionalization would include a deliberate expansion of the areas of lay practice, including conveyancing and advocacy. Demystification would take the process a step further, by equipping the ordinary citizen, to a more significant degree, to handle his own legal problems. At a mimimum, this process would enable him to deal with his lawyer on quite a different footing than he presently does.

These are the sorts of changes which are likely, if any are, to stimulate – for good or evil – radical transformation of a profession whose history and future are generally portrayed in colours of cautious conservatism.

Conclusion

The unstated assumption of this essay is that the legal professions in England, and in the other countries mentioned, might and should serve their respective societies better than at present. The explicit question, which remains unresolved, is whether improvements can be effected by changes in the institutions of regulation and self-regulation, or whether they will result only from dramatic changes imposed legally, or by social forces, from outside.

There is some evidence, in the British experience, that professional self-government shields lawyers from influences which might promote change. However, as the Benson Commission seems to agree, it is at least arguable that any interference with strong professional self-government might lead to a breakdown of the ethical standards and of the devotion to *noblesse oblige* upon which the English and Commonwealth Bars pride themselves. The Canadian experience, and critics in Australia, force us to question at least the latter argument. Institutions designed to promote accountability seem entirely consistent with the preservation of professional independence, and its supposed benefits. But whether they also perform their intended function of facilitating change and sensitivity to the public interest is not clear. Do we conclude, on the basis of American experience, that overt controversy and active contention between the organized profession and its individual and institutional opponents are necessary to secure meaningful reforms? And if so, how do we calculate the costs of such adversarial relationships?

These questions are, of course, impossible to answer; indeed, they are usually put rhetorically. The connections between the behaviour of lawyers and the forms of professional regulation are probably not so easily described. Surely lawyers' behaviour, as a group or as individuals, must be affected by such factors as the profession's demography, education, size, clients, roles and rewards. Moreover, what is desirable change is not self-evident. What may appear as a virtue from the perspective of one society may seem quite wrong from the perspective of another. For example, the close affinity of the English bench and Bar, which promotes conciseness, conscience and candour in advocacy, may seem to a North American to involve the sacrifice of the client's interests and the obscuring of broader social issues potentially raised by litigation. These are questions not so much of professional behaviour as of social policy.

But then the same might be said of all questions relating to legal services. Do we opt for relatively scarce, and expensive, legal services of high quality, or for relatively cheap and accessible paralegal services? Do we try to protect people's rights by sophisticated substantive and procedural laws requiring professional intervention, or by the promotion of informal social processes which depend upon self-reliance and mutual help? Until these higher-order issues are resolved, we lack a sense of the context within which the derivative issue of professional government should be resolved. The tail of professional government will not, in my view, wag the dog of social policy.

Acceptance of this fact, however, does not dispose of the accountability issue. I view accountability as a modest measure to be undertaken as a matter of principle, rather than in the expectation that it will accomplish radical (if any) change. The legal profession has long understood the notion that a lawyer must be willing to give to the client a full account of the way in which professional obligations have been discharged. Moreover, it has come to believe that faithful service to one's client can be squared with a sense of professional integrity and personal autonomy. To the extent that these cherished aspects of legal–professional culture are in fact accepted by individual lawyers, they should have no difficulty in translating them to the level of the responsibility of the profession as a whole. Accountability is the necessary implication of accepting a social trust; and it is compatible with the profession's independence.

A Royal Commission which cannot bring itself even to consider accountability (to say nothing of more far-reaching institutional options) is unlikely to find that its prescriptions for the future of the legal profession are regarded as an important, or even adequate, response to its mandate.

Notes

1. Benson 1979, e.g. p. 30 (rules of conduct), p. 62 (manpower policies), p. 288 (competence).
2. This recommendation drew one of the few dissents directed towards the issue of accountability. Benson 1979, p. 806. See Edmondson N. D., 2–10, 11.
3. Benson 1979, p. 387 (Law Society), and similarly for the Bar, pp. 438–9.
4. Castonguay, C. (Chmn.) (1970), *Report of the Commission of Inquiry on Health and Social Welfare Part V*, (Quebec). An account of the Commission's recommendations, and subsequent developments, is found in Issalys 1979.
5. Stat. Quebec 1973, c. 43 as amended.
6. I have described the growth of public accountability more fully elsewhere. Arthurs 1971.
7. Law Society Act, RSO 1970, c. 238, s. 26(1), repealed by S.O. 1973, c. 49.
8. *Ibid*, s. 26 (as amended).
9. *Ibid*, s. 23*a* (as amended).
10. The Committee did recommend strongly that the Society abandon its restrictions on advertising, or be legislatively compelled to do so, Recommendations 10.1 and 10.2.
11. POC Report, 1980, Recommendation 2.9.
12. *Ibid*, Recommendations 2.17 and 2.18.
13. E.g. *Rondel v. Worsley* (1967) 3 All E.R. 993 (HL) (barrister not liable in negligence for the conduct of litigation).
14. E.g. *Brown v. Inland Revenue Commissioners* (1965) AC 244 (HL) (despite custom or implied agreement, solicitors may not retain interest earned on client's trust accounts); *Saif Ali v. Sydney Mitchell Co.* (1978) 3 All ER 1033 (HL) (barrister's immunity does not extend to negligence in failing to join proper defendants in pleading).
15. For the testimony of one such 'demonic' agent, see Zander 1979.
16. These are referred to in Benson 1979, p. 29, table 3.1.
17. See e.g. *Banks v. Reid* (1978) 81 DLR (3d) 730 (Ont. CA); *Demarco v. Ungaro* (1979) 21 OR (2d) 673 (Ont. HC); Prichard 1977 and Belobaba 1979.
18. Canadian Bar Association, Code of Professional Conduct (adopted 1975), C.II, Competence and Quality of Service.
19. See e.g. Swan 1978 and Hurlburt 1979.
20. Combines Investigation Act, RSC 1970, c. C–23, s. 32 (as amended).
21. *Jabour v. Law Society of British Columbia* (1980) 98 DLR (3d) 442 (BCSC), rev'd. (1980, BCCA, unreported).
22. 371 US 415 (1963).
23. 433 US 350 (1977).
24. 421 US 733 (1975).
25. Benson 1979, pp. 809–11, Haines ND 4.1, 6, 7, 8, 9, 13.

References

Arthurs, H. W. Authority, accountability, and democracy in the Ontario legal profession, 49 *Cdn. Bar Rev.* p. 1.

Belobaba, E. (1980), Civil liability as a professional competence incentive, *Working Paper for the Professional Organizations Committee*, Ontario.

Benson, GBE Sir H. (Chmn.) (1979), *Royal Commission on Legal Services: Final Report*, CMND. 7648, London.

Economic Council of Canada (1969) *Interim Report on Competition*.

Foundation of Law Societies of Canada (1973), Independence of the legal profession, *Bulletin of Fed. of Law Soc. of Can.*, April, (hereafter Federation).

Hurlburt, W. (ed.) (1979), *The Legal Profession and Quality of Service*, Edmonton, Cdn. Inst. for the Admin. of Justice.

Issalys, P. (1978), The professions tribunal and the control of ethical conduct among professionals, 24 *McGill Law J.* p. 588.

Johnstone, Q. & Hopson, D. (1967), *Lawyers and their Work: An Analysis of the Legal Profession in the United States and England*, Indianapolis, Bobbs-Merrill, Ch. 2, especially pp. 42 ff.

Law Society of Upper Canada (1979), *Submission to the Professional Organizations Committee*, Ontario (hereafter Law Society).

McRuer, Hon. J. C. (Chmn.) (1968), *Royal Commission Inquiry into Civil Rights: Report No. 1, Vol. 3*, Ontario (hereafter McRuer).

New South Wales Law Reform Commission (1979), *The Legal Profession, Discussion Paper No. 1, General Regulation* (hereafter New South Wales).

Prichard, J. R. (1979), 'Professional civil liability and continuing competence in Klar' (ed.) *Studies in Canadian Tort Law*, Toronto, Butterworths.

Professional Organizations Committee (1980), *The Report of the Professional Organizations Committee*, Ontario (hereafter POC).

Reiter, B. (1979), Discipline as a means of assuring continuing competence in the professions, *Working Paper for the Professional Organizations Committee*, Ontario.

Swan, J. (1978), Continuing education and continuing competence, *Working Paper for the Professional Organizations Committee*, Ontario.

Trebilcock et. al. (1979) *Professional Regulation. A Staff Study of Accountancy, Architecture, Engineering and Law in Ontario*, Prepared for the *Professional Organizations Committee*, Ontario.

Williams, B. (1979), Abuse of power by professional self-governing bodies, *Law Society of Upper Canada Annual Lectures*, 345.

Zander, M. (1979), Promoting change in the legal system, 42 *Modern L. Rev*, p. 489.

Zemans, F. (1978), Legal aid and legal advice in Canada, 16 *Osgoode Hall L. J.* p. 663.

CHAPTER 8

The Benson Report and Legal Education: a Personal View

William Twining

The complexities of the subject of legal education probably outweigh its social importance in most parts of the world.[1] The structure of our system of legal education and training adds some local dimensions to this basic complexity. There are important differences in organisation, methods of financing, content and in tradition between the three jurisdictions of the United Kingdom. In England and Wales some features of the present situation make it difficult to describe, to analyse, to debate or to change. Several of these features are relevant to this paper, notably: a split profession; the variety of autonomous and semi-autonomous institutions providing legal education or training (universities, polytechnics, institutions controlled by the profession, colleges of further education, commercial tutors, schools, etc.); the different stages through which intending lawyers have to pass (the academic stage, a vocational course, in-training, restricted practice); the different routes to qualification for practice (law graduate; non-law graduate; mature student; para-legal; school leaver); the multiple functions of law degrees and of mixed degrees in which law is a major component; a diversity of approaches to the study of law, reflected in what may be termed the new pluralism in academic law; and the relatively rapid increase in both scale and innovation in legal education since World War II, especially since 1970.

It is not surprising that visiting foreigners are baffled, that specialists in education have steered clear of studying the system and that those who are professionally involved rarely have a clear perception of more than one section of the whole. One has some sympathy for the members of an already over-burdened Commission, which contained no academic lawyer, when confronted with these complexities. To have re-opened some of the fundamental issues raised before the Ormrod Committee would have been a daunting task.[2] The Commission was daunted. It decided to restrict itself to a limited number of issues within the existing structures and patterns. The approach adopted in the chapters under review is, as we shall see, selective, gradualist, largely exhortatory and strikingly parochial. The outcome is an up-dating and a gloss on Ormrod, eight years on.

The purpose of this paper is to provide a critical commentary on chapters 38 and 39 of the Report.[3] Pressure of space precludes consideration of all the issues considered by the Commission. In particular, I shall not say much directly about a common system of training, because little progress can be expected unless and until other changes have taken place; nor about pupillage, on which the Report recommends only very minor adjustments; nor on the important subject of continuing legal education, on which the Report does little more than recommend an evolutionary approach.

The Historical Context

Chapter 38 of the Report starts with a brief overview of the history of legal education in England and Wales. It purports to be little more than a *précis* of the account in the Ormrod Report, followed by a brief *resumée* of its recommendations and the extent to which they have been implemented. As history, both of these accounts are narrowly focused: they make little attempt to set preparation for the practice of law in the context either of the total picture of legal education in England and Wales, or of the methods of financing tertiary education in this country, or of international trends and developments which have been increasingly influential in the last decade. Such omissions can lead to misperceptions, e.g. of the social functions of the legal education system, to misjudgements, e.g. of the prospects of securing public funding for professional training, or to missed opportunities, e.g. to establish a structure which maximises the potential contribution of universities to the whole system of legal education without threatening academic excellence and innovation. There are plenty of examples from recent history of the dangers of adopting a narrow perspective in this area.

Ormrod Re-visited

When the Ormrod Committee was set up in 1967 important changes
in legal education were already under way. Old patterns were being
increasingly criticised, new ideas were being aired and there was a
body of experience from home and overseas on which people could
draw. Above all the scale of legal education was increasing at a
remarkable rate. The Ormrod Committee provided a forum for a
fundamental reappraisal and an opportunity for the two branches of
the profession and the universities and polytechnics to explore how
far they were prepared to co-operate in devising an integrated
system of preparation for practice. After prolonged, often difficult,
deliberation the Committee submitted a report containing 43 conclusions and recommendations.[4] Although it was clear from the
Ormrod Report that full integration of legal education and training
on the model of medical schools had not been accepted and that
there were still some important unresolved differences (notably
about the role of universities), there was nevertheless agreement on
a fundamental structure and on many points of detail. Since 1971
most of the debate and nearly all proposals for change bear the
imprint of the Ormrod Report.

It is sometimes suggested that the Ormrod exercise ended in
failure. In particular, disenchantment is the predominant tone of
academic comments on a decade of protracted debate, piecemeal
change and dogged assertions of autonomy by the main interest
groups.[5] Yet many of the concepts and recommendations of the
Ormrod Report have been accepted, at least in principle, and most
of its predictions, including some pessimistic ones, have proved to
be correct. Change has been slow, but it has nearly all been in the
direction charted by the Ormrod Committee, which itself favoured
an evolutionary approach.[6] The very existence of the Commission
may have helped to accelerate the process of implementation.

The Ormrod Committee's conclusions and recommendations are
reflected, at least in theory, in many present arrangements. In
particular, a three stage pattern (academic, vocational, continuing)
of preparation for practice has been established (recommendation
4);[7] the principle of multiple routes of entry has been entrenched (4,
12); a law degree is on the way to becoming the normal mode of
entry to the profession (6); the Bar has accepted the principle of
graduate entry (with minor exceptions); the proportion of non-

graduates qualifying as solicitors has declined significantly and the proportion of entrants who are law graduates is rising (6, 12); the general objectives of legal education and of the academic stage suggested by the Ormrod Committee form the basis of a fairly widespread, but not universal, consensus about strategic learning objectives (3 and 5);[8] the notion of 'core' subjects as the basis for recognition of degrees and/or exemptions has been implemented (5 (1), 8) with some modifications (see below); the target of about 2,000 law graduates *per annum* has been exceeded by over 50 per cent (7); 80 out of a possible 98 degrees, including all first degrees in law in England and Wales, have been recognised as providing the academic stage and ten more provide a basis for partial exemption (10,11); the list of alternative forms of qualification to a law degree has been accepted (12), with the addition of the Law Society's school leavers' scheme; courses leading to a common professional examination have been established, but the period for non-law graduates has been reduced to a year (13,14); new vocational courses have taken the place of the old-style cram courses and some attempt has been made to develop them along the lines indicated by the Ormrod Committee although this process has some way to go. In particular both branches of the profession seem likely to continue to place more emphasis on the study of substantive law, and less on direct teaching of skills, than was advocated by Ormrod (15, 17, 18, 22, 29); some adjustments have been made to the style and methods of assessment in the vocational stage, although these do not yet go as far as the Ormrod Committee proposals (15, 18, 35); vocational courses for intending solicitors, but not for Bar students, have been established in different centres in the North and the Midlands, as well as in London and the South (21, 28 (ii)); the Committee's more gloomy predictions about the prospects for public funding have been fully realised (26, 28 (iii)) and its optimistic exhortations to local education authorities have not been heeded (27); 'sandwich' courses have not developed on a significant scale (3); in 1978 the Senate issued guidelines for pupillage and abolished pupillage fees (31); significant progress has been made in developing continuing legal education and a Law Society working party is at present considering the subject (39); the Ormrod Committee's attempt at suicide was treated as having succeeded and it was replaced in 1972 by an Advisory Committee on Legal Education, with conspicuously different terms of reference (9, para. 186).

Of course, not all of the Ormrod Committee's recommendations have been implemented. The most important examples are as follows: (i) academic and vocational legal education are not closely integrated into a coherent whole (1); (ii) almost no progress has been made towards a common system of training beyond the academic stage in respect of vocational courses (20); (iii) no vocational courses are planned or offered at universities, but seven polytechnics are providing such courses for the Law Society (24, 25); (iv) the extent of public funding of vocational courses and professional training is even less than the Ormrod Committee had hoped or feared (26, 28 (iii)); (v) no Institute of Professional Legal Studies has been set up in England, although one has been set up in Belfast (40);[9] (vi) the system of articles has not been *replaced* by a vocational course and a period of three years' restricted practice; instead the Law Society proposes that articles should be improved, with restricted practice *additional* to a vocational course and articles; (vii) a number of specific proposals have either been rejected or have not been fully implemented in substance or in spirit.[10]

The Royal Commission Report

The Report takes the Ormrod exercise and its aftermath as its starting-point and, by and large, treats the main features of preparation for practice as settled. It concentrates largely on structural and administrative issues affecting the vocational and in-training stages and says little or nothing about the content, methods or personnel involved in each stage. It makes some comparisons with training for other professions, but makes almost no explicit reference to other jurisdictions.

Entry

The discussion of entry, though short, is potentially one of the most important sections in the chapters on legal education. The Commission takes clear positions on a number of important issues: it is for the educational system rather than the profession to redress the social imbalance in the numbers of those qualifying to enter the academic stage (39–5); the provision for multiple routes of entry is confirmed in order to ensure that recruitment is from 'as wide a reservoir as possible'; the Report is sanguine that demand will not significantly exceed availability of places for education and training, and it prefers to leave the regulation of the size of the profession to market forces after qualification, rather than to a system of quotas at any stage during education and training.[11]

I suspect that the issues in respect of numbers are much more complex than is suggested in the Report. I suspect, too, that problems of bottlenecks, quotas and selection for at least some of the stages of legal education and training are likely to become central issues of concern and controversy during the 1980s.[12] However, in the absence of reliable statistics and projections and any detailed analysis of the problems, it is rather difficult to make enlightened comment on this section of the Report.

The Commission's views on the social imbalances within the legal profession and what can be done about them are likely to occasion controversy. So, too, for rather different reasons is its endorsement of the principle of keeping open several routes for entry, especially the school-leavers' scheme. I confine myself to a few brief comments. One advantage, not mentioned in the Report, of having both a multi-functional system of undergraduate legal education and multiple routes of entry, is that it enables people in the 18–22 age group to defer important decisions about their careers. The young person who reads for a degree in law has the chance to opt out of a career in legal practice at almost any time from his or her first day of law study until after qualifying as a barrister or solicitor, without necessarily feeling that the time spent learning has been wasted. Thus one of the social functions of legal education as currently organised is to provide an opportunity to postpone final career decisions. Conversely, those who have failed to get undergraduate places to read law or who decide later on that they would like to enter practice, may not be substantially disadvantaged in respect of *opportunity* (whether they have been deprived educationally is another question).[13] There is widespread support for providing opportunities to 'mature persons' of various kinds to qualify. The grounds for the Law Society's special scheme for school-leavers are more questionable. The Report mentions no justification for what some may suspect is, or might become, a back door method of entry into the profession.[14]

The Academic Stage

The treatment of the academic stage is brief and highly selective. The Report notes that 80 degrees have been recognised as satisfying this stage, ten have been accepted as providing a basis for *pro tanto* exemptions, and eight have been rejected for this latter purpose; the proposal that the Open University should offer a law degree course is supported, as it was by the Ormrod Committee; the decision to allow non-law graduates to take the Common Professional Examination after only one year is also endorsed. The Commission considered it premature to pass comment on the arrangements for the Commom Professional Examination and the Solicitors' First Examination. It makes no comment on the content, length or other aspects of undergraduate degrees.

The treatment of the delicate topics of recognition of degrees and of exemptions for particular subjects is also rather cursory. The Report notes that there has been criticism of the manner in which control over the academic stage has been exercised, but it fails to state with precision the exact nature of the complaints. Instead, it reaffirms that 'the freedom of academic studies should not be inhibited'[15] and that non-legal material can properly be included in the curriculum, but it considers the present system to be satisfactory.

This misses the point of academic concerns about existing ways of dealing with the problem. These might be stated under three main heads. First, there is the problem of 'the creeping core.' After much debate the Ormrod Committee deliberately restricted the list of 'core subjects' to five. Subsequently trusts was added, first by the Bar, and recently by the Law Society. That made six. Courses on the English legal system or its equivalent may fairly be regarded as a seventh core subject *sub silentio*. From time to time the Advisory Committee on Legal Education or some other body commends a subject as being particularly important for intending practitioners, for example the law and institutions of the European Economic Community, French law and language, company law, welfare law, revenue law. Most readers will be familiar with the recent storm in a teacup over administrative law. Universities and polytechnics have been criticized for slowness in developing the teaching of such subjects as legislation, computers and the law and human rights. Academic lawyers point out that some subjects, which have been developed at undergraduate level in recent years, may be just as central to an understanding of law, or to preparation for practice, as those which are rather unsystematically commended by the profession from time to time. Why, for example, does the Commission single out company law and welfare law for commendation as important, without even mentioning labour law, family law, EEC or planning?[16] The essential concern about the 'creeping core' is that in time the list of required core subjects may grow; that the list of commended subjects will also expand, thereby threatening the viability of other options which may have at least as good claims for emphasis on educational grounds; and that the manner of identifying required and important subjects will continue to be as *ad hoc* and capricious as it has been during the seventies.

It is reassuring to hear that the Advisory Committee on Legal Education has recently affirmed that there is no intention to increase the number of core subjects. Academic lawyers are all too well aware that the undergraduate curriculum has increasingly come under pressure from a variety of sources, of which the relatively mild pressure from the legal profession is only a small part. The cumulation of pressures to include more and more subjects in the undergraduate curriculum is one of the reasons, but by no means the only one, for the establishment by the Committee of Heads of University Law Schools of a working party on four year degrees.The academic community will strongly resist further attempts to increase the proportion of three-year degrees that has to be devoted to particular subjects for the purposes of recognition or exemption.

The second ground for concern has been the manner in which the system of recognition and exemption has sometimes been exercised. There have been several specific complaints, particularly in respect of attempts to prescribe methods of assessment or examination.[17] Underlying these complaints is a general concern that there has been an insidious shift away from the spirit of the Ormrod Report which recommended *recognition of degrees*[18] (at least in respect of single honours and mixed degrees) to a detailed concern with coverage of particular subjects. This is symbolised by a shift from the language of *recognition* to the terminology of *exemptions*. This rather tiresome issue is more like a niggling and persistent border dispute than a serious conflict over territory. The record suggests that the scale of the problem can be exaggerated. No single subject law degree has yet been refused recognition and there has been a good deal of give-and-take on both sides. Perhaps the representatives of the universities and polytechnics on the Advisory Committee have adopted too defensive or passive an attitude over these issues. If, instead of responding *ad hoc* to particular instances, they had managed to persuade the professional bodies to accept some general *principles* for the quite separate issues of recognition of degrees and *pro tanto* exemptions, much conflict might have been avoided and the attention of the Advisory Committee might have been directed to other more pressing issues affecting legal education.[19]

A third ground for concern relates to innovation. The Report quotes with approval the following statement by the Senate:

Though the Council of Legal Education will wish to know the general structure of the degree so as to be able to assess what proportion of the total teaching is allocated to core subjects, it also believes that the universities must be free to develop the other part of the degree in the way they choose. Indeed the Council of Legal Education *welcomes in the non-core area the development of new ideas and approaches.*[20]

The spirit of this statement is welcome, but is the precise intention clear? *Expressio unius, exclusio alterius?* Can this mean that new ideas and approaches in the core area are not welcome, or that the academic community should have waited on news from the profession that tribunals are important, or that there is some connection between trusts and revenue law or that insurance and other systems of compensation for accidents are relevant to the study of negligence? Is it seriously suggested that our more innovative scholars and teachers should confine their attention to those subjects that the legal profession considers inessential? Hopefully, neither the Senate nor the Commission is to be taken as having intended what they said.

On most of the current issues in undergraduate legal education the Report is silent. There is no mention, for example, of clinical legal education, of student involvement in advice to, and representation of clients, of four-year degrees, of degrees with an orientation towards Europe, of sandwich courses nor, in this connection, of the EEC nor computers. Nor, more generally, is there any attempt to describe, analyze or comment on the new pluralism in undergraduate legal education. There is no mention as such of socio-legal studies nor, more surprisingly, of the potential role of postgraduate work in the academic stage and in continuing education, particularly in respect of training of specialists. Moreover, the Report has almost nothing to say about academic lawyers as a sub-branch of the legal profession and the relationship between academic law, legal training and legal services. Whether or not this silence is welcome, it is fairly typical of the essentially unsystematic and selective approach adopted in this part of the Report.

Vocational Training and In-training

The sections on vocational training and in-training are dominated by one central issue: the future of articles. In the course of developing its argument about this question, the Commission deals briefly with a number of inter-connected topics. It may be useful to dispose of these first. The Report notes that the provisions for the vocational stage for each branch of the profession are in a state of transition and that it is too early to make a detailed appraisal of the new schemes. The Commission accordingly restricts itself to re-emphasizing familiar points arising from criticisms of the old system: the importance of adequate accomodation; the need for part-timers to take their teaching commitments seriously; the importance of developing methods of teaching and assessment which discourage cramming. After reviewing the latest adjustments to the system of keeping terms, it suggests that unless further improvements are made and are found to work satisfactorily, the compulsory eating of dinners should be abolished; it makes proposals for improving the system for arranging pupillages, commends the abolition of pupillage fees, re-emphasizes the importance of a direct personal relationship between master and pupil, makes some suggestions about the timing of authorisation to practice at the Bar and supports the Senate's proposals for establishing a method of ensuring that adequate standards of oral English in court are achieved. Finally, with a few relatively minor adjustments, the present system of pupillage is commended.

The Report is less complacent about the future of articles. The Commission's view is summarized in two paragraphs:

A well-monitored, comprehensive period of articles following a period of vocational training might well be the best way of combining theory and practice in legal education. But the present system of articles is often haphazard, one-sided, and insufficiently monitored. The questions to which we directed our attention were therefore: what would have to be done in order to improve the present system of articles sufficiently to make it acceptable? If such an improvement should turn out to be impossible, what alternative system of training is there? (39–27)

The argument hinges to some extent on an assessment of the capacity and readiness of the profession radically to improve articles. We were impressed by the attempts of the Law Society to reform vocational training both at the institutional and the in-training stage. We were, however, also struck by the resistance which the professional organisations have encountered in the past from their own members. The proposals of the Law Society, published in November 1978, to bring into force an improved system of training during articles are on the right lines but they do not go far enough and we make proposals in paragraph 39–76 for further improving the system. Unless these improvements are made, we consider an alternative system of vocational training to be necessary (39–28).[21]

This statement needs to be seen in its historical context. After widespread criticism of the system of articles and much internal debate, the Law Society proposed to the Ormrod Committee that articles should be *replaced* by a vocational course followed by a period of restricted practice. There was some resistance to this proposal within the Law Society at the time, notably from the Birmingham Law Society. After some hesitation the Ormrod Committee accepted the Law Society's proposals.[22] After many twists and turns during the period 1971–7,[23] the outcome was the rejection at a late stage of an experimental vocational course intended as a *substitute* for articles. Instead articles survived, and the shelved course evolved into the new vocational course, which began in October 1979 as a substitute for the old Part II, but not for articles.[24] Among the factors which appear to have influenced the change of mind by the Law Society are: (i) a belief on the part of many solicitors that articles are the best mode of training; (ii) the failure to secure either substantial public funding or financial support from the solicitors' profession to finance a full-scale vocational course;[25] (iii) an increase in the numbers of applicants (law graduates and others) for places on vocational courses; (iv) doubts and uncertainties about what could be achieved by new methods of professional training.

One factor not mentioned directly in the Report is the allegation, commonly made in the past, that articles survived because articled clerks represented a pool of 'cheap labour' for some solicitors.[26] The Report seems to proceed on a quite different assumption, *viz* that if graduate articled clerks (who have already completed the vocational stage) are adequately remunerated and given proper training, then by and large the employment of such persons will be more of a burden than a benefit to the employer, at least in the short-term.[27] According to the Ormrod Committee the main reason for the Law Society's original proposal to substitute articles for vocational training was that 'experience in other countries suggests that so long as new entrants are regarded as apprentices they will not receive (proper professional) remuneration.'[28] Clearly there is a regular conflict between employment and training within an apprenticeship system; for example it is generally the case that the wider the range of work the apprentice has the opportunity to experience, the less likely is he or she to be immediately useful to the employer. Such matters are, of course, difficult to quantify and to some extent defy generalisation. But economic factors need to be taken into account when considering the relative costs and benefits of a satisfactory system of in-training and of a properly conducted substitute.

Economic factors are equally important in respect of vocational courses: full-time formal education or training is expensive; formal vocational training of the kind envisaged by Ormrod is much more expensive than traditional cramming: it is labour-intensive; it needs highly-skilled teachers, most of whom should also be experienced practitioners; it may need special equipment and accomodation; and other overheads *may* be greater. To date neither the Bar nor the Law Society has been able to find the resources needed to develop this kind of training at a high level of excellence – the present vocational courses are widely regarded as being 'Ormrod-on-the-cheap'.[29] My hunch is that articles will survive not so much because of any putative superiority as a method of training for a career – opinions about that may change as methods of vocational training develop – but because the net cost is less, some of the costs are hidden and the burden is more easily distributed quite widely. But this is at best a guess by someone who is not an economist. It is a matter of regret that in considering the main alternatives of articles, full-time vocational training and various mixed systems, the Commission did not attempt to make a systematic analysis of the economics of professional training in order to give answers to such questions as – who would pay? how much? for how many? – in respect of each possible strategy. Such an analysis is also a precondition for making a cogent case for increased state support for professional legal training, or to persuade the profession to provide the necessary funding themselves.

The approach adopted by the Commission is to consider the Law Society's proposals for improvement of articles, to recommend a number of further improvements and to set a deadline for the implementation and assessment of the new scheme. The arrangements are to be introduced within two years and should be finally assessed at the end of a further three-year period. If the scheme is not introduced or if the review shows the results to have been inadequate, an alternative scheme involving two years' vocational training should be introduced.[30]

There is little doubt that the implementation of the two sets of proposals would constitute an improvement on present arrangements.[31] Whether these improvements, taken in conjunction with the new vocational course, will go far enough to reduce significantly the force of the criticisms of the old system remains to be seen. The new scheme will increase the burdens on principals; it is a matter for speculation whether sufficient solicitors will be found who will be willing to offer articles and to conform to the spirit and the letter of the new scheme. What is clear is that the Commission has, in effect, extended the life of articles by at least eight to ten years. For the proposed review would take place after five years; it may take one or two years to conduct the review and to debate its conclusions and, if the final decision is that articles should be entirely replaced by an extended period of vocational training, it is likely to take at least three more years to phase in such a scheme.

A lot may happen during the next decade. Accordingly it was probably sensible for the Commission to refrain from making detailed propsals for an alternative system. Instead they content themselves with specifying the main characteristics of such a scheme. In essence these would be: (i) an academic stage, followed by a two-year vocational course (including a period of placement), (ii) leading to a degree, possibly called LL.B. (Vocational), (iii) to be organised by the College of Law and any university or polytechnic, (iv) to be followed by a period of restricted practice; (v) the vocational stage should make 'maximum use of the system of state support for costs of education'; and (vi) students would (*sic*) qualify for mandatory grants; and (vii) placements might be financed by a training levy on those firms which do not either assist with placements or employ a quota of solicitors during their period of restricted practice.[32]

Thus the message of the Commission to the solicitors' profession is in essence: 'Improve articles, or else . . .'. But it is a conspicuously weak 'or else'. Presumably if in 1985–6 the Joint Committee is not satisfied with the operation of articles, it will only be able to *recommend* their abolition and re-open the debate which took place during and after the deliberations of the Ormrod Committee (1967–74). Moreover, the new type of vocational training would not be feasible without considerable support from public funds through mandatory grants *and*, almost certainly, direct or indirect funding for both capital and recurrent costs. There is no assurance that public funds will be made available in the foreseeable future to support an extended period of vocational training for the legal profession.

The approach to articles adopted by the Commission has one great advantage: it buys time. This is important in two respects. First, by 1985 a considerable body of experience of institutional vocational training will have been built up in this country, as well as internationally. It will therefore be much easier to make an informed appraisal not only of the operation of the new system of articles, but also of the educational possibilities and the cost-effectiveness of alternative types of training. Secondly, during a period in which tertiary education generally will have been going through a phase of adjustment, this will provide both the profession and legal educators with an opportunity to devise and make the case for proposals which have a reasonable chance of gaining at least partial support from public funds, if the financial climate allows. To date such a case has not been made in a cogent and realistic manner. It is conspicuously lacking in the Report.

Given the generally evolutionary and pragmatic approach of the Report, it is surprising to find articles and extended vocational training being advanced as mutually exclusive alternatives for all intending solicitors. One of the main obstacles to improving the system of articles is likely to be the difficulty of finding sufficient firms that are both able and willing to conform to the more stringent requirements. If an extended vocational course were to be introduced for a limited number of intending solicitors (as a substitute for articles *for them*) this would have several advantages: it would relieve the pressure on places for good articles; it would give an opportunity to gain experience of the operation of such a course; and it would introduce an element of flexibility into the system. It is

difficult to believe that a satisfactory course for all could be introduced overnight, should the present attempts to improve articles be
judged to have failed. The introduction of such a course in the near
future, for limited numbers and on an experimental basis, besides
having the advantages already mentioned, might also help to ensure
that the objective of developing a system of good articles is
achieved, by reducing pressure on places. An experimental course
is entirely compatible with an evolutionary and pluralistic
approach. There seems to be no good reason why this initiative
should wait on the proposed review of articles in five years' time.

The Economics and Politics of Legal Education

Up to this point I have been only mildly critical of the chapters
under consideration. It is understandable that the Commission was
unwilling to try to canvass *ab initio* the whole range of issues
considered by the Ormrod Committee; it is sensible to suspend
judgment on innovations which have only recently been implemented or accepted. Nearly all of the recommendations, albeit
modest, seem to me to be sensible and worthy of support. But the
underlying weakness of the approach adopted in the Report is all
too apparent in the sections on finance and on the Advisory Committee on Legal Education. Our system of legal education and
training is flawed by two crucial weaknesses: inadequate resources
and lack of co-operation between the main interest groups. By
underplaying the importance of economic and political factors in
the system, the Commission failed both to diagnose the main
reasons for its flaws and to prescribe adequate remedies or
palliatives.

Finance

Much of the history of discussion of legal education could be written
in terms of a failure by those involved to pay adequate attention to
economic factors. It took American law teachers more than a
generation to perceive that the success of the Langdellian system
was due as much to the fact that it was an extraordinarily cheap form
of graduate training, as to its putative educational value. Only after
the pattern had been firmly settled did American law teachers wake

up to the fact that they typically had the worst staff–student ratio among graduate schools and that the law school was often subsidising the rest of the university.[33] In this country the present lack of mobility between academic law and legal practice, and many other aspects of the relationship between academics and practitioners, also have economic roots. It is now widely acknowledged that the Achilles heel of the Ormrod *Report* was that it did not explore in sufficient detail the financial implications of the structure it was proposing. With the wisdom of hindsight it is possible to state that it failed to bring out sufficiently clearly four propositions:

(i) that most new forms of legal education, especially formal institutional vocational training, are almost inevitably more costly than traditional methods;

(ii) that the best, perhaps the only, hope for obtaining substantial public funding for the vocational stage was through the University Grants Committee. That is why Scotland and Northern Ireland now have substantial support from public funds for professional legal training and England and Wales does not;

(iii) that it is quite unrealistic to expect state support for professional legal education and training unless (a) proposals for schemes of training fit within existing policies and rules governing the tertiary sector of education;[34] and (b) some limits are set on the *scale* of the system at the vocational stage. In other words, it is not realistic to expect an open-ended commitment of public funds to meet unchecked demand for places at post-first degree level.

(iv) Even if a substantial financial contribution is made by the legal profession towards the cost of legal training, whether by levy or otherwise, it is extremely unlikely that this will be sufficient to finance a large-scale, good-quality, full-time system of vocational training, even with the retention of an element of apprenticeship.

Thanks largely to the perceptiveness of its chairman, something like these propositions formed the starting-point for the approach adopted by the Armitage Committee in Northern Ireland. One of the lessons of the Armitage exercise is that it is possible to devise a framework of professional legal education within the university system which leaves ultimate control over entry with the profession and does not interfere with academic autonomy at the degree stage.

It is a matter for regret that these lessons do not appear to have been learned in England and Wales.

Grants

The section on finance in the *Report* is confined very largely to discussing the urgent problem of improving provision for grants at the vocational stage. Even this is not adequately analyzed. Long before the Ormrod Committee reported, both the profession and the law schools had been pressing for mandatory grants for vocational courses. The Ormrod Committee, recognizing that it would require special legislation to extend mandatory grants to professional schools, criticized the existing provisions, but contented itself with urging that the local education authorities which were withholding discretionary grants for professional legal training, should reconsider their policies. The Report adopts, with only slight modifications, the arguments put forward in Ormrod, but proposes mandatory grants at the vocational stage. It also recommends that the CPE and the first six months of pupillage be covered by mandatory grants.

The case advanced by the Commission is based on the grounds that under the present system only those who can afford to pay are assured of being able to enter the profession, with the result that it maintains the existing social imbalances and results in the loss of 'good recruits.' It is right to make the case mainly in terms of the public interest, but there are additional arguments which can be advanced. The situation has deteriorated since the Ormrod Committee reported, in that courses have become compulsory, have increased in length and relative expense and, especially since the last round of public spending cuts, the operation of the system of discretionary grants has become even more capricious.

It is in the public interest that public benefits, which are in short supply, should be distributed as far as possible in accordance with principles of justice. At present two such principles are being violated: first, policies with regard to discretionary awards vary from one local education authority to another; some are quite generous, some are unpredictable, some have adopted a policy of not giving grants for professional legal training. The result is that eligibility for awards depends on where one lives; it is not just, as the Report suggests, that some authorities make a grant conditional on accepting a place at a local polytechnic; some local education authorities (LEAs) are not giving *any* discretionary awards to intending lawyers.

Secondly, some students who have embarked on a law degree course in the settled expectation that they will stand a good chance of obtaining a grant for the next stage (provided at least that they do sufficiently well) have found on graduation that they are no longer eligible, either because of shortage of funds or because of a change in policy by their LEA. Some examples of such disappointed expectations are attributable to the arbitrary manner in which policies of cutting public spending have been carried out at a higher level; but sometimes it appears that expectations have been disappointed for other reasons, some of which may be open to challenge on legal grounds. The legal profession and academic lawyers can unite in giving support to the Commission's proposals in respect of mandatory grants, even if this requires special legislation.[35] Pending such a change, steps should be taken to reduce the indefensibly capricious operation of the present system.

What has to be faced is that even if the Report's recommendations on mandatory grants were accepted *in toto*, which is unlikely in the near future even if the case were made more cogently, this would fall far short of the likely capital and recurrent needs of an adequate system of professional training. The Report is misleading in implying that the only source of public funds for educational purposes is local education authority grants.[36]

The section on finance is the weakest section in the Commission's treatment on legal education. The lessons of Ormrod and Armitage are not brought out; no attempt is made to assess how much it would be reasonable to expect the profession to contribute towards costs of training; as was mentioned above, no analysis was attempted of the relative costs of articles and of alternative methods of providing vocational training; no consideration is given to the remuneration of law teachers nor to other factors that make good vocational training expensive; no indication is given of the *forms* which have to be adopted to maximize chances of public support. Finally, by ignoring the relationship between numbers of students and the costs and quality of a system of education and training, the Commission was able to beg the delicate and complex question of whether and how to control numbers at the vocational stage. If this criticism seems harsh, some cold comfort is to be found in the thought that underestimation of economic factors is an endemic weakness of most discussions of legal education. The subject is too complex to be left to lawyers.

The politics and diplomacy of legal education:
power, responsibility, accountability and non co-operation

Anyone connected with legal education can hardly fail to be aware of recurrent disagreements and tensions within the area. The economics of legal education are regularly ignored; there is a greater degree of awareness of the political dimensions, but they are not often openly discussed. To put the matter simply: there are seven main interest groups involved in preparation for legal practice: the Bar, the solicitors' profession, the universities, the polytechnics, aspiring practitioners (students and others), local and central government and the community at large. All of these might be thought to have a common interest that there should be at least an adequate, preferably an excellent, system of legal education and training, suited to its varied purposes and social functions. Over time several of these sectors have managed to carve out fairly distinct spheres of influence: each branch of the profession has maintained primary control over training and entry after the academic stage; the universities have retained a fair degree of autonomy over the content and methods of the academic stage and have been unwilling to take on the task of providing professional instruction on terms indicated by the profession – they have not been interested in providing a service on a basis which would involve responsibility without power. The situation of the polytechnics is rather more complex: for example, there is the complicating factor of their relationship with local authorities and the Council for National Academic Awards, (CNAA). Recently some polytechnics have judged it to be in their own and the public interest to participate in the Law Society's vocational courses. The judgment of history may well be that by doing so they stole a march on the universities. Successive governments have given a low priority to improving the quality of professional legal training, through financial support or otherwise, and they have so far not been willing to treat law differently from other professions. They have also by and large upheld the traditional claims of both branches of the practising profession to their spheres of influence, including control over entry and training. These claims have now been endorsed by the Commission. In this view, recent trends have confirmed the separation of these various spheres of influence. In particular the sharp differentiation by the Ormrod Committee between the various stages is plausibly interpreted as being based more on political than on educational grounds. The separation of the spheres of influence was thereby recognized and reinforced. Since 1971 the universities and, to a lesser extent, the polytechnics have retained primary control over the academic stage and have taken the opportunity to branch out in a variety of directions. Undergraduate legal education is more diverse that it has ever been here and more so than in most other countries. From an intellectual and educational point of view there is much to be said for this pluralism. However, a heavy price is paid for the present structure: the universities play virtually no role in the later stages of the process of preparation for practice and of continuing education, and there is a steadily increasing gap between academic law on the one hand and vocational training and legal practice on the other. Whether the universities have opted out, have been excluded or have stayed out by mutual agreement, depends on one's interpretation of recent history.

The fact is that they are now only marginally involved in professional legal education and training, and certain structural features in the situation (notably the binary system of higher education, criteria for academic advancement and the scales of remuneration of university teachers) confirm this trend. The two branches of the profession have also gone their own separate ways. Fear of fusion, perhaps combined with other factors, seems to have dampened any possible enthusiasm within the two branches for a common system of training even at the vocational stage. Recent developments have further entrenched this separation.

During and immediately after the Ormrod exercise there was a possibility that a sufficient degree of co-operation might have been achieved to make it possible to have a single integrated structure for preparation for practice through the development of law schools analogous to some medical schools. Even before the Ormrod Committee reported, it was apparent that a full integration of the total process was not acceptable to the main interest groups. The best that could be hoped for thereafter was a reasonable level of co-operation through negotiation and diplomacy rather than *fiat*.

The level of co-operation achieved to date has been strikingly low. Earlier I listed seven respects in which the objectives of the Ormrod Report have not been realized; the integration of the total process of preparation for practice; a common system of training; vocational courses located at universities; public funding of the vocational stage; the establishment of an Institute of Professional Studies in England and Wales; the replacement of articles by formal vocational training; and a number of specific proposals. A common thread links the first five items on the list: a relatively high degree of trust and co-operation between the main interest groups was an essential precondition for their implementation. Such co-operation was not forthcoming. The two main consequences of this have already been noted: the almost total exclusion of the universities from the system of legal education after the academic stage and the minimal level of financial support from public funds for the last three stages of professional training – vocational, in-training, continuing education. These two features are closely linked. It is no coincidence that Scotland and Northern Ireland have established systems of vocational training within the university system *with* substantial public finance.

What are the reasons for this difference between the three jurisdictions of the United Kingdom? Surprisingly the Commission barely notices the fact and attempts no explanation. Since it is fundamental to an understanding of the present situation, and since the reasons do not seem to be widely appreciated, it is necessary to try to spell them out. While it is true that there are important differences between the three jurisdictions in respect of history, relative prosperity and above all, size, the crucial reason for the different schemes which have been adopted is rooted in the politics of legal education and the system of financing tertiary education in the United Kingdom. The latter factor has already been dealt with.

What about non-co-operation? The main factors militating against co-operation between the three branches of the profession are: a fierce concern for *autonomy* on the part of all three groups: barristers, solicitors and academics; on the part of practitioners, fear of fusion, lack of confidence in the practical *competence* of academics and, perhaps, unease with the approach of academic lawyers in their role as critics; on the part of academics, a distrust of the *educational conservatism* of practitioners and a desire to conserve the classic values of liberal education. None of these attitudes provides a good reason for non-co-operation in legal education. In respect of autonomy, the constitution of the Institute of Professional Studies in Belfast shows how vocational training can be set up within a university framework with minimal surrender of autonomy over traditional spheres of influence by the interested parties. In Northern Ireland each branch of the practising profession retains ultimate control over entry; all three branches are represented on the governing body of the Institute which is quite separate from the Law Faculty at The Queen's university; the latter retains the same control over the content and the methods of teaching and examining its degree courses as it had previously.[37]

In respect of *competence*, it is first of all important to distinguish clearly between *individual* and *institutional* competence. No academic lawyer is likely to disagree with the proposition that it is essential that those involved in teaching vocational courses and supervising in-training should be competent to do the job properly. The problem of formal vocational training is *how* to achieve this objective: this is a matter of devising satisfactory employment policies for full-time instructors, with adequate provision to enable them to keep in touch with practice and of exploring ways of making effective use of part-timers. Again the Belfast Institute – and vocational schools in Dublin, Canberra and elsewhere – show what can be done. In Belfast, four experienced practitioners have been specially recruited as full-time teachers and extensive use is made of part-timers, including members of the judiciary. It would be difficult to maintain that a university or a polytechnic cannot provide a satisfactory *base* for a programme of vocational training; the least that such institutions ought to be able to provide is various kinds of facilities, expertise in educational administration and methods, and the advantages of belonging to a broadly-based academic community. They might also provide ideas and the expertise of specialists.

The academics' deeply rooted distrust of practitioners' educational attitudes relates mainly to courses at degree level. The Belfast Institute again provides a model as to how such concerns can be respected. Given the relative newness of formal vocational training in law and continuing legal education, fear of educational conservatism at this level is, perhaps, out-dated. The *situation* encourages innovation and experiment, admittedly within a fairly constricted framework; moreover, the development of a network of international contacts has already ensured that this is one of the more interesting and lively sectors of legal education.

It is difficult to accept that many people believe that the university community has nothing worthwhile to contribute to the development of vocational training and continuing legal education. It is also unlikely that many people think that the increasing divorce of academic law from ordinary legal practice is entirely healthy. It is difficult to believe that the costs of co-operation (in terms of independence, diplomatic self-restraint and time) outweigh the benefits, given the common interest of all groups in the development of a good system of legal education. If the above analysis is correct, then there is something badly wrong with the present situation in England and Wales.

On all these matters the Report is almost completely silent. What can be done to improve the situation in the aftermath of the Report? My personal opinion is that things have gone too far to make it realistic to think in terms of a radical restructuring of present patterns or of any sharp changes in direction. Moreover some of the attitudes referred to above are too deeply entrenched to disappear overnight. Nevertheless, I wish to suggest four ways in which the potentially disastrous effects of the present structure may be mitigated:

(1) The proposed Joint Committee on Legal Education should be given sufficient status, resources and support to enable it to be effective both in promoting co-operation between the various parties or interest groups and in monitoring the operation of the system;

(2) support should be given to the proposal of the Ormrod Committee that a committee should be set up, perhaps by the Lord Chancellor, to prepare a detailed scheme for the foundation of an Institute of Professional Legal Studies or some similar institution. The Institute should be seen, *inter alia*, as providing a means of involving the universities and the polytechnics in developing legal education at all stages after the academic stage;

(3) thorough study of the financial aspects of developing a satisfactory system of preparation for practice should be undertaken by or on behalf of the Joint Committee and realistic proposals should be worked out regarding ways and means of providing resources adequate to the task;

(4) that the basic strategy for legal education and training during the next phase should continue to be evolutionary and pluralistic; in particular the professional bodies should be responsive to proposals for new initiatives – for example, the pre-emptive development by some institutions of new types of course which integrate academic and vocational aspects, such as the idea of a five-year LL.B. (vocational) which was floated in the Report.[38]

These proposals are put forward for discussion, against the background of the foregoing analysis of the financial and political factors underlying the present structure of legal education. They are intended as a supplement to the recommendations of the Commission. Enough has been said already about the reasons for the last two proposals. It may be helpful to conclude this paper by elaborating on proposals (1) and (2).

A Successor to the Advisory Committee on Legal Education

The Ormrod Committee was originally set up as a standing committee with wide terms of reference.[39] The Ormrod Committee recommended its own abolition, to be replaced by an Advisory Committee on Legal Education and a committee to draw up a scheme for an Institute of Professional Studies. As was noted above, the second committee was not set up. The Lord Chancellor did, however, establish a standing Advisory Committee on Legal Education, which has met since 1972 under the successive chairmanship of two distinguished judges, Lord Cross and Lord Justice Lawton, with much narrower terms of reference, and only the most tenuous connection with the Office of the Lord Chancellor.[40]

The Report states: 'the overall impression we have been given is that the Advisory Committee has not achieved its main purpose of providing a forum in which professional and academic lawyers may meet to discuss mutual problems, of reaching conclusions which command respect on both sides and of bringing together the profession and the academic world'.[41] The Report gives no reasons why such an impression may have been created. It rejects the suggestion that an independent authority should be set up, such as a legal training board, with powers of control or supervision. Instead it recommended little more than a change of name, and the appointment of a non-lawyer as chairman. The new committee should issue regular reports, and occasional reports on specific topics, as well as being given the task of monitoring the new system of articles.[42]

This seems to be a clear example of weak prescription based on no diagnosis – at least no overt diagnosis. It is difficult to assess the positive achievements of the Advisory Committee because it has largely confined its public announcements to six reports on particular topics. On the basis of rather fragmentary information, one gains the impression that it has largely concentrated on matters of detail – the operation of the system of recognition and exemptions and the teaching of particular subjects. In addition it has discussed some proposals for change made by the Senate and the Law Society and it has provided a forum for airing criticisms and concerns of the various groups represented – a forum for conciliation or for diplomatic skirmishes. It has not been entirely useless, but the Commission's overall impression would probably be confirmed by most of the interested parties.

What went wrong? One can suggest a few reasons: it lacked both power and status; it conspicuously lacked official backing;[43] it lacked resources; no major initiative was taken by the Committee; it was not *used* by the groups represented, indeed there are doubts whether all members looked on themselves or behaved as *representatives*. So far as one can judge, the attitude of all parties has been largely one of defensive apathy, bolstered by concerns for academic freedom and professional autonomy.

If the objective is to provide a body which effectively promotes co-operation and monitors the operation of all phases of legal education, the Report's proposals do not go nearly far enough. It is probably right that a fresh start is needed, but much more positive steps could be taken to strengthen the Committee. Short of giving the Committee some powers, in addition to an advisory role, the following might be considered: its terms of reference could be made closer to those of the Ormrod Committee in its role as a standing committee; modest resources should be provided from public funds to enable it to carry out its functions with the support of an adequate secretariat; the membership of the Committee should be strengthened in respect of expertise and representation of all the main relevant interests including the committees of heads of university and polytechnic law schools; there should be close official connections with the Lord Chancellor's Office and the Department of Education and Science; routine matters should be delegated to sub-committees; the Committee should be consulted on matters of policy at an early stage, before plans have crystallized; the chairman should be a person of high standing, familiar with the legal profession and the system of tertiary education, such as a present or retired lawyer vice-chancellor. Such limited measures might help to make the new body rather more effective than its predecessor. But so long as such a body is only advisory, its success or failure depends almost entirely on the willingness of the main parties to co-operate.

No committee, however powerful and effective, can reasonably be expected on its own to perform the function of developing regular co-operation between the three branches of the profession. If this objective is to be taken seriously more substantial institutional arrangements are needed. Between 1846 and 1913 there were several attempts to establish a legal university or other national institution of legal education which would perform the function of bridging the gap between academic law and legal practice.[44] From time to time since then the idea has revived in different forms. One of the best known was the proposal by Harold Laski that there should be established an English counterpart to the Harvard law school. The most recent was the recommendation of the Ormrod Committee that the Lord Chancellor should establish a committee with a view to establishing an Institute of Professional Legal Studies, which would be concerned with continuing legal education.[45] These proposals have come to nought.

In view of this unhappy history, much of which is outlined in the Ormrod Report, it may seem fanciful to raise the idea once more. Nevertheless there are several features in the present situation which suggest that such an institution could play an important role in developing legal education at all levels and in involving the universities in the process. Much of what is happening in legal education is relatively new. Undergraduate legal education is changing rapidly; the demand for instruction in law is increasing at all levels – the Commission itself has given a boost to the trend towards providing legal education for all; formal training in professional skills has developed on a significant scale internationally, as well as in this country, only during the past decade; if apprenticeship is to survive in any form it will need to adjust as well as to improve; if it is to be replaced, a high degree of educational professionalism will be required in designing and implementing satisfactory alternatives. Continuing legal education is still in its infancy. Little has been done about the training of specialists. The collation of even elementary data about legal education has been left to the sterling individual efforts of Professor Wilson and Dr. Marsh. Virtually no serious reaserch on legal education has been undertaken in this country. A national institution, with strong links with the universities, the polytechnics, the practising profession and with specialists in training and education, might contribute a great deal to the evolution of a more suitable and better integrated system than we have at present. It might build a few bridges between the different spheres of influence. And it might introduce some educational professionalism into an area which has become too complex to be left to amateurs. The precise form such a national institute might take would need to be carefully considered; but its primary functions should be relatively clear: to promote research and development in respect of all aspects of legal education and, through co-operative enterprises, to counter some of the centrifugal tendencies which the structure of legal education and training continues to foster.

Conclusions and recommendations

The following conclusions and recommendations are advanced as a basis for discussion:
(1)   It is probably realistic to accept that the basic structure of legal education and training has been established for at least another decade and that no fundamental changes or shifts of direction are to be expected in the near future.
(2)   The chapters on legal education in the Commission's Report should be treated as representing a gloss upon the analysis and recommendations of the Ormrod Report, which will remain the *locus classicus* for public debate and decision for the foreseeable future.
(3)   The present structure of legal education, as it affects preparation for practice has two basic weaknesses: inadequate resources have been provided for the task and the universities play virtually no role in the stages after the academic stage. These weaknesses are linked by virtue of the rules and policies governing public funding of education and training for the professions. One result of the present

structure is a strengthening of the divide between the academic and professional stages and between academic law and legal practice.

(4)   The recommendations for change put forward in Chapter 39, although modest, deserve support except as follows:
(i) a more positive approach than is suggested in the Report to establishing a common system and shared facilities for the vocational stage should be urged on both branches of the profession; (ii) the possibility of introducing and developing an extended vocational course as a substitute for articles for *some* intending solicitors should be considered without waiting on the assessment of the new system of articles; (iii) the proposed Joint Committee on Legal Education, whether or not it is given any powers in respect of entry and training for practice, should be strengthened; (iv) the recommendations respecting mandatory grants should be supported; pending the introduction of such a change, the relevant authorities should be requested as a matter of urgency to review the operation of the system of discretionary awards as they affect intending barristers and solicitors.

(5)   A committee should be set up, perhaps by the Lord Chancellor, to consider and prepare a detailed scheme for a national Institute of Professional Legal Studies, which would be concerned with all aspects of the development of legal education and training.

(6)   The system of recognition of degrees and of *pro tanto* exemptions should be governed by a set of principles; once these have been established, the task of considering specific problems as they arise should be delegated to a sub-committee of the proposed Joint Committee on Legal Education.

(7)   The basic strategy for legal education and training in England and Wales should continue to be evolutionary and pluralistic.

Acknowledgement

I am grateful to Jill Cottrell, Michael King, Avrom Sherr, Christopher Snowling and Geoffrey Wilson for helpful comments on an earlier draft of this paper. Although it is written from the perspective of an academic lawyer, my views should not be taken as representative of those of my colleagues in England and Wales. Indeed, my main direct experience of policy making in legal education has been in other jurisdictions, notably as a member of the Kenya Council of Legal Education, of the Committee on Legal

Education in Northern Ireland (the Armitage Committee) and of the International Legal Center Committee on Legal Education in Developing Countries.

Notes

1. See *Legal Education in a Changing World* (1975), International Legal Center, New York, *passim*.
2. *Report of the Committee on Legal Education* (Ormrod Report) (1971), Cmnd. 4594 London, HMSO.
3. There are a few mentions of legal education outside Chapters 38 and 39, notably: 4–25, 26 (teaching law in schools), 20–6 (employed lawyers), 29–13(a) (standards for solicitors), 31 (training of legal executives) and in the Notes of Dissent (notably by Harper, Marsden-Smedley, Oppenheimer and Seligman). This paper does not deal with the section on Northern Ireland, except to point to some lessons of the Armitage Committee (*Report of the Committee on Legal Education in Northern Ireland* (1973) Cmnd. 579 London HMSO), and to the Belfast Institute of Professional Legal Studies as possible models. The *Report of the Royal Commission on Legal Services in Scotland* (the Hughes Report) (1980), Cmnd. 7846, London HMSO was published after this paper was written. Apart from giving an up-to-date account of the rather different structure of legal education and training in Scotland, the relevant chapters in the Hughes Report are noteworthy for the strong support given to four-year degrees and the extensive treatment of education and training for 'other providers of legal services.' (Ch. 17).
4. *Loc. cit.* n. 2.
5. E.g. Goode, R. (1979), Legal education after Benson, 129 *New Law Journal*, Nov. 15, pp. 1117–8. Gower, L. C. B. (1978), Looking back, Presidential Address, 14 *JSPTL (NS)* p. 156. 'Whatever happened to Ormrod?' was the theme of a Panel Discussion at the Society of Public Teachers of Law, SPTL Conference in 1974. See (1975) 13 *JSPTL (NS)* 199; not all of the contributors expressed disenchantment with developments since 1971.
6. Thomas, P. A. & Mungham, G. M. (1972), English legal education: a commentary on the Ormrod Report 7 *Valparaiso University Law Rev.* 87, p. 114.
7. Brackets in the text refer to the Summary of Conclusions and Recommendations, Ch. 9 of the Ormrod Committee Report, *loc. cit.* The three stages have sub-divisions: e.g. the academic can be divided into undergraduate, post-graduate (legal), common professional examination (CPE) and Solicitors' First Examination (SFE); the vocational stage includes both vocational courses and in-training; the Law Society's working party on continuing training has divided the area into five main sectors. The above categories are not exhaustive and are subject to change.
8. This is a controversial and complex topic. In particular many people would question how far legal education as a whole has gone in the direction of providing students 'with an understanding of the relationship of law to the social and economic environment in which it operates' (5(ii)) or 'with the intellectual training necessary to enable him to handle facts . . .' (5(iii)).
9. This is described in the Report at 42–85 ff.
10. In addition to points already mentioned in the text, see especially conclusions and recommendations 19, 28 (ii) (Bar), 35, 40, 42, 43.

11. The Report states: 'an intending practitioner may also encounter difficulty from a shortage of places at universities or institutions providing academic or vocational training. This has been a source of problems in the past, but there appear at present to be sufficient places to satisfy demand' (39–6). This is ambiguous and possibly misleading. If demand includes demand for places at the academic stage, this is inaccurate – there is competition for places at the academic stage and most universities and polytechnics operate quotas. If 'demand' refers to the number of law graduates seeking places in vocational courses, then *at present* the problem may not be acute, but demand may fluctuate. If 'demand' includes some notion of the absorptive capacity of the profession or the need for recruits to the profession, the argument is muddled. Little is known about the extent to which the academic stage operates as a filter. On the one hand, it seems likely that a significant number of potential recruits to the legal profession may be deterred by the image of law being competitive; on the other hand, new law schools and courses still continue to appear, in spite of, sometimes because of, the economic climate. The likely effect of the proposed Open University course on numbers is also unclear.

12. The story of the difficulties and developments in Northern Ireland in respect of numbers since 1973 makes an illuminating study in miniature of the problem in England and Wales. The difference in scale between the two jurisdictions may make for more flexibility in England, but the microcosm of Northern Ireland brings out more vividly some of the main factors which bear directly on the problem.

13. The opportunities for non-law graduates to qualify as barristers or solicitors are subject to the vagaries of the system of discretionary grants. It seems that in many parts of the country the non-law graduate is even less well off in this respect than the law graduate. On discretionary grounds, see *infra*, n. 34.

14. 39–15.

15. 39–19.

16. 39–48.

17. Gower, L. C. B. 'Looking Back' *op. cit.* n. 5, p. 159.

18. See esp. para. 108 of the Ormrod Report.

19. The writer has proposed a draft set of principles to the SPTL representatives on the Advisory Committee on Legal Education. These would, if accepted, represent a return to the spirit and, in most respects, the substance of the Ormrod recommendations.

20. 39–20 (italics supplied).

21. 39–27, 28.

22. *Op. cit.* para. 161.

23. See 'Whatever Happened to Ormrod?' *op. cit.* n. 5.

24. The new vocational course places much less emphasis on simulation than the pilot course; if anything, it appears to represent a step back from the Ormrod conception of vocational training which the pilot course sought to implement.

25. Members of the Law Society were unwilling to pay approximately £4 a head for the Vocational Year Pilot Scheme, which was dropped in 1974 (see 13 *JSPTL (N.S.)* p. 203). The argument presented in this paper is based on the premise that an adequate vocational training course, which concentrated on skills training and which catered for all aspiring practitioners would be an expensive enterprise. Even a substantial training levy could only be expected to cover a small proportion of the costs. The College of Law takes pride in having made its vocational courses almost self-financing, while maintaining fees at a relatively modest level (£820 in 1979–80; £960 in 1980–81).

26. For a discussion of financial barriers confronting prospective solicitors see Thomas and Mungham, *loc. cit.* n. 6, p. 99 *et seq.*
27. Esp. 39–76.
28. *Op. cit.* para. 161. In January 1980 the Council of the Law Society approved a new scheme for the remuneration of articled clerks and this was implemented in August 1980.
29. See, e. g. R. Goode *loc. cit.*
30. The main proposals are the keeping of a diary, exposure to at least three main fields of professional work, increased provision for study courses during in-training, closer supervision of the terms and conditions of articles, including regulation, a conciliation and arbitration procedure for principals and articled clerks, and an improved placement system. There is no specific mention of regular monitoring and inspection of articles.
31. On the new arrangements for articles introduced in 1980, see *supra.* n. 28.
32. 39–80.
33. See Stevens, R. B. (1971), Two cheers for 1870: the American Law School, 5 *Perspectives in American History*, p. 405.
34. See esp. The Education Act 1962 (as amended) and regulations thereunder. The main obstacles to a change at the present time appear to be: (i) that courses of professional training for barristers and solicitors do not fall within any of the categories which the Secretary of State may designate for mandatory awards under Section 1 of the 1962 Act; (ii) one of the main principles governing awards is that a student shall have only one opportunity as of right to an award for a course leading to a basic qualification; (iii) present policy is not to distinguish between law and other occupations in respect of awards; any change would have to be considered in the context of this general policy; (iv) in the immediate future government policy is to cut rather than increase public spending on education and training; (v) *semble*, while a single four, five or six-year course within a University or Polytechnic, such as the LL. B. (Vocational) mentioned in the Report might attract mandatory awards, any arrangement requiring more than one stage and qualification would probably require a change in the law.
35. See n. 34.
36. 39–94. This overlooks, for example, capital grants, earmarked grants for recurrent expenditure and access to funds such as equipment funds, within the UGC system of funding.
37. See 42–84 *et seq.* Of course, this structure has not eliminated all disagreements about legal education in Northern Ireland, as some recent experience confirmed; nevertheless it is suggested that it provides both a sound basis for eliminating unnecessary conflicts and a useful forum for trying to reconcile different interests and attitudes.
38. 39–80.
39. *Loc. cit.* para. 1.
40. 39–117.
41. 39–114.
42. 39–115–117.
43. *The Times*, April 10 1972 (Lord Cross); see Thomas and Mungham, *op. cit.* n. 6, pp. 129–30.
44. Ormrod Report, paras. 22 ff.
45. *Loc. cit.* recommendation 40 (paras. 174–6).

CHAPTER 9

Research Into Legal Services: Response and Reappraisal

Colin Campbell

It is not my remit to comment on the recommendations made by the Royal Commission on Legal Services. Some of the changes that are called for please me – others not. Many matters I would have liked to see attended to are ignored or dismissed in perfunctory fashion. (Since the Report as a whole is largely 'amoral', concentrating on the economy and efficiency of traditional and conventional arrangements, rather than on underlying principles, the omissions are not surprising.) Yet the relationship between research findings and the substantive recommendations does interest me. The deficiencies of much of the research done into 'legal services' are revealed by the Report; the failure by the Commission itself to overcome the shortcomings is notable;[1] yet in the data collected for the Commission may lie the raw material which researchers need to provide superior understanding of lawyers and their role in society. With the passage of time, we may well regard Volume II of the Report as considerably more valuable than Volume I. Further inquiry is necessary, as the Commission admits, and even more vitally, 'sense' has to be made of the evidence as it becomes available.

The Commission recommended there should be a Council of Legal Services with an adequate research capacity. (Some would regard this as tacit admission by the Commission of its own failure to do the job it was set up to do.) Whether such a Council comes into being or not, discussion of future research priorities is worthwhile. I shall indicate some areas that merit clarification and the reasons why there should be extensive further investigation. I begin with aspects of the Report – the discussion of legal services and lawyers' work – then widen compass to touch on policy issues and rather basic problems which remain unresolved not only in the Report but also in academic commentaries. The areas identified are a personal selection. The orientation is largely pragmatic, and while some passing remarks about general theoretical notions are offered, I have eschewed the 'sociology of sociology' approach which has been so popular (and often delightfully malicious) for so long. The self-indulgence of commentaries of this ilk has become clear to researchers disappointed by the lack of impact academic writings had on the Commissioners.

Responsive Research

With the benefit of hindsight it is clear that a small number of publications, which appeared in the late 1960s established new points of departure for legal research activity. Zander's *Lawyers and the Public Interest*, the two pamphlets *Justice for All* and *Rough Justice* and the books by Abel-Smith and Stevens titled *Lawyers and the Courts*, and *In Search of Justice*, stimulated considerable research interest. Charitable foundations and research councils showed preparedness to underwrite new inquiries. Surveys of lawyers, interviews with clients, monitoring of courts and tribunals, analysis of demographic, judicial and legal aid statistics, and experiments with 'alternative' legal procedures, proliferated. The focus was on the delivery of 'legal services' and the concern was the 'unmet need' for such services among certain individuals, groups or classes.[2] Many legal academics were attracted to work in this area – using empirical methods was relatively novel, the work was relevant to 'people', it helped to decant a zeal for reform that had been bottled up, it allowed ventilation of opinions critical of lawyers, prevailing laws and the legal system as a whole. At the end of a decade of inquiry and debate the Report appeared, and from it can be seen how much remains to be done. Four topics are discussed.
1.   The first, and most obvious, priority is to clarify what is meant by 'legal services.' It may seem anomalous, but little serious attention has been given to defining the term so as to minimize ambiguity and provide a base for comparative and evaluative statements. Academic literature and public commentary (e. g. by The Law Society and The Law Centres Federation) take it for granted that 'we know what it means.' Let us look at the Commission's approach:

There can be no precise definition of the extent of legal services. Lawyers in private practice may be found who are willing to give advice on a variety of matters which have no close connection with the law, but about which previous experience has given them expert knowledge. It is entirely a matter for any professional advisor personally to decide to what extent he is willing to give advice for which he accepts professional responsibility (2–2).

We regard legal services as being concerned with advice, assistance and representation which is required by a person in connection with rights, duties and liabilities of a legal character (2–2).

A legal service may be described as any service which a lawyer performs for his client and for which professional responsibility rests on him. No precise definition has been put to us and none is needed for our purposes . . . Services which are legal in the sense that a lawyer would perform them in the ordinary course of practice may also be performed by non-lawyers. In some instances a person may act on his own behalf without seeking the support either of a lawyer or another layman (4–16).

It has been questioned whether the activities of some law centres are directed to the provision of legal services . . . there is no settled definition of legal services and lawyers in private practice accept professional responsibility for activities which would not normally be categorized as legal services. Some law centres whose staff undertake work which is not directly concerned with legal rights, duties and liabilities, argue that in the case of law centres a definition of legal services should be applied which is broader than the conventional meaning of the words (8–9).[3]

How are we to interpret such statements? What is intended by the reference to 'rights, duties and liabilities'? What does 'of a legal character' add to or subtract from rights, duties and obligations? Is the practising lawyer's discretion to provide advice purely personal and unconstrained? How does its exercise relate to rights etc. of a legal character? What are the limits, if any, in non-lawyers offering legal services 'in the sense that a lawyer would perform them in the ordinary course of practice'? What is meant by a definition of legal services 'broader than the conventional meaning of the words'? Are there *no* criteria for determining whether a lawyer's time should be devoted to an issue as against that of a non-lawyer? How can public expenditure on 'legal services' (e. g. on the legal aid and advice schemes) be explained? Why are some areas of work confined to practising solicitors or barristers and not opened to all-comers?

While there are many uncertainties, some points are clear.[4] The Commission occasionally offers further glosses on meaning and invokes the term 'legal services' to make programmatic and evaluative statements about different practices, institutions and requirements. Yet the definitions used are inadequate, unclear, inconsistent and confusing, as is the discussion that rests on their use. To insert the 'definitions' for the phrase defined makes passages in the Report, some of which are indeed important, impossible to follow.

The shifts of meaning in terms used turn out to be crucial to some of the Commission's recommendations, particularly when they move from the security of discussing lawyers in private practice, to more novel forms of provision of legal services. We have seen that legal services are what lawyers do, but they may also be offered by non-lawyers. Yet law centres are described as doing community work that is not *really* a legal service. The Commission recommends that citizens law centres should be established.

to provide legal advice, assistance and representation to those in its locality . . . A distinction should be drawn between providing legal services in the way described and in carrying out general community work. At present some law centres concentrate on community work and for this purpose employ one or more community workers without legal training or qualifications. These centres like to work for the community at large or sections of it rather than for individuals. They often seek to attack the roots of the problems . . . or to promote changes . . . We consider that this type of work is not appropriate for a legal service (8–19).

Commentators sympathetic to law centres have attacked the Commission recommendations about citizens law centres as hostile and apathetic to valuable work. It may be more accurate to conclude that the Commission did not comprehend the rationale for community work (or test cases or group actions) because it never managed to define legal services. It failed to grasp or clarify the various techniques or skills used by lawyers, the range of procedures or strategies employed and the reasons for selecting different options. This prevented such congruence as there is with the work of others, who serve as active or passive advice-giving intermediaries for individuals or groups, being understood. Lawyers in private practices do 'all sorts of things' and some have close parallels to test case and group action and certainly some represent, albeit in a different environment, the diagnostic, catalytic and combustible work that is involved in law centre community work.[5]

A related illustration of failure to achieve clarity is provided by the Commission's comments on the work of existing law centres. It is important, now and in the future, to be able to determine whether public funding of law centres generally is justified, to monitor the performance of specific centres, and to make comparisons with other agencies. The amount and quality of work done must be relevant in this regard. But the tabulated data are somewhat less than helpful. For example, we discover that Tottenham Law Centre (9 full-time workers) dealt with 670 cases per annum, Newham (8 full-time workers) dealt with 808 cases, Benwell (6 full-time workers) dealt with 136 cases. Yet Brent Law Centre (7 full-time workers) dealt with 5,000 cases per annum, Camden (9 full-time workers) 6,198 cases, and Manchester (12 full-time workers) 13,000 cases. The Commission observes 'the definition and type of *cases* vary considerably: the answers therefore may not be directly comparable' (II Section 3, p. 74). Elsewhere the Commission refers to citizens advice bureaux handling three million *enquiries* in one year, and that a survey revealed one third of enquiries 'had a legal component.' Also 'it appeared that about 250,000 enquiries a year were referred from bureaux to solicitors' (7–7). Where public funds are involved, accountability for expenditure is required, and there is the popular concern with 'cost effectiveness.' But how can sensible judgments or comparisons be made if there is no understanding of a 'case' or an 'enquiry' as the component parts of the work? There have been arguments in the past about devoting money to law centres, CABx or enhancements to the legal aid, advice and assistance schemes. Is it not essential (as with 'legal services') that we clarify, for researchers and policy makers alike, the nature, type and amount of work that should be subsidized?

The Commission's discussion of law centre activity shows the price of inconsistency. In the future, law centres should concentrate on providing 'legal advice, assistance and representation to those in its locality, with special emphasis on social welfare law.' (8–3). Yet in discussing social welfare law the Commission notes that a feature of cases (*sic.*) in this area of law is 'that legal problems do not arise in isolation and that in many instances, although a legal element exists, personal and social problems predominate and call for appropriate skill and knowledge in those who deal with such cases' (2–10).

My purpose in alluding to the lack of precision in the use of terms is not merely to draw attention to sloppy or careless drafting. The terms prove to be pivotal in the substantial reasoning of the Commission. The ambiguity therefore detracts from and subverts the recommendations on the subject of the arrangements which should pertain in determining the deployment of lawyers and access to the law. This becomes most obvious when the Commissioners discuss the 'unmet need' for legal services. They say: 'the need for legal services may be estimated in a number of ways but its extent cannot be precisely quantified . . . However restricted is the definition of need for legal services, such services are, in some areas and for certain classes of society not available' (4–21).[6] It is difficult from this point in the Report to understand what, in the Commission's view, requires to be done in the future and for what reason. Some further remarks about the 'need' for legal services will be necessary but two observations are pertinent at this stage. First, discussion about 'legal services' is clearly based on some vague understanding of what solicitors in private practice say they do and tend to do, i. e. the conventional categories of work.[7] The contingent and accidental nature of these categories is neither appreciated, nor are the historical, economic or political influences which helped to shape them, scrutinized. Second, however, the lack of clarity in the Report is matched by the signal failure of academic researchers to do better. For over a decade reports on empirical research and discursive commentaries have exhibited indelible attachment to arguments about 'the unmet need for legal services'[8], even though the phrase has remained pathologically ambiguous.

2. A second priority must be to endeavour to improve and refine understanding of lawyer's activities, and thereby to evaluate their contribution to different purposes, interests and values espoused by individuals and groups in society. The evidence collected will be a valuable resource for future inquiries. Some researchers will aim single-mindly to enhance theoretical appreciations of the legal profession; others will want to carry out research that may lead to policy changes or to reform. Whatever the objective (and the two may be combined) a degree of re-orientation seems desirable. Some truly central characteristics of legal practice have not been given, in the past, the attention they deserve. This has inhibited the development of sophisticated explanation and has done little to engage the attention of practising lawyers or policymakers.

I do not disparage the research that has been accomplished so painstakingly, but I suggest researchers should 'respond' to the Report in three ways. First, by conscientiously collating and re-examining research evidence already available – including the Commission findings; second, by being prepared to reformulate existing theoretical concepts or constructs; third, by admitting, in principle at least, that overarching accounts of 'all things legal' from the emergence of capitalism or the advent of industrialization *may* lack close correspondence to, or sensitive grasp of the operation of law today. Such accounts are at a level of generality so removed from current problems that their application must depend on theoretical and empirical work at intervening levels of generality. There is a tendancy in the literature to encapsulate the 'essence' of some limited contemporary legal phenomenon by placing it in pride and triumph in juxtaposition to some notion drawn from the writings of Weber, Marx or Durkheim. The analysis provided by the classical writers of earlier historical periods were magnificent in their power and insight, but casual repetition and application to current practices can deride and deny the purposes of research.[9]

The research findings published by the Commission can, of course, be criticized, and constitute 'no more than the beginning.' Yet they contain systematic data and materials previously unavailable. If culled, analyzed, and properly developed, they may help to provide more accurate explanatory accounts of lawyers, their work and their role in society. A couple of examples, concerning solicitors in private practice, serve as illustrations.

The concentration on some types of legal work by the solicitors' profession as a whole is remarkable. Conveyancing, probate, wills, trusts, company and commercial work keep the profession going. (Indeed conveyancing and probate are the vital areas for all but the very large, predominantly city, firms who deal with the commercial work.) Together they provide 73.4 per cent of the gross fee income of the profession – conveyancing alone contributing almost half the income, i.e. £300 million at 1975–6 prices. This dependence, for revenue, on property transfers and work for corporate bodies can appear staggeringly high when the available range of legal work is contemplated – contentious and non-contentious, eligible under the statutory legal aid and advice schemes, etc. Other data published by the Commission help to explain the concentration. As regards individual members of the public, it is clear the clientèle of solicitors are drawn from higher socio-economic groups, those who own their own homes, and the better educated. The modes of establishing and maintaining contact with solicitors (and thus access to their skills) favours such groups. The matters on which solicitors are consulted (i. e. occupying their time as well as generating most revenue) reflect the massive concentration on the acquisition and transfer of property rights. Purchases and sales between the living, and transmission of the estates of the dead, pre-occupy the practice of law today. Examination of matters diagnosed as legal problems but not taken to solicitors, corroborates the systematic and self-perpetuating bias in the law being rendered to different groups and classes in society.[10]

Some may exclaim they suspected or knew all this and that aspects of the general picture had been identified in prior research.[11] But the Commission's findings are important – they are less tentative and more comprehensive, systematic and up-to-date than anything hitherto. They also pose as many questions as they answer. Before turning to the relevant questions, however, some features of legal practice on the ground should be mentioned – those which, it appears, have been given insufficient attention previously.

Solicitors in private practice continue, predominantly, to organize themselves in small units (partnerships) and they are wedded still to the traditional notion of being general advisers or people of affairs. What is called 'general practice' does include 'miscellaneous' matters but as the Commission has shown, the preponderance of work handled by solicitors is defined and restricted by demographic, organizational and economic factors. It would be better to describe solicitors as engaged in 'indiscriminate practice' in holding themselves out as competent in all areas or types of legal work. Next, legal firms are geared to financial profitability – a notion which apparently offends some researchers, although it is only too obvious to others. Devotion to reliably remunerative areas of work (and types of client) is therefore strong – even though other work which will or might provide significant income is accepted readily. It follows from this, like it or not, that solicitors will base their organization and represent attitudes (publicly and privately) to protect or enhance their livelihood. Next, the skills and facilities which solicitors provide on a mundane level are of a much less elevated or esoteric nature than outsiders – including academic researchers – often appreciate. Legal practice comprises largely routinized, pragmatic, business-like work and attention to irritating and trivial logistical detail, which must all be organized to ensure a steady flow of business (this includes keeping clients happy) but will avoid, or spread, risk of loss to the firm itself. It would be better if these aspects were emphasized in the literature, legal learning and research and technical legal skills being demoted accordingly to reflect the small part they play in lawyers' work. Last, the typical workstyle of solicitors approximates to that of most middle or low managers – trying to keep above water, make the decisions that are necessary, deal with constant interruptions and pressure, keep pace with competitors and outside influences in the market, and maintain or increase profitability.

Such features of legal practice would, I suggest, be endorsed by most self-conscious practitioners. Some of them have been noted in the existing literature on the legal profession. Yet if these features are not treated as merely tangential, they have often been seized on as causes for criticism of practitioners – apparently because they subvert or contradict idealized portraits of the legal profession.[12] Thus there are sardonic or sarcastic references to such features as cynical counterpoints to published self-justifications by the profession. In other cases the attention given to contemporary legal practice (as characterized) exhibits serious faults of omission. There is a failure to relate the features mentioned to important contextual and structural influences. The latter include the fundamentally important and unique division between solicitors and barristers, the massive concentration on conveyancing and probate, the organization of the legal system, obstacles in the way of pursuing actions through courts and tribunals, and the state of the law itself. It may well be that admiration of the achievements of law and society research in the USA has resulted in undue reliance on the categorizations of American lawyers, in a way which has inhibited investigation of the indigenous operation and practice of law.

My suggestion is that, without jettisoning all prior literature, much research effort should be devoted to providing fuller and richer accounts of lawyers' actual work, and legal practice, in ways which may establish links with wider structural arrangements and help to explain 'the system.' Some changes in emphasis and tone will be necessary. Thus, less stress should be laid on the need for change until the present position, and the reasons for its development, are better understood. Greater hesitation should be shown before untoward bad faith or manipulative selfishness are imputed to practitioners – not only because their point of view may be insufficiently understood but also because engaging their attention, sympathy or support, may improve explanation and the cause of reform. Indeed, less attention should be given to 'disproving' the conventional rhetoric celebrating the learned professions, and to the public statements of the professional bodies. Surely socio-legal researchers have heard of 'the presentation of self in everyday life'? Lawyers are not alone in using public relations. Certainly the actions and influence of the professional bodies are important (*vide* Royal Commission Report!) but more is revealed by their concrete decisions, by their practice rules, and even directions on charging methods, than the necessarily ponderous apologias for the profession and its role as guardian of the rule of law.

The range of statistics and survey data collected by the Commission should be mined for information, and longitudinal studies should be undertaken. The data should be used as a baseline, allowing further inquiry and, as trends are identified, stimulating further research. Many of the tasks ahead are arduous. Plotting and describing different aspects of legal work, changes in legal practice, the structure, composition, and remuneration levels of firms, stratification within the profession, the pervasive influence of the divided profession on the provision (or stultification) of skills available to clients – all these will take time. So too will analysis of fee-charging methods (to private clients and under publicly financed statutory schemes) as well as the consequences of regular advertising of lawyers' services, and extension of legal aid and assistance provisions. But these are the variables which should help to explain why legal practice is as we find it now, and why those solicitors who might like to devote their time and talents otherwise, are constrained or prevented from doing so. Wider organizational and economic realities profoundly shape the possibilities open to legal firms. Regrettably, the developed literature about 'lawyering' in the USA (and splendid typifications of solo practitioners, mega-lawyers etc.) cannot be transplanted readily.[13]

In suggesting significant changes of orientation in future inquiry, I do not wish to undervalue what has been achieved. But it is only by responding to the Commission commentary (and data) that the questions which deserve to be asked seem likely to gain a hearing. Only further research will give us insight into otherwise inexplicable features of the legal process. Perhaps some of the interesting questions (about legal work and about legal practice) may be mentioned.

(i) Legal Work

Lawyers have become locked into conveyancing and probate work.

(Continuation of the conveyancing monopoly by the Commision can, at a simple level, be understood as recognition of the profession's 'dependence for survival' on the remuneration it generates.) How did this come about? How irretrievable is the present position – what alterations would be necessary to dilute the dependence? Is symbiotic attention to property rights justifiable? If so, do 'property rights' require re-definition and in what ways? If not how may the bonds be broken? If lawyers spend so much time on what are, after all, routinized and unchallenging tasks, what jobs might they undertake that would be of value to others or of greater contribution to society? The naivety of the last question is, I believe, apparent only since public finance supports legal practice in various ways (e.g. education and training, legal aid and advice), so having some say in the return seems fair. There is a legitimate public interest in the optimization of expensive legal training and skills. In any event some laws are passed with social purposes in view. What *changes* to the rights of audience before courts, to legal aid provisions, to restrictive practices between the two branches of the profession, would be necessary to 'open up' legal practice to more people and to different problems? What incentives (e.g. economic) and relaxations (e.g. practice rules) would allow solicitors to concentrate on disenfranchized areas of law (and the people typically affected), for example on welfare law, civil liberties, and public interest law? If lawyers serve such a restricted clientèle on such restricted matters – what about the rest?

(ii) Legal Practice

Do partnerships remain a viable mode of organization for legal practice? Should 'indiscriminate practice' be allowed? How can small units achieve and maintain competence in increasingly complex and specialized areas of law? Should lower limits to partnership size be enforced? Should specialization in some areas (only) be required? Should client or issue dedication – allowing interprofessional associations — be developed? How may the quality of 'legal services' be measured, monitored and controlled?[14] Is independent scrutiny possible or does the model of the 'medical audit' deserve application? To some, such questions might seem odd or anomalous, but recourse can be made to the organization and operation of large city firms. There, deliberate and discriminating decisions have been made about the work that will be handled and that which will not; specialization is encouraged and appropriate staff are employed – a specific clientèle is offered a high-quality, dedicated expert service. These decisions are partially in response to such questions and the rationality of the response derives from analysis of the economics of practice, and the state of the law itself.

Such questions are merely illustrative of areas where further work would be interesting and should enhance understanding of the legal profession and the role of law. Some of the questions have been ignored, others are familiar – although reformulated to point up their relevance or to avoid attachment to concepts or assumptions which have proven sterile or misleading. Attempts to find answers would pose further questions but would provide core knowledge on which scrutiny of other services – by voluntary and statutory agencies and other organizations and groupings – could be based. This might allow evaluation and exploration of alternative provisions. By confining illustrative questions to traditional legal activities I do not imply a restriction of inquiry, far less do I assume the *status quo*; on the contrary, such work should contribute to the analysis and evaluation of current arrangements *and* comparison with the efficacy of 'alternative' provisions. The refusal by the Commission to answer such questions may be because they were not 'properly put'.

Attention to the areas mentioned should help to overcome some shortcomings in academic commentaries on the legal profession. The literature is at its most impressive in dealing with 'the rise of professionalism' and in contrasting the rhetoric and reality of emergent professions. Analysis, however, of the current position is less profound. Johnson (1972), whose rather pat account of occupations in general has enjoyed considerable popularity, even remarks 'professionalism may be in decline' (p. 47). Whether because of undue reliance on knowledge of the 'lawyering process' in North America or otherwise, we have insufficient understanding of lawyers in Britain today. It would be disappointing if contemporary changes and influences had to await the next generation for coherent sense to be provided. It might seem harsh to suggest that socio-legal research has established what the legal profession is *not* like, but has been unable to portray what it *is* like. Yet regarding much of the work so far as mainly negative would at least help to explain the Commission's lack of attention to the literature.

3. A third priority must be to participate in policy discussions about the operation of law and its dissemination to members of the public.[15] If it is once accepted that law, as a series of normative statements, cannot be neutral, then it follows inescapably that neither can the administration, availability and use of the law be neutral. Academic researchers *should* attempt to stimulate open discussion of policy implications. They have no particular mandate (and are elected to speak for no-one) nor have they any less freedom to speak than any other citizen. They often have the skills to collect and interpret systematic data, to penetrate complex technicalities and to offer exogenous accounts of unrevealed or accepted practices. The well-known justifications of a free press based on a broad 'balance of powers' approach are sufficient to persuade me that academic researchers should involve themselves actively in debates about legal policies. It is a matter for profound regret that the tradition in the UK represented in the attitudes of those holding administrative responsibility and ossified in swingeing laws – remains dedicated to maintaining closed and private consideration of matters of genuine public interest.

Of course there have been policy discussions – and some public rows – about the provision of legal services. But with some impressive exceptions, the impact of research findings on policy decisions is poor. Researchers may be criticized for naivety, ingenuousness and lack of perspective in failing to appreciate the problems policymakers face. A partial response at least, however, is that this is a direct result of the closed style of administration which prevails. Yet the tone of academic criticism has sometimes been off-putting. Those wishing to change the orientation of legal practice should not be suprised if they fail to gain supporters among lawyers when they indict the whole profession, top to bottom. The institution of marriage perhaps provides an analogy. Many men and women are married, maintain common law marriages or otherwise contrive stable relationships. The institution of marriage and the nature of these relationships is inadequately explained by mocking stories of true romance *à la* Barbara Cartland, and pointing to instances of brutish wife battering as general reality! Such remarks would be irrelevant of course were it not for the dismay expressed by so many researchers at the failure of the Commission to treat seriously some of the arguments for reform to which they were so deeply attached. In any event some priorities for policy-orientated work may be mentioned.

First, efforts have to be made to attract attention to the fraught issue of allowing researchers access to the data they require and to the institutions of the law. The severity of the difficulties experienced by socio-legal researchers in pursuing the legitimate purposes of research have been great. The climate maintained by the threatening provisions of the Official Secrets Act, and compounded by the extent of the rules of contempt of court and the attitude of the pofessional bodies, has prevented investigation in many areas which deserve scrutiny. Problems in gaining cooperation from private practitioners, voluntary associations or members of the public, deserve to be tackled in the normal way; but additional obstacles should not be placed in the way of researchers seeking a right of entry into the public institutions of the law nor to their recorded proceedings. That the operation of courts and tribunals, for example, should be accepted as a matter of public concern justifying ready access for researchers, seems to follow clearly from the notion that 'justice must be seen to be done.' The data on the operation and administration of the law should be public and not private. Of course if controversial *exposés* result from the collection of data, both sides can have their say – but ready access should be provided. No-one who noted the treatment afforded Baldwin and McConville for their only moderately provocative findings in *Negotiated Justice* can be sanguine about the future of socio-legal research, unless different arrangements can be made. It is dispiriting that the Commission ignored this point (even while calling for more research) and it may be that the parameters for empirical research will remain restricted and confined. But that researchers (individually, in combination or with the relevant research councils or foundations) should seek to improve access arrangements, seems vital to the development of research into the provision of legal services.[16]

Second, the precise nature, operation, administration and costs of the publicly financed legal aid advice and assistance schemes deserve close examination. Here, researchers should be able to rely on the good sense of the Commission which, apart from its recommendations about existing provisions, made perceptive comments about the scheme as a whole. It was accepted that, given the expenditure involved, the available information about the operation of the scheme is woefully inadequate. The annual reports produced by the Law Society do *not* provide – as they should – clear descriptions of the nature of work done, types of work handled, take-up by the public, nor do they allow judgements as to justifiability of the schemes in operation. The Commission says as much and even recommends a statistician be made available (at public expense) to improve the position.Hopefully this will happen. It is not just that annual votes of money have been made without anyone (including the Lord Chancellor's Advisory Committee) knowing precisely how it is spent. It is also that accurate tracking should provide researchers with valuable data in an area which will remain central to most discussions about the provision of legal services.

Third, attention should be given to monitoring the penetration and mobilization of laws. The Commission calls for systematic research and updating of their findings. Clearly this will require funding and a continuing responsibility should be to monitor knowledge, awareness and take-up of different laws – those already on the statute book and others as they are passed. A simple objective will be to discover which laws 'work' and why. This may include attention to resource provision, administrative policies etc. Of course many statutes are passed for complex reasons and not all of them are intended to result in concrete action. But some legislators, or policy makers, *are* concerned that laws should bring about results and monitoring their implementation would be valuable. Researchers in the UK have looked askance at the Knowledge and Opinion of Law (KOL) studies so popular in continental Europe. It may be we should rediscover the motives and interests which guided KOL studies in a way which will provide direction.

From the few available studies it can be seen that knowledge about different laws, and the ability to take up opportunities provided can vary massively throughout the community. More information, in further areas, is required. First, such material should be of direct relevance in providing the data on which informed policy making may rest. Second, significant problems of communication between researchers and the practising profession might, thereby, be overcome. Practitioners tend to base their views on pragmatic experience of the presenting clientèle and their problems, and they may, thus, underestimate what other work is not brought to them. Consequently they may regard discussions of the distance between the law and some sections of the community as plainly critical of the profession. Researchers, relying on data collected, but failing to explain its meaning or the extraneous influences which maintain the distance, can conclude wrongly that it is all the legal profession's fault. Finally, monitoring the mobilization or penetration of laws ought to assist in painting a clearer picture of the legal system in operation.

Following Galanter, many researchers tended to dismiss inquiries into the 'gap' between law and society; this dismissal was, I believe, premature.[17] Identifying where there are gaps and where there are not, how the gaps are bridged or traversed, should help to explain different laws, their administration and their relevance in society. Examination of law's achievements of purposes, where and why different effects occur, and what people are affected, would be valuable. It may be that our *a priori* theoretical notions are inadequate. Lack of attention to the operation of laws may confine socio-legal work to exactly the sort of formalistic analysis in traditional jurisprudence which it has been so determined to escape.

Some years ago in a different context the Lord Chancellor accepted that since the state makes the laws which govern and regulate people's lives, it is under a reciprocal obligation to make these laws readily available. It might be worth emphasizing this approach and reformulating questions about the operation of the law on the essentially democratic justification of law making. Access to and collection of information on the 'performance' of laws and legal institutions would allow those interested in legal policy making the material they need to make sensible judgements. Scrutiny of the extent and availability of legal aid and advice might throw up different issues if the obligation on the state to render laws available were stressed. It is important to insist that the law cannot be a secret and, by its nature, few people can afford to regard it as a luxury.

4.   Since the end of the 1960s there has been constant reference to 'the unmet need for legal services.' *Justice for All* made play with the evocative phrase. The study by Abel-Smith, Zander and Brooke (*Legal Problems and the Citizen*) was devoted entirely to examining and 'quantifying' the extent of the need. Reports of the Lord Chancellor's Advisory Committee are replete with references to 'unmet need.' After more than a decade in popular use, the phrase is enshrined in official thinking and in the Report – yet its meaning remains unclear and seriously problematic.

Fitzgerald has suggested that the modern resuscitation of the notion 'need' can be explained in terms of the reaction, in the social sciences, against the prevailing value of neutral orthodoxy and as echoing the call for relevance, significance and action. He also suggests, admitting to some oversimplification, that academic commentators on 'needs' tended to divide according to political criteria. Thus radical theorists were 'pro-needs', stressing the legitimating purpose of government in the satisfaction of human needs, while conservatives tended to be 'anti-needs', emphasizing the function of government being to respond to expressed wants and demands, and sometimes arguing that emphasis on needs could carry authoritarian implications. Fitzgerald's most important point however is stated as follows:

the very ambiguity of the concept 'need' in large part explains its plausibility in use. The notion 'need' has such currency, especially among popularizers and propagandists, and gains such persuasive force, because on one hand it involves imperatives and on the other because it appears to root them in common sense and in empirical reality. Once we have called something a 'need' in common usage, it would be odd without considerable explication either to deny that it is good or that it should not be satisfied . . . But to talk in terms of 'needs' involves smuggling in a view of what ought to be under the guise of what is, or what can be as a matter of fact. Built into the word 'need' is a notion of necessity and one is unsure whether what is meant is an empirical or factual necessity, a logical and analytic necessity, or a normative necessity (1977, pp. 195–6).

The relevance of this to the arguments about enhancing the provision of legal services seems considerable. Attention to the unmet need for such services, like socio-legal studies in general, coincided with calls for relevance among legal academics. At that stage too, something of a political division was also noticeable. Time has passed, however, circumstances have changed, and the phrase 'the unmet need' has become a benchmark for most academic and policy-related discussions about lawyers and their activities. The question remains whether use of the phrase 'unmet need' partakes of the ambiguity and confusion Fitzgerald alleges to exist in discussions of need in general.

How *do* needs relate to or contrast with 'wants', 'demands', 'preferences', 'predilictions', 'choices', 'desires', or 'deserts'? How does a researcher reliably distinguish one or more persons' needs from the wants, demands, etc, of others? Which 'needs' deserve to be treated as real, human or important and not artificial, contrived or trivial?[18] Even assuming such questions are resolved satisfactorily, what 'needs' should be met and for what reasons?

Empirial studies to data have been largely devoid of *any* attention to such questions.[19] Commentators have noticed the problematic nature of research procedures in this field and referred to the more subtle insights gained from American research. Philip Lewis raised the questions directly at an early stage, but while the importance of his argument was formally acknowledged, no constructive solutions were found. Lewis wrote:

if certain problems are spoken of as legal ones and official support is given to legal methods of solving them, that is to take a particular attitude to problems of that kind, problems which may be seen by those most closely concerned as best solved in another way. For instance if a tenant of a flat has a leaking roof he may be regarded as having a legal problem; does his lease provide that the landlord should do the repairs, and is the mechanism of the courts adequate to ensure quick action? But he may choose to get a ladder and not a lawyer, and we can argue whether it is better that people should be made to fulfil their legal duties or that they should be encouraged to take practical steps to avoid material damage regardless of their legal responsibilities (1973, p. 79).

There have been two broad types of reaction to the nagging points raised by Lewis. The first has been exhibited by those determined to increase the availability of law to all members of society, and the second by professional bodies and policy makers responding to calls for the extension of publicly-financed schemes. Both admit the logic of Lewis's view, but the first reaction was to maintain the calls for reform by illustrating the value of the work that can be done, and by pointing to the possible or probable *serious* consequences that might ensue from lack of legal intervention. Thus the Law Centres Federation rehearse dramatic instances of help being given to clients by law centre workers – this is what we are doing, they say, this is the 'need' we are meeting. The seriousness of the client's predicament allows the insistence that something must be done. But even if we take an extreme example, this may be inadequate. Thus, does a youth of seventeen accused of multiple murder and held on remand *need* a lawyer. Most people would say yes, but members of the Provisional IRA often reject any lawyers and refuse to recognize the court. Even in the most serious cases the difficulties remain.

The second type of reaction has been manifested both in antagonistic and defensive ways. Initially the ambiguities or un-certainties involved in references to 'the unmet need' were seized on in pejorative fashion. That value judgments were or might be involved was stressed, sometimes to provide a 'realistic' perspective (you can take a horse to water but you can't make it drink) or to impugn the protagonists of reform for being radicals, political activists or agitators. Some local authorities and local law societies adopted this approach. The more defensive variant on this reaction – calmer and more restrained – was to query where arguments based on the 'unmet need' might lead. The Commission puts the view elegantly: 'a society in which all human and social problems were regarded as apt for legal remedy or susceptible to legal procedures would not be one in which we would find it agreeable to live' (2–2 8). Attractive as this view may be, it fudges the issue by failing to articulate or make explicit those problems which do and those which do not deserve legal consideration.

It is clear that neither of these reactions overcomes the difficulties identified by Lewis. Neither addresses directly questions concerning at what point lawyers become relevant, in what way, in what sort of circumstance, and why they should be made available to people, if necessary at public expense. It is even more disappointing that the problematic phrase has now been elevated into official discourse and used to determine the availability of lawyers in the future. Two courses of action, both suggested in Fitzgerald's discussion of 'need', might be pursued in further research inquiry.

The straightforward, but radical course, would be to develop Fitzgerald's own argument and admit 'the concept of "need" operates as a mechanism to camouflage imperatives under an empirical guise,' (1977, p. 201) and conclude that since 'need' is inherently ambiguous, no clear understanding – no empirical research and no empirically grounded theory – is likely to be constructed on its base. This course would require the development of other approaches and other concepts would have to be put to service in future research. The other course, instead of rejecting the concept of need, is to embrace it – and go further. Value judgments and policy considerations are inextricably involved in discussing needs. But whatever the difficulties, attention to 'needs' is probably inescapable when decisions about the allocation of benefits have to be made in an unequal society where there is a moderate scarcity of resources. To attribute a need to a person or group is to recognize that they do not have, or are unable to enjoy, some resource or opportunity which they should have, to achieve or fulfill a legitimate goal or condition. 'Need' is distinguished from 'want' in that 'to talk of need implies the lack of something which prevents a person reaching or maintaining some state defined by the norm.'[20] The concept is of a teleological nature, so let attention be turned to the relevant purposes and policies. Discussion of the 'unmet need for legal services' should then relate the incidence of use and experience of lawyers, to the normative statements of the law while, in parallel, wider consideration is given to the goals and purposes in view in using the law. This will involve clarification of the role of law itself.[21]

Reappraisal

The efforts expended in researching the provision of legal services has been considerable. The Commission has reported its findings. Yet, understanding of even basic terms is primitive, essential information about lawyers and their work (and indeed about others who use or interpret the law) is not available, there has been a sad but continuing distance and lack of co-operation between researchers and policy makers, and quite fundamental and elementary concepts adduced in argument, have remained vague and ambiguous even where they have not been plainly abused or distorted. Put another way, it is these areas of weakness or confusion which should be tackled in future inquiries, in response to the Commission's call for more and better research (!) or straightforwardly to gain a firmer grasp of the operation of law in contemporary society.

The areas selected for discussion ('legal services', lawyers' work, policy considerations, and analysis of 'the unmet need') bear the separate arguments for clarification and re-orientation. But together, taken only as aspects of a more general topic, they help to identify an underlying difficulty – one which helps to explain the shortcomings of completed work – the lack of adequate theory concerning the operation of law in society. There appears to be no coherent view on the role and remit of law maintained by policy makers. If there were, researchers could respond, and there has been no guiding theory according to which they could interpret and present empirical findings. The lack of an explicit theoretical framework concerning the operation of law has stifled the development of legal services research. This is what requires attention and suggests there should be a reappraisal.

The metamorphoses of the law, the legal system, its courts and tribunals, which has occurred in the last few decades has been remarked on by many commentators. The amount of law has increased seemingly exponentially, and the number of lawyers has grown accordingly. The strategies and methods, direct and indirect, used in law making has increased in range. The number and type of courts and tribunals – formal and informal – to encourage the resolution of conflict has increased. Yet neither from the legislature nor from the administration is there any discernible justification of the appropriateness of law as a tool of policy, nor (through a Ministry of Justice or the guaranteed protection of fundamental freedoms, e.g. in a Bill of Rights) is there any means of regularly focusing attention on the changes underway. The incoherence of understanding of the contemporary legal order in the UK is truly remarkable.

Available theoretical approaches reveal paradoxes. The prevailing orthodoxy in jurisprudence remains analytical jurisprudence and legal positivism. This 'school' bases its reasoning on the coercive element in the law and proceeds, thereafter, to formalistic and exquisite analyses of detailed norms and legal precepts. The lack of relevance of this approach to the actual operation, administration and use of law in society is stupendous. In sociology of law, however, the orthodoxy is represented by a series of variants on theories of conflict, which achieves its greatest sophistication in Marxist theory. Here, the major properties of law include mystification, legitimation and repression. This is often[22] difficult to square with the call for 'law for the people.'

The lack of theoretical appreciation of the legal order, stems from the lack of clear linkage between data collected on the ground (most legal services research so far) and overarching theories which explain all things legal at this particular point in the development or demise of capitalism. The familiar call for linkages between different levels of theory (general and more particular) has no greater relevance than for sociology of law in the UK today. Researchers cannot continue to explore the provision and use of legal services if they are informed only by some vague understanding of law that emphasises its coercive or repressive functions. The *use* of law can highlight where law is (also) a resource or a facility, it suggests law may protect and regulate, it may be valuable and progressive; it may guarantee security or allow individual purposes to be achieved; it can safeguard or help to realize interests.

Systematic attention to the use of law in different contexts, and by different individual groups and classes, should serve to achieve important objectives even though the process will take time. It should help to clarify the nature of 'legal services', which in turn might allow discussion of the adequacy of their provision. The uses for particular purposes and goals may clarify discussion of the need for services. Attention to lawyers' work and the economic costs of law is relevant because, necessarily, choices will have to be made about the priorities to be recognized in deploying legal services. By concentrating on establishing reliable linkages between generalized analyses and empirical findings, our understanding of the legal order and the social order will be improved. Existing macro-theoretical approaches should achieve greater subtlety and explanatory power. Some broad constructs will have to be amended no doubt, and others refined.

The greatest failure of researchers and the Commission was to locate consideration of the availability of legal services in the wider context of some understanding of the role of law in contemporary society. It is a daunting prospect to begin the construction of new theoretical accounts. The argument is that this is necessary, and attention to the areas identified should allow a productive start to be made to the painstaking construction of new theories. The development of theory should be in conjunction with and in relation to concrete problems and empirical research.[23]

Acknowledgement

I am grateful to Ray Geary, Paul Phillips, Paul Wiles and Malcolm Wood for comments on an earlier draft of this paper.

Notes

1. Unlike the RCLS, the Royal Commission on Criminal Procedure (1981) seemed to appreciate the need for research on many topics within its remit at an early stage, and sponsored and used research in an effective way.
2. The strong influence of US research interest in 'the delivery of legal services' was obvious from the outset (cf. *Justice for All*). As will be seen this was to prove important.
3. It is interesting to compare the approach of the Royal Commission on Legal Services in Scotland which states: 'It is tempting to say that 'legal services are services provided by lawyers' but we reject this for two reasons. Firstly not all work done by lawyers falls into the category of a legal service . . . Secondly not all legal services are provided by lawyers . . . Accordingly when we speak of legal services we mean advice, information or assistance involving a knowledge

of rights and obligations conferred by law and of legal procedures whether provided by a lawyer or otherwise.' (1–19).

4. That *two* Royal Commissions on Legal Services laid significantly different emphases on the topic of their enquiry is notable (cf. Note 3 *supra*). The discussion here focuses on the Report dealing with England, Wales and Northern Ireland.

5. I appreciate that there are different conceptions and justifications of 'community work' – and indeed of test cases and group actions. These are important but do not affect the point discussed here.

6. The Scottish Royal Commission however states: 'ideally the use made of legal services would express the total need for legal services. However, not all need results in use of legal services and in some cases the service provided may, *by its inadequate quality or supply fail to meet the whole need*. The total need for legal services is the sum of actual use plus unmet need.' (1 pp. 20–21, italics added).

7. It is indeed anamolous that there is little published material which actually charts and explains 'what lawyers do' even though the topic is eminently researchable.

8. Cf. in particular Abel-Smith, Zander and Brooke: *Legal Problems and the Citizen.*

9. This is especially so where there is a vulgar refusal to recognize that *any* sociological theory needs constant development on relation to changing social reality.

10. See RCLS Report II, especially Sections 8, 16 & 22.

11. If such points *were* known and identified in prior research, the failure to impress the relevance and meaning of the knowledge on the Commission is even more remarkable.

12. Admittedly there are exceptions i.e. where contrasts between actual work and rhetorical utterances are pursued because of theoretical interests in linguistic analyses, communication of social symbols etc.

13. The written constitution, the power of judicial review, the organization of the profession, the rules of ethics and the economics of practice make 'lawyering' in the USA different. It is sad that language barriers inhibit comparisons and exchange of research findings within Western Europe and Scandinavia. Certainly the organization of the legal systems and legal professions vary but economic and politico-ideological contexts throw up similar problems and interestingly variant responses.

14. Cf. the recognition by the Scottish Royal Commission of the relevance of the *quality* of work done in discussing 'the need for legal services' (Note 6 *supra*).

15. Paradoxically the two books by Abel-Smith & Stevens which helped to stimulate research interest in 'legal services' had such an orientation. The research continued without sufficient attention to the organizing approach and tone of these early discussions.

16. Certainly if there is to be a Council of Legal Services (cf. RCLS Report, Ch. 6) it should have power to demand access to data required for its work.

17. Cf. Galanter (1973). Having made as many disparaging remarks about research into the 'gap' between law and society as most (*mea culpa*) this view clearly reflects a marked change of mind.

18. Much of the literature on 'needs' in general, concentrates on endeavours to classify and explicate those needs which are important, real and true (and thus deserving of satisfaction) and which are not. Cf. Fitzgerald (1977) *passim*.

19. Sadly, but unsurprisingly, the two Royal Commissions on Legal Services have nothing sensible to offer on the nature or meaning of the 'need' for 'legal services'. The Commission in Scotland showed cognizance of the problems

involved, whereas the Commission in England and Wales simply ignore the issue.

20. Cf. Fitzgerald (1977), p. 196.
21. The difficulties involved in discussions of need apply generally and not merely to 'legal needs'. Despite the problems, 'need' does seem to be central to political vocabulary and theorizing. Much of the relevant literature on 'need theory' shows recognition (implicit or explicit) of the importance of relating 'needs' to the aims in view in seeking to satisfy them. Achieving 'Freedom' has remained a *lietmotif* from Marx to Marcuse.
22. There are honourable exceptions e. g. E. P. Thompson (1975), Ch. 10.

References

Abel-Smith, B. & Stevens, R. (1967), *Lawyers and the Courts*, London, Heinemann.
Abel-Smith, B. & Stevens, R. (1968), *In Search of Justice*, London, Allen Lane.
Abel-Smith, B., Zander, M. & Brooke, R. (1973), *Legal Problems and the Citizen*, London, Heinemann.
Baldwin, J. & McConville, M. (1977), *Negotiated Justice*, London, Martin Robertson.
Fitzgerald, R. (Ed.) (1977), *Human Needs and Politics*, Oxford, Pergamon Press.
Galanter, M. (1973), 'Notes on the future of social research on law', *Mimeographed paper presented to Conference on Developments in Law and Social Science Research*.
Johnson, T. J. (1972), *Professions and Power*, London, Macmillan.
Morris, P., White, R. & Lewis, P. (1973), *Social Needs and Legal Action*, London, Martin Robertson.
Report of the Royal Commission on Legal Services (1979), Cmnd. 7648, HMSO.
Report of the Royal Commission on Legal Services in Scotland (1980), Cmnd. 7846, HMSO.
Society for Conservative Lawyers (1968), *Justice for All*, London.
Society for Conservative Lawyers (1968), *Rough Justice*, London.
Thompson, E. P. (1975), *Whigs and Hunters*, London, Allen Lane.
Zander, M. (1968), *Lawyers and the Public Interest _ A Study in Restrictive Practices*, London, Weidenfeld & Nicholson.

Index